Understanding Property Law

Understanding Property Law

Edited by
Ezekiel Dickson

STATES
ACADEMIC PRESS
www.statesacademicpress.com

Published by States Academic Press,
109 South 5th Street,
Brooklyn, NY 11249, USA

ISBN: 978-1-63989-544-1

Cataloging-in-Publication Data

Understanding property law / edited by Ezekiel Dickson.
p. cm.
Includes bibliographical references and index.
ISBN 978-1-63989-544-1
1. Property. 2. Possession (Law). 3.Things (Law).
4. Wealth. I. Dickson, Ezekiel.

K720 .U53 2022
346.04--dc23

For information on all States Academic Press publications visit our website at www.statesacademicpress.com

STATES
ACADEMIC PRESS

Contents

Preface

It is often said that books are a boon to mankind. They document every progress and pass on the knowledge from one generation to the other. They play a crucial role in our lives. Thus I was both excited and nervous while editing this book. I was pleased by the thought of being able to make a mark but I was also nervous to do it right because the future of students depends upon it. Hence, I took a few months to research further into the discipline, revise my knowledge and also explore some more aspects. Post this process, I begun with the editing of this book.

The area of law that controls the various types of ownership in personal property and real estate is known as property law. Property indicates the legally protected claims to resources like land, personal property and intellectual property. It can be exchanged through contract law. If the laws of property are violated, one can sue under tort law in order to protect it. The concept, idea and philosophy of property form the basis of property law. There are two views on property rights. These views are the traditional view and the bundle of rights view. The traditional view believes that there is a core and inherent meaning in the concept of property. The bundle of rights view believes that the owner of the property only has bundle of permissible uses over the property. This book unfolds the innovative aspects of property law which will be crucial for the progress of this field in the future. It provides significant information of this discipline to help develop a good understanding of the property law and related fields. The topics covered in this book offer the readers new insights in the field of property law.

I thank my publisher with all my heart for considering me worthy of this unparalleled opportunity and for showing unwavering faith in my skills. I would also like to thank the editorial team who worked closely with me at every step and contributed immensely towards the successful completion of this book. Last but not the least, I wish to thank my friends and colleagues for their support.

Editor

1

Assignations of All Sums Securities

Dr Ross G Anderson

> No appointment was ever more successful and none illustrates more clearly the desirability of having as a professor one who is conversant with the practice of the branch of the law he is called on to teach. To set a man to teach conveyancing who is not engaged in large practice, and who only knows the subject from books or historically, is like making a man professor of surgery who has only read about it and who never performed an operation.[1]

A. The Chair of Conveyancing

(1) Introduction

Robert Rennie was appointed the Professor of Conveyancing in 1993. During a tenure marked by indefatigable industry, Robert's chair became, in the eyes of the profession, the face of the Glasgow Law School. With Robert's retirement, there comes the opportunity to reflect not just on Robert's contributions, but also on the place of the Chair he has held with such distinction in the Scottish legal profession, in legal education and in legal scholarship. So before addressing the technical topic I have chosen for my contribution, it is first to the history and context of the Chair that I turn.

1 D Murray, *Memories of the Old College of Glasgow* (1927) 236, describing the first holder of the Chair of Conveyancing, Professor Anderson Kirkwood.

(2) The first Conveyancing Chairs

2014 saw the Tercentenary of the appointment of the first holder of the Regius Chair in Civil Law in the University of Glasgow, William Forbes in 1714. But it was in the nineteenth century that the Universities of Glasgow and Edinburgh founded chairs of Conveyancing. If the word "conveyancing" is considered to be a word for which Scots lawyers have peculiar affinity, it may be because University Chairs in Conveyancing is a peculiarly Scottish phenomenon (although the basic idea which underlies these Chairs has a modern appeal in the United States, where all self-respecting law schools must have a Professor of "clinical legal education"). The creation of the Chair of Conveyancing in the University of Edinburgh marked a significant break with the effective monopoly exercised by the Faculty of Advocates on the chairs in law in that University, since the appointment to the Chair of Conveyancing would come from the ranks of the Society of Writers to Her Majesty's Signet. The notion of the "lower branch" of the legal profession – solicitors – being remotely qualified to found a University Chair was a source of considerable invective from members of the Faculty of Advocates, the politically conservative members of which found the appointment of the leading Whig, and future editor of the *Edinburgh Review*, Macvey Napier, as the first holder, almost too much to bear.[2] One of the most prolific contributors to the contemporary conservative periodical, *Blackwood's Edinburgh Magazine*, himself an advocate, pointedly observed how, in England, conveyancing was in the hands of the bar:[3] the English, he ventured, would "laugh" even to hear even of a *lectureship*, never mind a *Professorship*, of conveyancing in a University.[4] The "abstruse science" of

2 "Franciscùlus Funk," "The Pluckless School of Politics, No 1" (1823) 14 *Blackwood's Edinburgh Magazine* 139-44. Funk was the pseudonym of John Cay, Advocate: see A L Strout, *A Bibliography of Articles in Blackwood's Magazine: volumes I through XVIII, 1817-1825* (1959) 110. Cay was sheriff at Linlithgow from 1825 to 1865. Cay was one of the oldest friends of John Gibson Lockhart (for whom see n 4): D Douglas (ed), *The Journal of Sir Walter Scott, from the original manuscript at Abbotsford* (1890) (reprinted 2013) I, 22, n 1. For the background to the Edinburgh Conveyancing chair in the WS Society's lectures, first given by Robert Bell, brother of George Joseph, see my "Introduction" to G Watson (ed), *Bell's Dictionary and Digest of the Law of Scotland*, 7th edn (1890) (reprinted 2012) xviii-xxxi.

3 As it remains to this day: see, for instance, the references to "conveyancing counsel" in the English Civil Procedure Rules, r 40.18 and 40.19 and Practice Direction 40D.

4 "C.N.," "Tail-Piece" (1823) 14 *Blackwood's Edinburgh Magazine* 144. "C. N." = Christopher North, the pseudonym of a number of contributors, often John Wilson, Advocate and Professor of Moral Philosophy in the University of Edinburgh, but in this case Strout (n 200) attributes this tail-piece to John Gibson Lockhart, Advocate, but best known as a satirist and as the biographer of his father-in-law, Sir Walter Scott.

conveyancing,[5] in so far as it related to deeds, according to this disaffected and "nearly fee-less advocate" was insufficiently learned to justify the erection of a University Chair; and *esto* there was a need for such a chair – as advocates say – only a member of the Faculty of Advocates would be sufficiently respectable to hold it.[6]

The background to the Glasgow Conveyancing chair is no less without human interest. As in Edinburgh, the local professional association – of which a good proportion of Glasgow's law graduates have become members – the Faculty of Procurators in Glasgow,[7] finding the instruction of the University Professors out of touch with the needs of aspiring writers,[8] took matters into its own hands. The Faculty of Procurators appointed, in 1816, one of its own, James Galloway, to give a series of lectures on Conveyancing. Galloway's lively lectures, though now largely forgotten,[9] display considerable learning and a palpable enthusiasm for the subject.[10] Eventually, the Faculty of Procurators agreed to endow a chair in the University, on the Edinburgh model, in 1861.[11] The first holder was Anderson Kirkwood, of whom David Murray – someone well placed to judge[12] – wrote the words which introduce this contribution. The central importance to the University of a Professor with the invaluable experience of the law in action, as well as law in the books, is evident in the roles of the first two holders of the Chair, whose efforts were instrumental in organising the practicalities – funding, contractual negotiations and dealing

5 Cf G L Gretton, "Sharp Cases make Good Law" 1994 *SLT (News)* 313-14: "Feudal law is hardly a popular subject. Indeed, together with 'mediaeval' and 'Dickensian' it is an all purpose term used for condemning the grubby and unwanted survivals of an obscure and barbarous past. Of course, most feudal law has long since been abolished. But some parts remain, perhaps unloved, and perhaps unloveable, but law."

6 "Pluckless School of Politics" (n 2) 139 ff.

7 See D Murray, "The Faculty of Procurators in Glasgow" (1897) 13 *Scottish Law Review* 36. The Faculty received its royal patronage from His Majesty in 1950. For Murray, see n 12 below.

8 Compare the French *'écrivain'* and David Murray, "The Term 'Writer' as used in Scotland," *Glasgow Herald*, 15 March 1884.

9 D M Walker, *A History of the School of Law: The University of Glasgow* (1990) 41.

10 J Galloway, *Lectures in Conveyancing* (1838).

11 Ordinance of the Scottish Universities Commission, 15 June 1861, signed by John Inglis (then Lord Advocate): *Edinburgh Gazette* June 18, 1861, 792-93.

12 A remarkable lawyer, scholar (not just in law) and bibliophile, Murray was himself a conveyancer: see e.g. J Rankine, J L Mounsey and D Murray (eds) *The Scots Style Book* (1902-1905) 7 vols. A founding partner of Maclay Murray & Spens LLP, he was arguably the foremost Scottish legal scholar of the generations his long life spanned. He donated 24,000 items of this 40,000 volume library to the University of Glasgow. To this day, that collection, too little recognised, remains one of Glasgow's greatest resources. For Murray, see M S Moss, "Murray, David" *Oxford DNB* (2004-).

with the small matter of acquiring the site – for Sir George Gilbert Scott's unmistakable building at Gilmorehill.[13]

(3) The 1916 election to the Conveyancing Chair

The Emeritus Professor of Comparative Law at Oxford, Bernard Rudden, himself a qualified solicitor, once pointed out that academics are, from the nature of their position, risk averse, sometimes unsuited, and often little grounded, in the realities of commercial life.[14] And it is difficult to imagine any Professor, insulated from the pressures of daily practice, and whose knowledge of the law was derived only from the books, being able to offer to students Galloway's lively, if portentous, admonition that:[15]

> One single blunder in a deed, by which it may be rendered invalid and ineffectual – whether this may have arisen from ignorance, or carelessness – might have the effect to subject the unfortunate conveyancer by whom the deed had been framed, in damages, to such a ruinous extent, as might blast all his future prospects, and involve him in penury and misery during the remainder of his life…

But practical experience and scholarly achievement are not mutually exclusive: a point perhaps never better demonstrated in the 1916 election to the Chair of Conveyancing. The election would mark the first appointment of a professional academic in the modern sense to a law chair at a Scottish university. David Murray, whose words open the present contribution, was a colossus not just in the west of Scotland but of the Scottish legal profession as a whole. A former Dean of the Faculty of Procurators, he was a member of the Council of the Faculty of Procurators that made the appointment to the 1916 Chair. All of the applicants wrote to Murray personally and, characteristically, Murray has meticulously preserved each application for posterity.[16] The other members of Council who would have been eligible to vote were William Gillies (Dean), David Murray (Ex-Dean), James Mackenzie (Ex-Dean), Peter Lindsay Miller, John Mair, William

13 Murray (n 1).

14 B Rudden, "Selecting Minds: An Afterword" (1993) 41 *American Journal of Comparative Law* 481 at 486.

15 J Galloway, *Lectures on Conveyancing* (1838) 9. The student or academic reader who considers the warning overblown should reflect on *Lonedale Ltd v Scottish Motor Auctions (Holdings) Ltd* [2011] CSOH 4.

16 *Applications for Chair of Conveyancing* (1916) [GUL Sp Coll Mu21-a.3].

George Black, Thomas Alexander Fyfe, Andrew Mackay, James Graham, Daniel Munro Alexander, and Allan Maclean.[17]

(4) The candidates

In the election there were 13 candidates, all drawn from the local profession. For present purposes, historical interest immediately focuses on three of those candidates: Hugh Reid Buchanan, John Richard Cunliffe, and William Sharp McKechnie.

John Richard Cunliffe, a local writer with long experience, submitted a modest letter of application focussing on his practical experience and eschewing testimonials. Almost as an afterthought, Cunliffe mentions in passing that, since he was applying for a University Chair, it might be "not irrelevant to mention that I have done a good deal of literary work," referring to his editorial work on a number of English classics and his *New Shakespearean Dictionary* (1910). Having been spared the responsibilities of the Conveyancing Chair, Cunliffe would go on to produce *Blackie's Compact Etymological Dictionary* (1922) and the standard student text, *A Lexicon of the Homeric Dialect* (1924). To put the merit of that work in modern context, it was republished in the United States by the University of Oklahoma, in 1963, with paperback editions following in 1977 and, again, as recently as 2012.[18]

Hugh Reid Buchanan,[19] a prize-winning MA philosophy graduate, had proceeded to Germany, to study at Jena and Berlin, where he had spent two years studying philosophy and jurisprudence, before returning to take an LLB with distinction. He had been the University's lecturer in Roman law before becoming the solicitor to the Caledonian Railway Company and, at the time of his application, a partner with M'Grigor Donald & Co. His time at the Railway Company had made him valuable contacts with establishment figures: Buchanan's testimonials for the chair contained references from the Dean of the Faculty of Advocates (and future Lord President) James Avon Clyde, KC MP; a future Dean of the Faculty of Advocates and Court of Session judge, J Condie S Sandeman KC; and two

17 *Minute Book of the Royal Faculty of Procurators.*

18 In addition, Cunliffe compiled *Blackie's Compact English Dictionary of Current English* (1969) and the *Secondary School English Dictionary* (1969).

19 See 1912 *SLT (News)* 85 for a portrait. Walker, *School of Law* (n 9) 85 described Buchanan as a "vigorous and scholarly man."

future Lords of Appeal in Ordinary: H P Macmillan KC (Lord Macmillan) and William Watson KC MP (Lord Thankerton).

William S McKechnie[20] was one of Glasgow's limited number of DPhil graduates,[21] who had received his doctorate for his published work, *The State and the Individual.*[22] With that solid scholarly background, McKechnie, after working for a time as a writer,[23] took his first academic post at Glasgow University as the Lecturer on Constitutional Law and History. He was, during his time as a lecturer, extraordinarily productive: producing what, a century on, is still considered to be a fundamental study of the sources for *Magna Carta;*[24] a critique of Parliament's second chamber in *Reform of the House of Lords*[25] (which heavily influenced the Parliament Act 1911); and a monograph setting out the constitutional consequences of that far-reaching measure, *The New Democracy and the New Constitution*, in 1912.

As a professional academic, McKechnie had applied for a University Chair before. In 1909, McKechnie had applied for the Chair of Constitutional Law and Constitutional History in the University of Edinburgh. McKechnie submitted what were probably (at least at that time)[26] the most impressive

20 See J S Medley (revd J C Holt) "McKechnie, William Sharp (1863-1930), historian" *Oxford DNB* (2004-); 1911 *SLT (News)* 9 for a portrait; and 1916 *SLT (News)* 89.

21 Glasgow, like Edinburgh, St Andrews and Aberdeen, awarded the DPhil, as the arts and humanities research degree, until at least 1917 with the regulations being finally amended in 1919 to introduce the PhD as the higher research degree: *Regulations for the Degree of Doctor of Philosophy (University Court Ordinance No LXXIV (Glasgow No 21)), as approved by Order in Council, dated 18th August 1919*. The Ordinance is reproduced in A Clapperton (ed) *University Court Ordinances 1915-1924* (1925) 66-67. Ironically it was in 1917, just as the Scottish universities introduced the PhD as its standard "lower" doctorate, that the DPhil became the standard Oxford doctorate: R Simpson, *The Development of the PhD Degree in Britain, 1917-1959 and since: An Evolutionary and Statistical History in Higher Education* (2009).

22 W S McKechnie, *The State and the Individual: an introduction to political science, with special reference to socialistic and individualistic theories* (Glasgow, 1896). W Innes Addison, *A Roll of the Graduates of the University of Glasgow, 31st December 1727 to 31st December 1897* (1898) 674 and 681 records that 2 DPhils were awarded in 1896.

23 McKechnie had been admitted as a member of the Faculty of Procurators in 1890 after serving his apprenticeship with Roberton, Low, Roberton and Cross. He appears to have practised full-time until 1894.

24 W S McKechnie, *Magna Carta: A Commentary on the Great Charter of King John, with an Historical Introduction* (1905) (2nd edn 1914) (reprinted 1958); R H Helmholz, "Magna Carta and the Ius Commune" (1999) 66 *University of Chicago Law Review* 297 at 303. The full text of McKechnie's study has now been made available online by the Liberty Fund as one of the classic text's on liberty, available at http://oll.libertyfund.org/titles/338

25 W S McKechnie, *The Reform of the House of Lords* (1909).

26 Hector MacQueen has suggested that "the most distinguished field of candidates ever for a law chair in a British university" were received by the University of Edinburgh

set of testimonials ever compiled for a Professorial appointment to a Scottish law chair:[27] with a printed booklet containing glowing testimonials from scholars in Scotland, England, France, Germany, Austria and the United States, together with reviews from the *Times Literary Supplement, The Daily Telegraph, The Manchester Guardian,* some US newspapers, reviews in French and German journals, as well as the Scottish newspapers. But to no avail: the election to the Edinburgh constitutional Chair too was in the gift of the Faculty of Advocates and the Faculty, true to form, appointed one of their own, Hepburn Miller.[28]

An academic background, however, was no guarantee of election to the Glasgow Conveyancing Chair in 1916. For although his talents as a legal scholar were beyond question, some members of the Council wondered how McKechnie would manage to discharge the duties of the chair – which, after all, required the teaching not of constitutional theory, but the intricacies of feudal conveyancing; and, moreover, placed a heavy demand on the Professor for opinions and appointment in many title deeds as arbiter ("a kind of official referee," the English authors of his *Dictionary of National Biography* entry record). McKechnie did have conveyancing experience: he had practised full-time for four years after he qualified as a partner in the firm of McKechnie and Gray. And although, for the best part of twenty-five years, he had worked in the University, he had continued to practise and the firm remained in existence until 1915.

David Murray, for his part, though well qualified to judge McKechnie's scholarship, was of the view that McKechnie was not the man for the Chair, instead considering Buchanan "the best of all the candidates, followed by Cunliffe." The implication is that Murray placed

in 1938 for the Edinburgh Chair of Civil Law, which attracted Fritz Schulz, Fritz Pringsheim Adolf Berger, David Daube and F H Lawson: see H L MacQueen, "Two Toms and an Ideology for Scots Law" in E C Reid and D L Carey Miller (eds), *A Mixed Legal System in Transition: T B Smith and the Progress of Scots Law* (2005) 44 at 56. The Chair was in the gift of the Faculty of Advocates who nonetheless managed to elect one of their own, the "atrabilious" Matthew G Fisher KC (who had studied in Göttingen), for whom, see Sir Nicholas Fairbairn QC, *A Life is too Short, autobiography*, vol I (1987) 61 and A F Rodger, "David Daube 1909-1999" (2001) 118 *ZSS (RA)* xxi-xxii. Fisher's entire scholarly output appears to have been a single article mid-way through his two-decade tenure.

27 *Application and testimonials of William Sharp McKechnie, M.A., LL.B., D.Phil., Lecturer on Constitutional Law and History in the University of Glasgow, for the Chair of Constitutional Law and Constitutional History in the University of Edinburgh* [GUL Sp Coll MacLehose 688].

28 His father was a Lord of Session, Lord Craighill.

McKechnie third. But Murray's was not the majority view. For the end result, recorded by Murray, placed Buchanan only fourth; McKillop, third; and Cunliffe, second. "Leaving Dr McKechnie," Murray tersely noted, "as elected."[29] Murray's dissatisfaction may be reflected in his recording of contemporary professional gossip. "After McKechnie had been elected, it was remarked," Murray pointedly noted on the front of Alexander Donaldson's application (Donaldson came seventh), "that, as he [McKechnie] knew nothing about Conveyancing he should take a six month course with Mr Donaldson, so as to qualify himself."[30]

(5) Wider significance of McKechnie's appointment

It is a modern phenomenon that University Law Schools are often conspicuous for the absence of academic staff with experience of legal practice. It has long been suggested that there is much to be gained for legal scholars from obtaining at least the minimum experience of legal practice. But McKechnie's appointment is a rare example of a professional academic being elected by a professional body for a coveted post. He was, indeed, the first professionally trained academic – published doctorate and all – to be appointed to a chair of law in a Scottish university. He voluntarily created honours courses for advanced study. With his scholarly background, and his own experience of professional practice, it is near certain that McKechnie would have been intimately familiar with the history and tradition of the Chairs of Conveyancing in Glasgow and Edinburgh. There was thus an obvious subject for his inaugural lecture. So, in the autumn of 1916, McKechnie chose to address the matter of professional pride that had hung over the lecturers and professors of Conveyancing – members, to a man, of the lower branch of the profession – for over a century: "Conveyancing as a University Study."[31] It may be, in no small part, due to the stature of men like McKechnie in the twentieth century that the Chairs of Conveynacing have maintained, until now, such a central role in the Scottish Universities. But McKechnie's appointment was of wider significance still: McKechnie's career set the mould for the full-time professional legal academic in Scotland.[32]

---

29 The election took place on 2 March 1916: *Glasgow Herald*, 3 March 1916.

30 Murray noted this on the front of Donaldson's application. Donaldson, on the vote, was placed seventh.

31 Murray's collection (n 16) preserves a flyer for the lecture: Wednesday 18th October 1916 at 4.30pm.

32 W S McKechnie's son, Sheriff Hector McKechnie KC too would make a significant

(6) The end of an era

In 1970, the holder of the Chair was J M Halliday.[33] Amongst many other works, Halliday published a commentary on the Conveyancing and Feudal Reform (Scotland) Act 1970. The preface records that he was indebted to Mr Robert Rennie for being "largely responsible for preparation of the index."[34] I suspect this invaluable contribution to a standard text was what may have been, in University language, Robert's first "scholarly collaboration" (Robert, with characteristic modesty, described to me his input to that commentary more prosaically: "that's all you were allowed to do in those days"!) But however that may be, I have chosen to honour Robert's service as a worthy holder of a Chair which has had many worthy holders by delving into areas surrounding the practical operations of the assignation of rights in security.

B. Two Aspects of Standard Securities

The "accessory principle" is a well-known principle common to most European legal systems. The accessory principle applies, in particular, to securities, whether real securities (such as the landlord's hypothec) or personal securities (such as cautionary obligations). The accessory principle has a number of aspects. One is that the accessory, the security, cannot exist in the abstract, for it is parasitic to the principal. Discharge of the principal debt thus extinguishes, *ex lege*, the accessory security. Another aspect is transfer: where the principal goes, so too must the accessory security follow (*accessorium sequitur principale*).[35] Cautionary obligations and floating charges – the subject of Robert's PhD[36] – are good examples of where assignation may occur automatically.[37]

---

contribution to the study of Scots law in his work as the first Literary Director of the Stair Society.

33 Halliday himself was honoured with a valuable *Festschrift:* D J Cusine (ed) *A Scots Conveyancing Miscellany: Essays in Honour of J M Halliday* (1987).

34 J M Halliday, *The Conveyancing and Feudal Reform (Scotland) Act 1970* (1970) v.

35 *Selby v Brough* (1794) 2 Ross LC 661 at 666 per Lord President Campbell; *Watson v Bogue (No.1)* 2000 *SLT* (Sh Ct) 125 and *Trotter v Trotter* 2001 *SLT* (Sh Ct) 42.

36 R Rennie, *Floating Charges: A Treatise from the Standpoint of Scots Law* (PhD, University of Glasgow, 1971).

37 Assignation of standard securities, as will be seen, is covered by an express statutory provision: Conveyacing and Feudal Reform (Scotland) Act 1970, s 14, which innovates on the common law *accessorium sequitur principale* rule. The assignation of floating charges, in contrast, is regulated by the ordinary law of assignation and thus more easily effected.

As Andrew Steven has demonstrated, however, the Scottish standard security pays little heed to such fundamental doctrines as the accessory principle.[38] On Steven's examination the standard security proves not to be much of an accessory security at all.[39] But the problems to which the accessory principle seeks to provide answers often relate not to questions of property law – who holds the security – but to questions of debt:[40] which debts, incurred to which creditor, are covered? It is this general issue I wish to address in this contribution in the context of the assignation of all sums securities.

C. Further Advances

(1) Heritable securities pre-1970

Prior to the introduction of the standard security with the Conveyancing and Feudal Reform (Scotland) Act 1970, there were three ways of constituting a heritable security: (i) the pecuniary real burden; (ii) the bond and disposition in security and (iii) the *ex facie* absolute disposition qualified by back letter.[41] For present purposes, suffice it to say that one of the drawbacks of the bond and disposition in security was that it was security only for the sums advanced by the creditor on or around[42] the time the security was taken – further advances made after the security had been taken were liable to founder on the Bankruptcy Act 1696 which struck at "debts contracted for thereafter."[43] All sums securities could not therefore be effectually created over real rights in

38 A J M Steven, "Accessoriness and Security over Land" (2009) 13 *Edinburgh Law Review* 387.

39 Steven (n 38).

40 For the statutory definition of which, see n 55 below.

41 A pecuniary real burden, such as a ground annual, could also be used to create a *debitum fundi*, but normally only in favour of a predecessor in the feudal chain. It could not generally be used in order to secure a loan from a bank not already a party to the feudal relationship. It was accepted that the money need not be advanced until after the debtor had signed.

42 It was accepted that the money need not be advanced until after the debtor had signed the bond for the money: *Dunbar v Abercromby* (1789) 2 Ross LC 638 at 644 *per* Lord Eskgrove. "The limits of this rule," Gloag conceded, "are not very easy to define": Gloag and Irvine, *Rights in Security* (1897) 67. Today the issues often arise under the Insolvency Act 1986, s 245, for which, see *Re Shoe Lace Ltd* [1992] BCC 367 at 369-70 per Hoffmann J, affd [1993] BCC 609.

43 RPS 1696/9/57. It is necessary to appreciate the distinction between sasine and infeftment which, until the Infeftment Act 1845, were two separate procedures: see *Burnett's Tr v Grainger* 2004 SC (HL) 19 at para [91] *per* Lord Rodger of Earlsferry.

land;[44] moreover, according to Lord Justice Clerk Braxfield, an agreement to provide credit was not, for the purposes of the 1696 Act, a debt.[45]

But the law developed. From 1814, the creation of a revolving facility was permitted by way of the cash credit bond and disposition in security where credit to a certain sum was committed up to which limit the borrower could redraw even after the granting of the security.[46] Another development was the recognition that the security conferred on a holder of an *ex facie* absolute disposition was such as to cover further advances. The borrower under such a security was not the owner of the lands secured: the security holder became the owner and the borrower had a reversionary personal right to reconveyance of his property on repayment of the indebtedness to the security holder. And this right to reconveyance could itself be used as a security. So suppose Brian granted to the Bank of Scotland for "all sums due or which hereafter may become due" an *ex facie* absolute disposition to the Bank of Scotland. Having borrowed £1,000 from the Bank of Scotland at 8%, the Bank of Ireland offers him credit for a second ranking security at 7%. Brian assigns his reversionary right in security to the Bank of Ireland. Intimation of that security to the Bank of Scotland has the effect of limiting the existing security for the sums already advanced. Although not spelled out in the speeches of the House of Lords in *Union Bank of Scotland Ltd v National Bank of Scotland Ltd*,[47] the rationale for the rule where a second ranking security is constituted, was stated by Lord Chelmsford in *Hopkinson v Rolt* to be to ensure that no "perpetual curb is imposed on the mortgagor's right to encumber his equity of redemption."[48] The rationale is similar to that underlying the doctrine of catholic and secondary creditors: the catholic

44 *M'Lellan's Creditors* (1734) House of Lords, unreported: see Erskine, 2.3.50 and Bell, *Commentaries* (7th edn 1870) II, 730.

45 *Stein's Creditors v Newnham, Everett & Co* (1794) 2 Ross LC 648 at 650 (in which the Lord President sat as Lord President Probationer). See too Lord Braxfield in *Pickering v Smith* (1788) 2 Ross LC 645 at 647: "An infeftment is not to dance backward and forward; if extinguished today, it cannot revive tomorrow." Braxfield's view is not modern Scots law.

46 Payment of Creditors (Scotland) Act 1814 (54 Geo III, c 37) s 14. Statutory authority for such a revolving facility remains in the form of the Debts Securities (Scotland) Act 1856 (19 & 20 Vict, c 91), s 7 and, in addition, 1970 Act, s 9(6): "The Bankruptcy Act 1696, in so far as it renders a heritable security of no effect in relation to a debt contracted after the recording of that security, and any rule of law which required that a real burden for money may only be created in respect of a sum specified at the date of creation, shall not apply in relation to a standard security."

47 (1886) 14 R (HL) 1, following the decision of the House in an English appeal, *Hopkinson v Rolt* (1861) ER 829.

48 *Hopkinson* (n 47) 845.

creditor cannot be allowed to (ab)use his position to destroy the security of subsequent creditors. In modern terms, the policy could be stated to be to encourage competitive lending and to ensure that any attempts by the first creditor, in contract, to monopolise his position as lender to the borrower, is not supported by the general law.

(2) Clayton's case issues

In a case where there are two separate securities – one ranking after the other – the effect of notice of the subsequent security crystallises the sum due. Crystallisation is also important in order to apply the rule in *Clayton's case*,[49] that the earliest debit is extinguished by the earliest credit. In the event that the first creditor does not rule off the crystallised sum, and ensure any further advances (such as cheques honoured after the crystallisation date) are recorded in a separate account: otherwise any repayments made by the debtor will automatically reduce the secured (pre-crystallisation sum) rather than the unsecured sum (post-crystallisation advances).

(3) The modern law

But the modern statutory provisions allow the first ranking security holder to maintain his priority for "any future debt which, under the contract to which the security relates, he is required to allow the debtor in the security to incur."[50] The scope of the rule on further advances is thus much reduced under s 13. Moreover, with the abolition of the ranking preference afforded by an inhibition,[51] many of the issues surrounding further advances and which Robert explored in detail,[52] no longer arise. There is also the curious discrepancy between the provisions of the Conveyancing and Feudal Reform (Scotland) Act 1970 and the Companies Act 1985 on the case of further advances by second ranking security holder. Originally both acts contained the wording still found in the Companies Acts: where a second ranking security is taken which is intimated to the first ranking security

49 *Devaynes v Noble (Clayton's Case)* (1816) 35 ER 767 at 793. See further P Hood, "Clayton's Case and Connected Matters" 2013 *Juridical Review* 501-39.

50 1970 Act, s 13(1)(b). Unlike under Land Registration Act 2002, s 49 there is no need for the obligation to make further advances to appear on the register. For floating charges, see Companies Act 1985, s 464(5)(b): "future advances which he may be required to make under the instrument creating the floating charge or under any ancillary document."

51 Bankruptcy and Diligence (Scotland) Act etc 2007, s 154.

52 R Rennie, "Inhibitions, Standard Securities and Further Advances" (1994) 39 *JLSS* 52.

holder, the effect of intimation is to restrict the first-ranking security to the "advances" presently made or which he may be required to make.[53] The 1970 Act was, however, amended in 2003 in the course of the *Entfeudalisierung* of Scottish immoveable property law,[54] as a result of which "advances" was replaced in s 13 of the 1970 Act with the more readily intelligible "debts." "Debts" is defined in the 1970 Act to include any obligation, whether or not it is an obligation to pay money.[55] "Advance," in contrast, is limited to money claims. How the s 13 notice works in a case where there is a standard security in respect of a continuing obligation by the debtor to do something other than to pay money is obscure.

(4) Relevance to assignation cases

The point about further advances is that the authorities referred to relate always to the situation where there are two separate security rights. The modern legislation – s 13 of the 1970 Act and s 464(5) of the 1985 Act – now expressly sanctions the situation where the first ranking security holder (subject to the law of catholic and secondary creditors) can maintain his priority for further advances. That this position has been reached in the context of two securities is important when we turn to consider the policy and principle that should apply in the case of an assignation of a single security.

D. Assignation of All Sums Securities

(1) Gretton's article on all sums securities

Another contributor to this *Festschrift* in Robert's honour is himself an honoured member of that most exclusive club, dwindling – with Robert's retirement – to three members *ordinarius*, and known to Lords of Appeal in

53 Companies Act 1985, s 464(5).

54 Title Conditions (Scotland) Act 2003, s 111. The operation of s 13 of the 1970 is excluded in relation to the issue of perpetual debentures under s 736 of the Companies Act 2006: Redemption of Standard Securities (Scotland) Act 1971, s 2. Section 4 of the 1971 Act provides that the 1970 Act and the 1971 Act may be cited together as the "Conveyancing and Feudal Reform (Scotland) Acts 1970 and 1971."

55 1970 Act, s 9(8)(c): "'debt' means any obligation due, or which will or may become due, to repay or pay money, including such obligation arising from a transaction or part of transaction in the course of any trade, business or profession, and any obligation to pay an annuity or *ad factum praestandum*, but does not include an obligation to pay any … rent or other periodical sum payable in respect of land, and 'creditor' and 'debtor' shall be construed accordingly."

Ordinary as "the Professors of Conveyancing:"[56] Professor George Gretton. It was Gretton who first recognised the importance of Lord Dunpark's decision in *Sanderson's Trs v Ambion Scotland Ltd.*[57] Judgment was given in 1977 and, until it was belatedly reported in 1994, was not widely known.

(2) Sanderson's Trs

The case was unusual. S Ltd granted to H Ltd a standard security over development land. H Ltd then assigned its standard security to the trustees of a discretionary trust, in security, for a loan of £28,000. The standard security was granted for all sums due or to become due by S Ltd to H Ltd. The standard security and the assignation of it were recorded, in the order of standard security followed by assignation, on the same day. Following registration, the trustees made further advances to S Ltd. S Ltd then went into receivership. The trustees claimed that the further advances were covered by the standard security which they held as assignees. The trustees raised an action to enforce.

Assignations of standard securities are permitted by s 14 of the Conveyancing and Feudal Reform (Scotland) Act 1970. That section provides:

> Any standard security duly registered or recorded may be transferred in whole or in part, by the creditor by an assignation in conformity with Form A or B of schedule 4 to this Act, and upon such an assignation being duly registered or recorded, the security, or, as the case may be, part thereof, shall be vested in the assignee as effectually as if the security or the part had been granted in his favour.

Form A appeared to require specification of either (a) the certain sum for which a security is granted; (b) a maximum sum of £X, to the extent of £Y being the amount now due thereunder; or (c) other cases described in terms of a Note to the form.[58] In *Sanderson's Trs*, because the standard security

---

56 Lord Rodger of Earlsferry, *The Church, the Courts and the Constitution* (2008) 95: "That feudal law, which has a strong claim to being the real intellectual achievement of the Scottish judges, was unceremoniously binned by the Scottish Parliament, unmourned even by its supposed acolytes, the Professors of Conveyancing." Although, as Robert has pointed out, he is the last Professor to hold a titular Chair of Conveyancing: R Rennie, "The End of Conveyancing as we know it" (2003) 48(11) *JLSS* 15 and "A Tale of Two Systems" (2014) 59(11) *JLSS* 13.

57 1994 *SLT* 645 OH.

58 The Note is in these terms: "In an assignation, discharge or deed of restriction (1) a standard security in respect of an uncertain amount may be described by specifying

assigned was in "all sums" terms, it was argued that the assignation was not in Form A terms and thus ineffectual. That argument was shortly disposed of on the basis that "sufficient compliance" with the forms and procedure contained in the 1970 Act, provided that the assignation "so conforms as closely as may be."[59] But Lord Dunpark also provided a number of powerful rationales for why specification of the sum should not be necessary.

His Lordship did not find the pre-1970 law of much assistance. The Bankruptcy Act 1696, as we have seen, rendered invalid any attempt to extend a heritable security to a debt contracted after the recording of the heritable security.[60] The *ex facie* absolute disposition in security, Lord Dunpark recognised, "was the only pre-1970 method of creating a real security for future, as well as for past, loans, without limit of amount."[61] And where the creditor in such a case – the infeft owner – sought to transfer his position, by assignation (of the debt) and disposition (of ownership of the land), there was no requirement to specify the debt assigned.[62]

The next rationale identified by Lord Dunpark was that, in a case where the only party who has an obligation to make further advances is the cedent (the creditor of the outstanding sums) it makes sense for any assignation to crystallise the sums assigned. In such a case, where a creditor seeks to assign the claim presently owed to him with the security, it is necessary to specify the sum assigned. Cedent and assignee need to know what is being assigned. Suppose a facility of £1000 of which £500 is outstanding. Any assignation by the creditor has to specify the sum because the creditor as cedent. For having agreed to a facility of £1000, the cedent has an obligation to extend credit to that sum. The obligation to make further advances cannot be assigned. The case of further advances by a cedent, following assignation of an existing claim plus the security, is the inverse situation of further advances on a

---

shortly the nature of the debt or obligation (e.g. all sums due or to become due) for which the security was granted, adding in the case of an assignation, *to the extent of £X being the amount now due thereunder* and (2) a standard security in respect of a personal obligation constituted in an instrument or instruments other than the standard security itself may be described by specifying shortly the nature of the debt or obligation and referring to the other instrument or instruments by which it is constituted in such manner as will be sufficient identification thereof."

59 1970 Act, s 53(1).

60 Ibid, s 9(6).

61 1994 *SLT* 645 at 649H.

62 This form of security – *fiducia cum creditore* – suffers from the disadvantage that the creditor becomes the owner of the collateral. As a result, the creditor can transfer good title to a third party. The borrower, who pays back the debt, may not then be able to acquire a re-transfer of the property from the creditor, not least in the situation where the creditor has become insolvent.

second security being taken. With assignation, the cedent transfers away the first-ranking position. In a case where there are two securities, one ranking behind the other, the s 13 notice may crystallise the sum for which the first-ranking security holder maintains his first ranking security.

(3) The problems

It was Professor Gretton who highlighted the great practical difficulties which may arise on the assignation of all sums securities, in an article which accompanied the reporting of the *Sanderson's Trs* decision.[63] He used this example: a debtor grants an all-sums security to the Bank of Pictavia. Suppose the loan was originally for £100,000 but the indebtedness is now down to £1,000. The same debtor has unsecured indebtedness to the Bank of Dalriada for £100,000. As Professor Gretton pointed out, were the Bank of Dalriada to take an assignation of the security the debtor would now find himself with £101,000 of secured debt. Suppose, then, Professor Gretton asked, the debtor had concluded missives to sell his property, on the basis that the £1,000 would be discharged from the purchase price. Prior to settlement, the debtor learns that the Bank has assigned its security and that he will need to come up with a redemption figure that is now in six figures. Such a result, Professor Gretton argued, would be "absurd," for it could place the debtor in breach of his missives. Similarly, if the debtor were to be sequestrated shortly after the assignation of the security, the result would be that the Bank of Dalriada had managed to jump the unsecured creditors' queue, without being subject to the law of unfair preferences. For the law of unfair preferences applies only to acts of the debtor.[64] An onerous assignation by one creditor to another, in contrast, like a ranking agreement concluded between creditors, is challengeable neither under statute nor, probably, at common law.[65]

Nonetheless, I suggest that Lord Dunpark's decision was correct and that assignations of all sums securities are permitted. The result, I would suggest, is not absurd, for the following reasons:

63 G L Gretton, "Assignation of All Sums Standard Securities" 1994 *SLT (News)* 207.

64 Bankruptcy (Scotland) Act 1985, s 36(1).

65 Of course, there may be questions about the extent to which an assignation is valid. An assignation of an all sums security for £1,000 (the outstanding indebtedness) could be said to be valid only to the extent of £1,000 of debt.

(i) The debtor seeking to sell his heritable property is, *ex hypothesi*, doing so for a price. That price can be used to pay, in Gretton's example, the Bank of Dalriada (the assignee of the security) at settlement;

(ii) Even in the absence of assignation of the security, the Bank of Dalriada could use diligence by inhibition, the effect of which would cause the same problems as an undischarged standard security (diligence may, of course, not be possible if there has been no default on the unsecured loan to Bank of Dalriada, but if there has been no default somewhere, it is less likely that the BofD would be in the market for a security).[66]

(iii) The argument that the debtor's land "cannot be burdened by the extra £100,000 without his consent,"[67] ignores the fact that the debtor has already expressly, by his own deed, granted an all-sums security.

(iv) The effect of assignation of an all sums standard security is contained, as Gretton observes, in s 14 of the 1970 Act. Section 14 provides that, "upon such an assignation being duly registered or recorded, the security, or, as the case may be, part thereof, shall be vested in the assignee as effectually as if the security or the part had been granted in his favour." The effect of the assignation, therefore, curiously, is *ex tunc*: the security is deemed to have been granted to the assignee from day one.

(v) The assignation of the security would not breach a pre-existing negative pledge clause granted by the debtor: as Gretton himself perceptively observes, the assignation is not an act *of the debtor*. Moreover, the effect of s 14 is to deem the security to have been granted by the debtor to the assignee. If the security, as granted by the debtor, was not a breach of the negative pledge clause, neither is the assignation.

(vi) The assignation forms contained in Schedule 4 to the 1970 Act cannot supply a requirement not mentioned in s 14, namely that any all sum standard security is immediately converted into a security for a fixed sum. The wording of the style assignation in Schedule 4 does appear to envisage specification of a maximum sum for which the security is assigned. That may be for a fixed sum. But there is no good reason why the assignation may not be expressed to mirror the terms of the security itself: for "all sums due and to become due." As the Lord Ordinary held in *Sanderson's Trs v Ambion Scotland Ltd*, an assignation of a standard security is not necessarily disconform to the Act if it does not state the sum due to the cedent at the date of the assignation. The

66 The loan agreement between the debtor and the Bank of Dalriada – assuming the unsecured indebtedness arose under a loan – may contain a consent to preservation and execution clause, although, if the debtor is a consumer, Consumer Credit Act 1974, s 93A may prevent summary diligence.

67 Gretton (n 63) at 209.

Lord Ordinary in *Liquidator of Letham Grange Development Co Ltd v Foxworth Investments Ltd*,[68] also held that it is possible to have a hybrid Form A/Form B security. Strict conformity, with either the security or the assignation forms, does not appear to be required, providing the security is consistent with the operative terms of the Act.

(vii) Assignations of personal rights to payment occur without the consent of the debtor. At common law, accessory securities (in the wide sense, including personal securities, such as cautionary obligations) are transferred with an assignation of the claim even if there is no mention of the accessory securities. The debtor's consent to assignation of either the underlying debt or a security granted in respect of that debt is not therefore required.[69]

(viii) Indeed, under the law of catholic and secondary creditors (which applies admittedly as between two or more secured creditors) the law sometimes implies a transfer of securities between creditors, where the creditors, as well as the debtor, do not expressly consent.[70]

(ix) As Gretton observed, it was Professor Halliday's view that in order for an assigned standard security to cover further advances by the assignee, a formal variation of the security would be required.[71] The rationale is that such a variation would supply the debtor's express consent to the security covering post-assignation further advances by the assignee of the security to the debtor. But is the best evidence of the debtor's consent to those further advances being covered not, in fact, the debtor's consent to the acceptance of those further advances? It might be argued that, at the stage any such advances have been made, the debtor would not necessarily know that the security has been assigned, since s 14 envisages registration rather than intimation. But that point is an argument for requiring, as under the general law of assignation, intimation to the debtor in order to interpel the debtor with the effects of the assignation. Further advances by an assignee of the security is yet another situation where it is intimation that could

68 2011 *SLT* 1152 at para [101], *per* Lord Glennie (revd on a different point, [2013] CSIH 13; 2013 *SLT* 445, itself revd [2014] UKSC 41, 2014 *SLT* 775).

69 Even claims arising out of regulated consumer credit agreements which are not secured on land may be freely assigned by the creditor although may be assigned without the debtor's consent (although, between 1 February 2011 until 30 March 2014), Consumer Credit Act 1974, s 82A required the creditor to notify the debtor. The purpose s 82A, and Art 17 of the Consumer Credit Directive 2008/48/EC, was obscure given existing EU members states' private laws on the question.

70 *Littlejohn v Black* (1855) 18 D 207 referred to with approval by Lord Reed in *Szepietowski v National Crime Agency* [2014] UKSC 65, [2014] AC 338 at paras [81]-[84].

71 J M Halliday, *Conveyancing and Feudal Reform (Scotland) Act 1970*, 2nd edn (1977) para 9-07; *Conveyancing Law and Practice* (1987) vol III, para 40-19.

be said to play a central role: until the assignee has intimated the assignation to the debtor, any advances by the assignee will not be covered by the security.[72]

(x) Finally, and perhaps most tellingly, the permissibility of assignation of all-sums securities, in policy terms, can be tested by the mirror-image situation. Take the example of the Bank of Pictavia and the Bank of Dalriada referred to above. The Bank of Pictavia has an all sums security but only £1,000 of indebtedness, while the Bank of Dalriada has unsecured claims for £100,000. There is nothing wrong with the Bank of Pictavia taking an assignation of the Bank of Dalriada's unsecured claim. The effect would be that the all-sums security now covered the £101,000. The effect on any proposed sale by the debtor would be the same.

E. Practicalities

(1) The debtor who has granted an all sums security

All this having been said, however, the practical difficulties highlighted by Professor Gretton remain. Suppose the debtor has concluded missives to sell in the knowledge, in our example, that he has only £1,000 of debt outstanding to the Bank of Pictavia. After conclusion of the missives, he learns that the Bank of Dalriada, to whom he is already indebted to the extent of £100,000 now holds the security. Does this assignation render him in breach of the missives? Any breach of the missives relates to the warranty of "good and marketable title" not to acts of the seller, for, in our example, the seller has done nothing. The assignation is not an act of the seller. How then can the debtor under an all sums security protect himself? There are two practical responses: the first by transactional lawyers, the second by the courts.

(2) The need for intimation

Transactional lawyers seeking redemption statements from a heritable creditor that holds an all sums security need to seek an undertaking that no assignation of the security has taken place or will take place prior to

72 Cf Land Registration (Scotland) Act 2012, s 41. But that applies only to applications under s 21 or 29. An application to register the assignation of a registered standard security would fall under s 26.

settlement. The response of the courts must be to apply by analogy the traditional Scottish approach to intimation: although the assignation of the security may take place only on registration, that registration cannot affect the debtor, even with respect to existing indebtedness, unless and until the assignee of the security has interpelled the debtor by intimating the assignation of the all sums security to him. For because assignation takes place without the debtor's consent, the debtor cannot be prejudiced by that about which he does not know and about which he has no obligation to inquire. The result is that if a debtor concludes missives to sell, without having received intimation of the assignation of the security, the security, in any question with the debtor, cannot cover more than was due to the original creditor. The debtor, *qua* seller, has no obligation to run searches to check that the holder of his all sums security has not changed. That this is the correct analysis can be tested by asking the question of what would happen in the mirror-image situation where the creditors agree between themselves to assign not the security but the claim: the unsecured creditor assigns the claim to the holder of the all sums security. That assignation has effect against the debtor only from the date of intimation. If the debtor has entered into missives to sell the property, but between missives and settlement there has been a registration of an assignation of the security,[73] the seller cannot be prejudiced until the assignation has been intimated to him: he need redeem only to the extent of £1,000.[74] As a result of that payment, he is entitled to a discharge of the security from the assignee who, in turn, may have a claim against the cedent. The assignee *may* have a breach of warrandice claim against the cedent, but probably not. For the warrandice in an assignation of a claim plus security is only *debitum subesse*: the debt is due and owing. But for warrandice purposes, as for others, that warranty can be given only at the date of the assignation. Take again the example of £1,000 owed by the seller under a standard security, which is assigned to another creditor who has unsecured indebtedness

73 Of course, in most cases involving a sale, a registration of an assignation of the security prior to settlement will be picked up in the searches, alerting the buyer to the need for a discharge from the assignee.

74 The Scottish Law Commission is likely to recommend superseding intimation as a constitutive requirement for completing an assignation with registration: Scottish Law Commission, Discussion Paper on Moveable Transactions (2011) ch 11. But intimation will remain, as it does in other legal systems which allow for effective assignation without intimation, for practical purposes to "interpel" the debtor.

of £100,000. In ignorance of any assignation of the security, the borrower concludes missives to sell the property in good faith. The borrower cannot be prejudiced by the assignation and the assignee must be considered to have bought a claim only of £1,000, albeit with an all sums security. In order for the assignee of the security to interpel the debtor with knowledge that the assignee now has an all sums security which, because of pre-existing outstanding indebtedness to the assignee now encompasses £101,000, intimation by the assignee to the borrower is required.

(3) Further advances

The question often arises whether an assignee of an all sums security is secured for any further advances made by the security holder. Providing there is no competition with any other security holder, no problems will arise. As I have indicated, any problems which may be thought to occur with the assignation of an all sums security, can often be avoided if, as is often the case in corporate groups, that it would be possible to effect the assignation of the claim to the existing all sums security holder. This is often the easiest way to deal with further advances issues that may arise. In the event that the security is assigned then, depending as always on the terms of the documentation, it may well be that the provisions of s 14 – deeming, on registration of the assignation, the security always to have been held by the assignee – are sufficient to cover any advances that the assignee may propose to make.

(4) Practical results

In the result, therefore, although I have disagreed with some of the reasoning first offered by Professor Gretton in his pioneering article on the assignation of all sums securities 20 years ago, and with which all studies of this subject must begin, we are not far apart either on principle or in the result. The assignation of all sums securities – including cases involving the taking of standard securities over existing standard securities which sometimes incorporate assignations[75] – needs to be carefully thought through. I, for one, would not go quite as far as Sheriff Cusine in describing

75 See e.g. *UK Acorn Finance Ltd v Smith*, [2014] Sh Ct Banff 25 (14 July 2014).

the assignation of standard securities for a fluctuating amount, as in the case of an "all sums" security as "undesirable,"[76] although, as I have sought to highlight, the lack of careful thought leaves a potential mine field of problems for the unwary. But, with careful preparation, there may be a number of practical advantages, particularly in the corporate sphere, to be gained from taking the assignation of all sums securities. In most cases, however, if, at the outset, there is a likelihood for a need to assign or allow the possibility of further participation in the secured creditor's position, Gloag's advice, given over a century ago, remains good: the all sums security and indebtedness should be constituted in favour of a security trustee, with further participation taking place privately between the creditors.[77] The delights of partial assignations of all-sums securities may be left for another time.[78]

F. Conclusions

Robert Rennie's retiral marks not just the end of chapter of a busy professional life: it also marks a sad break for an institution which, for centuries, has maintained close contact with its own graduates in the legal profession in the West of Scotland. The University has paid Robert a back-handed compliment of sorts by deeming Robert to be irreplaceable and making no attempts to refill the Chair. The decision not to replace Robert brings an end to a significant chapter in the history of law teaching in the Scottish universities. What started with the appointment of Macvey Napier to the Edinburgh Conveyancing Chair in 1824 comes to an end with the retirement of Robert Rennie as the holder of the Glasgow Chair in 2014. At a stroke, vast numbers of arbitration clauses, tucked away in Deeds of Conditions to a significant proportion of Glasgow's tenement properties, appointing the Professor of Conveyancing in the University as arbiter, may be frustrated.[79] The professionalism of local practitioners is also likely to avoid the unseemly situation of other Professors of Law in the University, with considerably less experience of Conveyancing than even the great scholar McKechnie, being approached to accept an appointment to rule on

76 D J Cusine, *Standard Securities* (1991) para 6-11; D J Cusine and R Rennie, *Standard Securities*, 2nd edn (2002) para 6-06.

77 W M Gloag and J Irvine, *Rights in Security* (1897) 126, n 5.

78 See e.g. Gloag and Irvine (n 77) 126.

79 Anecdotal evidence suggests that these clauses are only infrequently invoked.

the finer points of the abstruse science. But I prefer to close by focussing instead on Robert's qualities as a man, in particular his industry, integrity and, above all, good humour.

The University of Glasgow without the waist-coated Professor Rennie will be a poorer place; but the University, without a Professor of Conveyancing at all, will be a poorer place still.

2

Completion of the Land Register: The Scottish Approach

John King

A. Introduction

Scotland can lay claim to the world's oldest, still running, public property register. Dating from 1617,[1] the Register of Sasines has witnessed the industrial revolution, the extension of the franchise and the spread of property ownership. It is a real success story; the authors of the Act got it right first time, and deed registration became a concept which was subsequently adopted, in various guises, across the world.

Scotland also has one of the most recent land registration systems by international standards. The Land Register was a late introduction to Scotland: the Land Registration (Scotland) Act 1979 ("the 1979 Act") commenced in 1981, albeit only for the operational county of Renfrew.[2] It took a further 22 years before the Land Register was extended to all registration counties in Scotland.[3] The 1979 Act has enabled the registration

1 Registration Act 1617.

2 Land Registration (Scotland) Act 1979 (Commencement n 1) Order 1980, SI 1980/1412.

3 The Land Registration (Scotland) Act 1979 (Commencement n 16) Order 2002, SI 2002/432, brought on to the Land Register the registration counties of Banff, Moray, Nairn, Ross and Cromarty, Caithness, Sutherland and Orkney and Zetland.

of over 1.5 million properties in Scotland but it has not been without challenge or criticism.

One commentator scathingly described the Act as "having all the intellectual sharpness of mashed potato."[4] Consequently, within 12 years of the 1979 Act operating throughout Scotland (though doubts persisted as to whether or not it also extended to Scotland's seabed as well as its land), it has been reformed and replaced, subject to transitional provisions, by the Land Registration etc. (Scotland) Act 2012 ("the 2012 Act").

One of the key policy aims that lay behind the 2012 Act was enabling the completion of the Land Register. No timescale for completion was provided in the Act, though the Economy, Energy and Tourism Committee recommended the "setting of a target and interim targets, even if aspirational, on the face of the Bill."[5] This was not an approach that found favour with the Minister responsible for the Bill.[6] However, other factors have subsequently influenced Scottish Ministers to set a timescale for completion.

In May 2014 the final report of the Land Reform Review Group was presented to Scottish Ministers.[7] Established by the Scottish Government in May 2012, the ground had a remit to consider a broad spectrum of land reform issues. One of the areas it considered was coverage of the Land Register and it recommended that:[8]

> ...the Scottish Government should be doing more to increase the rate of registrations to completion of the Register, a planned programme to register public lands and additional triggers to induce the first registration of other lands.

Following consideration of that report, Paul Wheelhouse MSP, the Minister for Environment and Climate Change, made the following announcement:[9]

> Along with my colleague Enterprise Minister Fergus Ewing, I have asked Registers of Scotland to prepare to complete land registration within 10 years, with all public land registered within five years

4 Professor George Gretton commenting on *Kaur v Singh*: see 1997 SCLR 1075 at 1085.
5 Scottish Parliament Official Report, Economy, Energy and Tourism Committee, 6 Mar 2012, col 58.
6 Land Registration etc. (Scotland) Bill: Economy, Energy and Tourism Committee Stage 1 Report – Scottish Government Response (2012).
7 Land Reform Review Group, *The Land of Scotland and the Common Good* (2014).
8 Para 32.
9 Scottish Government, "Target Set to Register all Scotland's Land" (news release), 25 May 2014.

So, some 33 years since land registration was introduced to Scotland, we now have a target for completing the Land Register by the end of 2024. This essay seeks to offer a definition of completion, considers the contrasting approaches to completion under both the 1979 Act and the 2012 Act, compares these with the English and Welsh experience and asks whether or not the legal tools exist to enable completion within the ten year target.

B. The Case for Completion

Setting aside discussion over the timescale for completion, the suggestion that a completed Land Register is desirable is likely to be met with general approval. That was certainly the emphasis of the evidence provided to the Economy, Energy and Tourism committee. They reported that there "was overwhelming support from witnesses for a Land Register that is reliable, secure and accessible and for the eventual closure of the Register of Sasines."[10]

The arguments in favour of a completed Land Register have been well rehearsed in recent years. The Scottish Law Commission (SLC) succinctly stated that "the short answer is that the Land Register is better than the Register of Sasines"[11] and then detailed why this was so. Similarly the Consultation Document on completion of the Land Register[12] ("the completion consultation document") lists the benefits. Indeed, glancing south of the Border, the website of Her Majesty's Land Registry (HMLR)[13] also lists near identical reasons why registration in the Land Register and the aim of a completed register is so desirable. So, what are the reasons?

The completion consultation document sets out four compelling reasons: transparency, cost, efficiency and national asset. Transparency is self-evident. A map-based register of title to land makes for simple interrogation and so provides ease of access to information on who owns Scotland. That, in turn, reduces the costs associated with examination of titles: it takes less

10 Scottish Parliament, Official Report, Economy, Energy and Tourism Committee, 6 Mar 2012, col 19.

11 Scottish Law Commission, Report on *Land Registration* (Scot Law Com n 222, 2012) vol 1 para 33.17.

12 Registers of Scotland, Completion of the Land Register Public Consultation (2014).

13 Land Registry, Practice Guide 1: First Registrations (2003) para 1.2, available at http://www.gov.uk/government/publications/first-registrations/practice-guide-1-first-registrations. One additional advantage they list is making large holdings of land and portfolios of charges more readily marketable.

time and effort to examine an entry on the Land Register than it does if a property is held under title deeds on the Sasine Register. Added to this, the SLC has highlighted[14] the growing issue that some younger conveyancers may not have the requisite knowledge of the workings of Sasine titles.

For a country of Scotland's size, it is inefficient to have two property registers. The Land Register makes it easier to transact with property, which in turn, facilitates the property market and makes Scotland attractive to foreign investment. At a macro level, transparency, ease of access and the guarantee of title adds value to the economy. That fits with the final reason provided by the completion consultation document for a completed Land Register being a national asset. Knowing who owns Scotland and having access to that information supports those public and private bodies and companies whose administrative and business activities require use of accurate title information. The Land Reform Review Group also commented[15] on the difficulties of having an informed discussion on land reform and land use in the absence of comprehensive information on land ownership in Scotland.

Though there is general consensus that a completed Land Register would be an unqualified positive for Scotland, the fact the journey to that end is set against the backdrop of a near 400-year old deeds register is to our advantage. It is more helpful to have two property registers than to simply have one incomplete Land Register. If a property is not on the Land Register, there is a very high chance it will rest on deeds in the Sasine Register. In short, except for an indeterminate but expected low volume of properties not on either register, it is generally possible, albeit at times with difficulty, to identify the title deed or potential title deed that relates to an area of land.

Contrast that with England and Wales. There is one national property register, Her Majesty's Land Register ("HMLR"), but it is not yet complete. Approximately 15% of the land mass of England and Wales is not on HMLR.[16] Tracking information on non-registered land is anything but straightforward; there may be some information in local registers or there may simply be no information available. So, as much as there are solid reasons for completing Scotland's Land Register, we should recognise that

14 Scottish Law Commission, Report on *Land Registration* (n 11) vol 1 para 33.18.
15 Land Reform Review Group, *The Land of Scotland and the Common Good* (n 7) Ch 23.
16 HM Land Registry, *Annual Report and Accounts 2013/14* (2014) 43.

other jurisdictions with incomplete Land Registers may look at us with envy over the continuing safety net that an old deeds register can provide.

C. What Constitutes Completion?

In being asked to complete the register within ten years, it is clearly essential that the Keeper sets out what this entails. This allows progress to be monitored and expectations to be managed. There are various interpretations that can be suggested.

First, completing the Land Register could be viewed as achieved when the Sasine Register is closed to new deeds of any type. RoS estimates that there are some 1.1 million property titles[17] remaining in the Sasine Register. The rate at which titles transfer from the Sasine Register to the Land Register has averaged at an annual rate of 40,270 first registrations over the last ten years.[18] On the designated commencement day for the 2012 Act, 8 December 2014 ("the designated day"), the Sasine Register closed to all dispositions. Over the last ten years, an average of 22,850 dispositions have been recorded each year in the Sasine Register.[19]

The 2012 Act contains powers under section 48(2) and (3) which, if used in full, could have the effect of closing the Sasine Register to all deeds. The mechanics and practicalities of this are discussed later. Of course that would not make the Sasine Register redundant; it would simply up the pace with which properties transfer on to the Land Register. In 2013-14 some 35,000 deeds were recorded in the Sasine Register, affecting an estimated 25,000 different properties and interests in land.[20] Notwithstanding the increased pace with which properties would move on to the Land Register, the fact remains that the two property registers would continue to co-exist for potentially many decades. So, closure of the Sasine Register to new deeds would not equate with a completed Land Register.

Secondly, taking the first interpretation a step further, completion could be viewed as achieved when all properties and interests held on title deeds recorded in the Sasine Register are brought on to the Land Register. Unquestionably that would be a significant achievement, as it would enable the Sasine Register to take a well-earned retirement amongst Scotland's

---

17 Registers of Scotland (RoS) estimates, current as of November 2014.
18 Based on Land Register intake figures from April 2004-March 2014.
19 Sasine Register Minute Book entries April 2004-March 2013.
20 Sasine Register Minute Book April 2013-March 2014.

national archives. However in terms of Scotland's new Cadastral Map there would still be gaps. In land registration parlance, there would still be tracts of land without a red edge delineating ownership boundaries. There would still be unregistered land and so the Land Register would not be complete.

Thirdly, the most comprehensive interpretation of completion combines interpretations (i) and (ii) and seeks to add to that the remaining unregistered land. That would provide a complete cadastral map for Scotland reflecting ownership of land, identifying long leases over land and also detailing ownership of separate tenements in that land. It is currently impossible to ascertain the full extent of land that does not fall within either the Land Register or the Sasine Register. Within RoS we have anecdotal knowledge of some such land, for example the original land holdings of St Andrews University and some City of Edinburgh Council land holdings in Edinburgh's Old Town. The full extent of unregistered land will only become apparent when all properties and interests held on title deeds recorded in the Sasine Register are in turn registered in the Land Register. Much of this land will have seen ownership transferred via charters and deeds that were executed prior to the establishment of the Sasine Register. It is also possible that some of this land will have been gifted as common good land, may be undivided commonty or may, if never alienated, remain with the Crown.

It is also inevitable that some of this notionally unregistered land will ultimately trace back to titles on the Sasine Register that were considered to have previously transferred to the Land Register. This is not surprising; aside from the difficulties in interpreting often vague Sasine deed descriptions, the prescribed application form[21] for a first registration under the 1979 Act invites the applicant to advise if they will accept the Land Register boundaries reflecting the occupied extent where that is less than the legal extent as set out in the deeds. Whilst this provision can often resolve what would otherwise be a boundary issue with a neighbouring property that also includes the same area within its title deeds, there are instances where slithers of land excluded from Land Register titles will not fall into any other titles.

An applicant may choose not to include land outwith their physical boundaries (fence, hedge etc.) within the Land Register title. This may

21 Land Register (Scotland) Rules 2006, SSI 2006/485, r 9(i)(a) (Part B question 2(a)).

satisfy the expectations of a purchaser in a first registration transaction but it does mean that the seller may remain, unwittingly in most cases, the owner of the excluded interest. It is not uncommon for such slithers to be considered abandoned and unused by anyone or to be possessed as part of a neighbouring property extent without being contained within the legal title for that property. Identifying and resolving these unintended consequences of the operation of land registration under the 1979 Act will be challenging, though it may be that the new 2012 Act provisions for prescriptive claimants[22] will provide a vehicle for bringing some of these strips of land on to the Land Register.

The completion consultation document sets the bar high. It favours the comprehensive interpretation. It is noted that even if this point is achieved, the cadastral map will not remain unchanged; it is a living map and registered extents will change to reflect sub-divisions and amalgamations of property.

D. Completion: Achievable or Unattainable?

All three of the above possible interpretations talk in terms of absolutes when considering what could constitute completion. The question that arises is whether or not it is practical to talk in terms of absolutes or is that an aspiration that is simply too high. The answer depends in large part on whether or not legal powers exist to enable completion or not. If the legal powers do exist, and there is a political commitment to maximising the use and effect of those powers, then absolute completion is not a forlorn aspiration. Equally, starting from a position whereby legal powers on their own would not be sufficient to achieve completion would suggest that any target ought to be more modest.

(1) England and Wales: the comprehensive register

There has long been an unsubstantiated anecdotal view amongst RoS registration staff that HMLR must be near completion. That view was informed by two factors (three if you include the absence of any research): first, the awareness that the Land Register stems from 1862,[23] and secondly the application of a little relative mathematics. The argument runs that if

22 Land Registration etc (Scotland) Act 2012, ss 43-45.
23 Land Registry Act 1862.

the Land Register has been in existence for over 150 years, it must be near complete if our own Land Register has 58%[24] of properties on it after a mere 33 years. Set in the context of a pub quiz for land registrars, it is doubtful if many would correctly answer 54.5% if asked to estimate the end March 2006[25] figure for land mass coverage of England and Wales. Clearly, our view has been wrong.

It has taken a considerable period of time for their Land Register to gain traction. Although the Land Registry Act 1862 established a land register for England and Wales, it did not back its introduction with any element of direct or indirect compulsion. Consequently, by 1868, only 507 titles were registered. The need for compulsion was recognised, albeit in a less than robust fashion by the Land Transfer Act of 1897; local counties could still veto the introduction of compulsory registration.[26] As a result, adoption was slow.[27]

Compulsion was to the fore in the Land Registration Act 1925, as provision was made for the Sovereign, by Order in Council, to make registration following a sale compulsory in any area.[28] It is reported that forecasts at the time suggested that compulsory registration would be extended to all areas by 1955. This was not to be and the remaining 14 areas were not brought within the ambit of the Land Registry until 1 December 1990.[29] At this point there were some 12.7 million registered titles whereas now there are some 23.8 million.[30] Before the introduction of computer mapping the Land Registry was not able to work out the percentage of land registered. So, the fully-operational English and Welsh Land Register is only some 13 years ahead of our own wholly-operational Land Register.

HMLR do now have a considerably more comprehensive range of legal triggers for registration, referred to under section 4 of the Land Registration

24 Registers of Scotland, *Completion of the Land Register Public Consultation* (n 12).

25 Land Register, *Annual Report and Accounts 2005/06* (2006) 14.

26 Under s 20(5)-(6), the Registry had to give 6 months' notice to the council concerned and if within 3 months the Council held a meeting with at least two thirds of councillors present that rejected compulsory registration, then the order could not be made.

27 In 1899 London County Council became the first area to adopt compulsory registration following a sale. An attempt to pass a motion to prevent this under s 20(6) was defeated by 73 votes to 35 (*The Times*, 16 Feb 1898).

28 Land Registration Act 1925 s 120.

29 Registration of Title Order 1989, SI 1987/1347, available at http://www.legislation.gov.uk/uksi/1989/1347/contents/made. These were the districts of Babergh, Castle Point, Forest Heath, Leominster, Maldon, Malvern Hills, Mid Suffolk, Rochford, St Edmundsbury, South Herefordshire, Suffolk Coastal, Tendring, Wychavon and Wyre Forest.

30 HM Land Registry, *Annual Report and Accounts 2013/14* (n 16) 11.

Act 2002 ("the 2002 Act") as the "requirement of registration." The approach under section 4 is to specify a comprehensive list of events, on the occurrence of which the title must be registered. In contrast to Scotland, the 2002 Act specifies that registration must occur within a specified time limit; namely two months from the date on which the trigger event occurred.[31] The penalty for non-compliance is severe: the transfer or grant or creation becomes void "as regards the transfer, grant or creation of a legal estate."[32] So trigger events will result in registration.

As in Scotland, the triggers that generate large volumes of registration applications are the transfer of a freehold estate or a lease for valuable or other consideration or by way of gift. A lengthy list of other triggers is provided for, some of which have proved to be significant in generating registration and countering circumstances where registration may otherwise be avoided. As an example of the former, compulsory registration applies on the creation by the owner of an estate in unregistered land of a protected first legal mortgage[33] unless it is a mortgage of a lease with no more than seven years to run. (A protected first legal mortgage is defined as one that, on creation, ranks in priority ahead of other mortgages affecting the mortgaged estate).

The latter is illustrated by the requirement for registration on what is termed an assent, including a vesting assent.[34] So the transfer by a trustee or executor to a beneficiary would necessitate registration; this is aimed at countering the situation that occurs in Scotland whereby properties can pass through generations of the same family without any impact on the property registers. Because of the way in which HMLR captures management information it has not been possible to obtain accurate figures to illustrate the impact of these triggers. Discussion with senior HMLR staff suggest both have had a major affect in triggering registration.[35]

There are two other legal vehicles open to HMLR to further completion. The Lord Chancellor may "add to the events on the occurrence of which the requirement of registration applies such relevant event as he may

31 Land Registration Act 2002 s 6.

32 2002 Act s 7(1).

33 Ibid s 4(1)(g).

34 Ibid s 4(1)(a)(ii).

35 John Peaden, Director of Operations. A sampling survey on first registration cases marked off on 1 September 2014 from Birkenhead, Coventry, Croydon, Durham, Fylde, Gloucester, Hull, Leicester, Nottingham and Peterborough offices showed that 11% were triggered by the assent provision.

specify in the order."[36] To date this power has been used once[37] to extend compulsory registration to partitions and most deeds of appointment of new trustees. The only other legal tool available to HMLR is to promote voluntary registration and this has been used with effect.

In 2002, HMLR adopted as part of its corporate strategy the achievement of a "comprehensive register."[38] It was explained that a comprehensive land register:[39]

> ...will include the majority of freehold land forming the surface of England and Wales. The register need not necessarily include leasehold land although we would expect to register those leasehold interests where the leasehold interest is a valuable interest. The register need not include the seabed and the foreshore. Land where the owner cannot be identified and roads, rivers, and other physical features where ownership is not determined by registration. Also, rent charges and certain rights that can be registered (such as the right to fish or hold a market) need not be included in the comprehensive land register. However, we would still encourage the registration of all these Interests.

The choice of the term "comprehensive" reflected the challenge of completion and the acknowledgement that although the legal framework for determining when registration was compulsory was extensive, it would not by itself lead to all properties being registered and to achieve a significant increase in the properties and land mass on the Land Register other steps would be necessary. Those steps subsequently centred around a marketing campaign to promote and encourage voluntary registration. Incentives in the form of a lesser registration fee (25% reduction) and partnership working whereby Land Registry staff were embedded in organisations to help prepare applications were offered. That campaign ran until 2012, when the decision was taken not to actively market voluntary registrations. The workforce in HMLR had been reduced to match registration intakes and an assessment of the costs against the benefits of registering the remaining land mass was considered too high. The decision was taken to allow the trigger provisions to bring on the remainder of unregistered properties, though voluntary registration would still be available.

---

36 Section 5 of the 2002 Act allows s 4 to be amended.

37 The Land Registration Act 2002 (Amendment) Order 2008, SI 2008/2872 which came into force on 6 Apr 2009. Available at http://www.legislation.gov.uk/uksi/2008/2872/introduction/made

38 See the 10 year Strategic Plan included in HM Land Registry, *Annual Report and Accounts 2002/03* (2003).

39 HM Land Registry, *Public Consultation – The Comprehensive Land Register* (2007) 10.

The voluntary registration campaign was a success. By end March 2012, some 23.3 million registered titles existed, accounting for some 79% of the English and Welsh land mass.[40] Notwithstanding that achieving the comprehensive register is no longer part of their corporate strategy, the land mass coverage has continued to grow; by end March 2014, some 84.3% had been registered.[41] HMLR's experience was positive and demonstrates that Scotland is perhaps sitting on an as yet untapped demand for voluntary registration. The volumes of voluntary and compulsory first registrations since 2007 are set out in the table below.[42]

Year	Voluntary FR	Comp FR	Percent Voluntary
2007-08	94,879	235,492	28.7%
2008-09	205,201	166,767	55.2%
2009-10	125,307	148,333	45.8%
2010-11	91,037	144,065	40.4%
2011-12	58,945	127,328	31.6%
2012-13	51,001	126,108	28.8%
2013-14	39,002	129,626	23.1%
Total	665,372	1,077,719	38.2%

(2) Scotland: aiming for the complete Land Register

The focus of the 1979 Act was not on a completed Land Register. More immediate concerns were to the fore, such as introducing land registration to a jurisdiction where the Register of Sasines, and all the conveyancing practices associated with it, had been largely unchanged for some 360 years. The focus was rightly on introduction and not completion of the Land Register, a sentiment strongly to the fore in the earlier Reid and Henry Committee Reports.[43] Notwithstanding that those reports acknowledged

40 Land Registry, *Annual Report and Accounts 2011/12* (2012).

41 HM Land Registry, *Annual Report and Accounts 2013/14* (n 16).

42 Figures provided by HMLR and derived from annual reports.

43 *Registration of Title to Land in Scotland* (Cmnd 2032: 1963) ("the Reid Report") and *Scheme for the Introduction of Registration of Title to Land in Scotland* (Cmnd 4137: 1969) ("the Henry Report").

the benefits of land registration they were both heavily influenced by the possible inconvenience that introduction could bring to those transacting with property and to the Keeper:[44]

> To prevent dislocation of the work of the Keeper and his staff we suggest that the only practicable scheme is to begin introducing registration of title in one Division and then extend it to other Divisions from time to time as circumstances permit. We regard it as impracticable to require the titles of all properties in a Division to be registered within a limited time. We think that the best method would be to make registration of title compulsory on the first transfer for onerous consideration of any property within a designated Division, and to permit registration of title of any property within such Division at any other time if the owner applies for it.

In favour of such an approach, the committee cited two reasons:[45]

> We do not think it would be reasonable to require an owner to incur the expense of registration except on such a transfer, when the title of the property will have to be examined in any event, and therefore the additional expense involved in registration of title will be small. Secondly, it would unduly increase the work of the staff in the Register House to require compulsory registration of title on other occasions.

The Henry Committee reached a similar conclusion.[46] History has shown that their concerns were not overstated: extending land registration to all of Scotland, provisionally timetabled for nine years, ultimately took some 22. This elongated timescale, and the associated build-up of first registration casework that accompanied it, has done much to influence the scepticism with which a number of practitioners view the target of completion within ten years.

The 1979 Act approach generally aligns with what were then the main routes on to the Land Register in England and Wales, namely a transfer for valuable consideration, grant of lease, or through the Keeper accepting a request for voluntary registration. One notable difference with the approach to registration in England and Wales is that the 1979 Act did not make any provision for a time period within which registration should take place after the occurrence of a particular trigger event. Consequently, registration is *prima facie* optional; section 2(1) provides that an unregistered interest in land "shall be registrable."

44 *Registration of Title to Land in Scotland* (n 43) para 91.
45 Ibid.
46 *Scheme for the Introduction of Registration of Title to Land* (n 43) para 11.

There is of course a sting in the tail should registration not be sought, for in the absence of registration no real right will be obtained. As the commentary to the Registration of Title Practice Book narrates, "the compulsitor is that there shall be no real right without registration."[47] There are other factors driving the time frame in which registration ought to occur: limited company standard securities over registered land require registration in the Land Register before they can be registered in the Register of Charges.[48] The protection afforded by letters of obligation and the new advance notices[49] in effect set a time-frame within which registration will, in the main, occur.

Requests for voluntary registration were permissible under the 1979 Act[50] and the Keeper was given the discretion on whether or not to accept such a request. The criterion by which the Keeper should consider such a request is that of expediency. In practice, for the period from 1981 through to the mid-2000s that criterion was tightly applied and voluntary registrations were rare. The emphasis was very much on the impact such a request would have on the Keeper and not on the needs of the applicant. As the Practice Book[51] explains: "the Keeper does not normally accept voluntary registrations unless there are obvious benefits to him." The main source of voluntary registrations related to transfers of a half *pro indiviso* share in a Sasine title. In those circumstances the Keeper would encourage voluntary registration of the remaining half share. The only other circumstance in which the Keeper would regularly accept a request was in connection with a builder or developer's title for which individual plots were about to be sold.

The reason for the reluctance to accept requests was simple: RoS was not coping with the volume of trigger-based registrations and did not want to add to the time it would take to complete those registrations. The Keeper's position began to change in the mid-2000s. There was growing acceptance that the balance of convenience was tipped too heavily in favour of the Keeper. A more relaxed and encouraging approach developed and culminated in a joint article[52] by the current Keeper and Fergus Ewing MSP, the Minister for

47 *Registration of Title Practice Book*, 1st edn (1981) para C02.
48 Companies Act 1985 s 410.
49 Section 58(1) of the 2012 Act provides an advance notice has effect for the period of 35 days.
50 1979 Act s 2(1)(b).
51 *Registration of Title Practice Book*, 2nd edn (2000) para 2.9.
52 F Ewing and S Adams, "All aboard the Land Register," 17 Oct 2011, available at http://www.journalonline.co.uk/Magazine/56-10/1010324.aspx

Energy Economy and Tourism, heralding an effective open door policy. The exceptions to that are limited and relate in the main to ongoing litigation affecting the property to which the request relates. In the last four years, RoS estimate that the volume of voluntary registrations has been in the region of 2000 applications per annum: about 4% of the overall volume of first registrations. That of course compares poorly with the volume of voluntary applications received by HMLR. The open door policy has been supported by some targeted marketing of voluntary registration, mostly around commercial and residential developers and large private estates.

The 1979 Act was not wholly oblivious to the future. The Act states that Ministers may provide:[53]

> ...that interests in land of a kind or kinds specified in the order... shall be registered; and the provisions of this Act shall apply for the purposes of such registration with such modifications, which may include provision as to the expenses of such registration, as may be specified in the order.

The provision has not been used. Commentary in the Practice Book describes this provision somewhat dramatically as "machinery for the elimination of the Register of Sasines."[54] In a nod to the current discussion on funding completion, the then Government did indicate the costs of closing the Sasine Register would, other than in trigger situations, be borne by the public purse.[55]

The problem with the 1979 Act approach is that it allowed for no middle ground. Triggers for registration were set in the legislation and no provision was made for the addition of further triggers. Instead, section 2(5) allowed Scottish Ministers to provide that at a certain point in time those remaining unregistered properties would be registered by the Keeper. Finding an explanation as to how this provision would work in practice is challenging. I am unaware of any detailed discussions within RoS as to its use and there were no plans to suggest to Ministers that it be used. Mindful of the costs associated with section 2(5), the Scottish Executive did suggest in 1999 that consideration of its use would be appropriate when most properties in a registration county had been registered through sale.[56] It indicated that would be the case after 10 to 15 years of land registration. That was an overly optimistic assessment of the pace of completion. In the event, the gap from a limited set of triggers to committing to full registration was considered a leap too far.

53 1979 Act s 2(5).

54 *Registration of Title Practice Book*, 1st edn (n 47) para C16.

55 HC Debs, First Scottish Standing Committee, 27 Mar 1979, col 13.

56 Scottish Executive, Land Reform: Proposals for Legislation (E/1999/1), Para 6.3.

Without question, the 1979 Act has advanced completion. In just under 34 years, some 1.5 million property titles have been registered, estimated at roughly 58% of all properties within Scotland.[57] This is a not inconsiderable figure given that it was April 2003 before all of Scotland was operational under the Act. For the registration counties that were first on to the Land Register, the title coverage is way in excess of the Scottish average; Renfrew stands at 76% and Dumbarton at 74%.[58] More recent converts to the Land Register, particularly those predominantly rural counties, have much less coverage. Both Ross & Cromarty and Caithness have fewest titles registered: an estimated 36%.[59] This is not surprising. Properties in the more economically active and densely populated urban areas change hands more frequently than properties in rural areas.

Under the 1979 Act triggers for registration, completion would simply not be achieved. Some properties never change hands and some transfer for no consideration. RoS forecast that registration counties would peak at around 90% title coverage based on the 1979 Act triggers.[60] Achieving 90% coverage would vary from registration county to registration county:

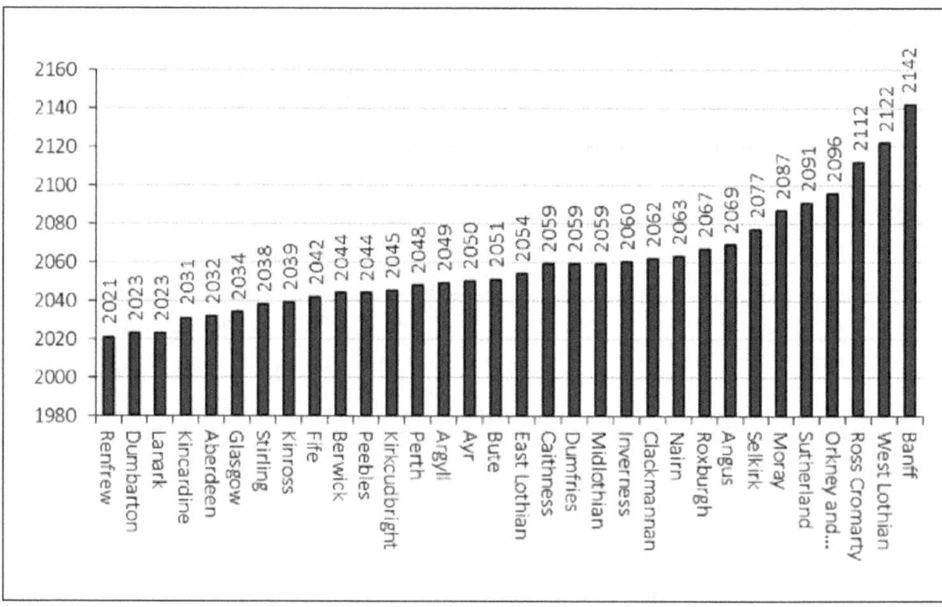

Projected completion rate with no changes

57 Registers of Scotland, *Completion of the Land Register Public Consultation* (n 12) para 16.
58 RoS, figures accurate to end Mar 2014.
59 Idem.
60 Registers of Scotland, *Completion of the Land Register Public Consultation* (n 12) para 26.

Between now and 2030. RoS forecast that only five registration counties would potentially exceed 90% title coverage. The majority of counties would take to 2060 to see 90% title coverage and for some of the more rural counties, such as Ross and Cromarty and Banff we could be waiting for up to 100 years and more. In short, completion would simply not happen and therein lies the driver for the changes introduced by the 2012 Act.

(3) The 2012 Act

The 2012 Act takes a markedly different approach to the bringing of properties on to the Land Register as compared with the 1979 Act. Not only does the Act provide the technical tools to further the goal of completion but underlying those technical provisions is a strategy to direct their use. The 2012 Act approach to registration moves away from the approach under the 1979 Act of listing transaction types the occurrence of which will require registration. Instead it lists those deeds to which the Register of Sasines is closed; the effect being that they must be registered in the Land Register.[61]

In an Act concerned with completion one might suspect that the list would be extensive. On the contrary it is brief. On the designated day the specified deeds to which the Sasine Register is closed number three; disposition, lease and assignation of lease. The door to the Sasine Register is left slightly ajar for those dispositions where recording in the Sasine Register is necessary for purposes of dual registration under the Title Conditions (Scotland) Act 2003.[62] Registration remains voluntary but as under the 1979 Act a real right cannot be acquired otherwise.[63]

The 2012 Act approach to registration makes no distinction between a disposition for value and a disposition for no consideration or value. Notwithstanding the additional 8500-10000 new registrations that RoS forecast will be generated by this approach, the impact on completion is marginal. The following table suggests that registration counties will achieve 90% completion earlier than would otherwise be the case but not significantly earlier.[64] Achieving 90% completion rates across Scotland would still take until the 22nd century. As under the 1979 Act, and indeed as is the case in England and Wales, some properties and interests will

61 2012 Act s 48(1).
62 Ibid s 48(6).
63 Ibid s 48(1).
64 RoS, Business Planning Forecast May 2014.

simply not change hands and so this new registration requirement will not deliver completion.

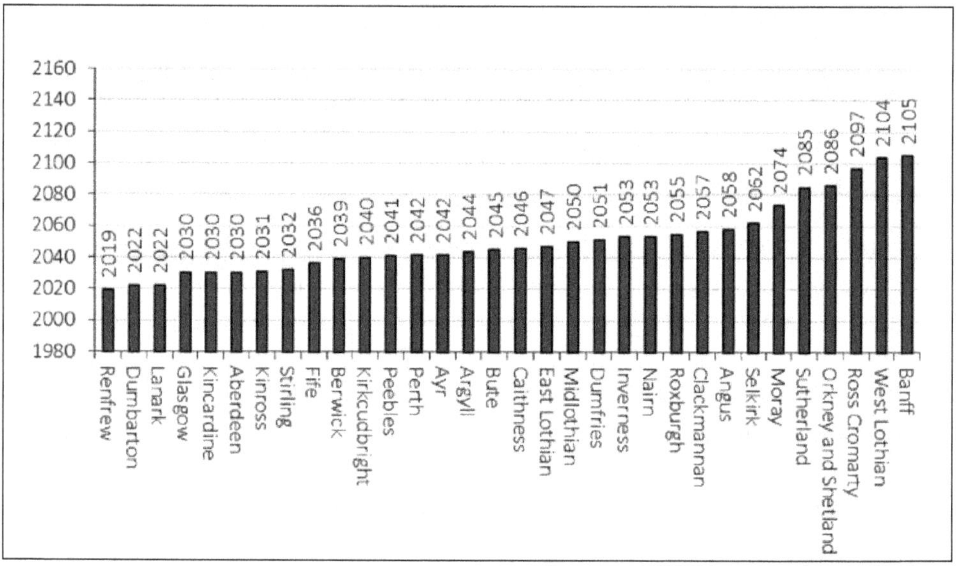

Projected impact of the 2012 Act

There is one further legislative change that the 2012 Act introduced that will aid completion, both in a direct and an indirect way. That change concerns leases. Leases are by their nature temporary. Under the 1979 Act, they enter the Land Register and then, at the end of their life, the associated entry on the Land Register is removed. The 2012 Act sets different legal requirements around leases and those requirements aid completion. It will no longer be possible to register a lease, a sub-lease or an assignation of an unregistered lease unless the plot of land to which the deed relates is also registered. Where the plot of land is unregistered, an application to register such a deed will induce registration of the owner's plot; termed "automatic plot registration."[65] On its own this will not have a major impact on completion – over the last ten years RoS has registered an annual average of 945 leases.[66] Where it will have more impact is on making landlords consider whether or not it would be more practical to voluntarily register

65 Automatic plot registration is required by the operation of sections 24, 25 and 30 of the 2012 Act.

66 RoS, Business Planning figures for the period January 2004-December 2013. From 1 January to 11 November 2014 some 1664 leased have been registered. The increase is in the main due to leases of airport car parking spaces.

all their land rather than simply the area affected by the lease. As a driver of voluntary registration, the impact of automatic plot registration could be significant, for it is only through voluntary registration that a landlord can retain control of the registration process for his or her land.

The 2012 Act brings about no immediate changes as far as applications for voluntary registration are concerned. The Keeper's discretion to accept or refuse such an application remains as does the test of expediency. So too does the Keeper's open door policy to voluntary applications. However, the Keeper recognises that more will be required than simply having an open door to voluntary applications if the ten year completion target is to be met. The volume of voluntary applications will have to increase substantially and the challenge for realising that will rest with the Keeper. Voluntary registration will have to be actively marketed and the Keeper will need to employ a range of different arguments to different sectors in aid of this. For some, the existence of the automatic plot registration provisions may offer an inducement to register; for others having certainty and assurance as to legal boundaries may be important: and for the wider public sector the catalyst to register will be the target set by Scottish Ministers to register such land within five years. It is the Keeper's understanding that the vehicle for this is voluntary registration.

Set against the benefits of voluntary registration will be cost. Costs will be a factor for many who are open to considering voluntary registration; the Keeper acknowledges this and the completion consultation document sought views on an appropriate level of financial incentivisation. Registration fees are only part of the overall costs; there will, in most cases, be legal costs. However, as the successful HMLR experience has demonstrated, costs are not an absolute barrier. The outcome of the consultation is not yet known.

The need to promote voluntary registration means that the legal discretion the Keeper has to refuse a request for voluntary registration is likely to prove theoretical rather than real. The 2012 Act gives Scottish Ministers the power[67] to prescribe an end to that discretion and it is thus perhaps no surprise that the Keeper favours its removal.[68] There are other strong legal reasons for ending that discretion and those reasons derive from the strategy for completion that the Act gives effect to. The completion toolkit set out in section 48 includes the power for Scottish Ministers, after due consultation with the Keeper and other appropriate

67 2012 Act s 27(6).

68 Registers of Scotland, *Completion of the Land Register Public Consultation* (n 12) para 30.

persons, to close the Sasine Register to standard securities on a county-by-county or all-Scotland basis. Closure of the Sasine Register in this way will create additional "triggers" that will increase the number of properties having their first registration onto the Land Register. Before this power can be enabled, section 48(7) requires that the Keeper's discretion to refuse an application for voluntary registration be removed.

The reason for this is perhaps best explained by an example. If the Sasine Register is closed to a standard security, the creditor's rights under the security can only be made real through registration of the security in the Land Register. To enable registration of the security, there must be a Land Register entry for the property. Thus, the property to which the security relates must be registered in the Land Register either before or at the same time as the security. As there is no statutory trigger for this the proprietor must apply for voluntary first registration in the Land Register. This power is helpful. Based on 2013-14 Land Register intake figures, some 6000 standard securities fell to be recorded in the Sasine Register. The table below shows the projected effect the addition of this provision to the completion armoury would have.[69]

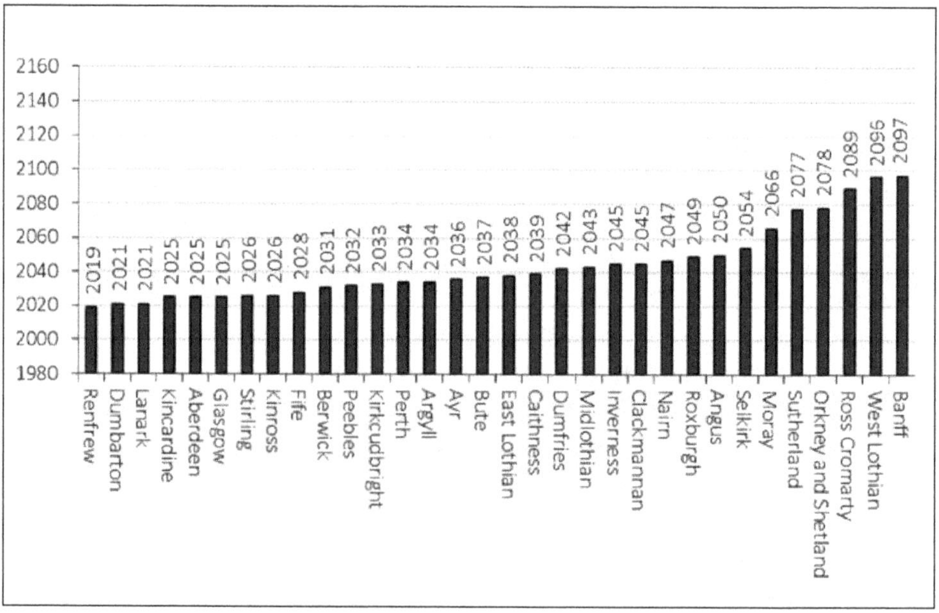

Projection completion rate inclusive of 2016 standard security changes

69 RoS Business Planning, May 2014.

The practicality of closing the Sasine Register to standard securities and other deed types has to be considered, and was one of the areas of focus in the completion consultation document. Certain standard securities are already a trigger for registration in England and Wales. That suggests that the market can accommodate the additional work associated with the registration of the property. In the commercial arena, the Keeper has noted that there is an increasing number of requests for voluntary registration arising from the unwillingness of certain lenders to make high end loans in the absence of a Land Register title. In any event, the fact that standard securities are dealt with specifically on the face of the 2012 Act reflects the Scottish Parliament's view that at some point consideration should be given to closing the Sasine Register to them; the issue is one of timing as opposed to principle.

Closing the Sasine Register to other deed types is more problematic and this is reflected in the completion consultation document. Many of the deeds recorded in the Sasine Register are drawn up and granted by a body other than the proprietor; the most common being discharges, improvement grants, and charging orders and the incentive to apply for voluntary registration does not exist in the same way as with a standard security. Although it is possible for automatic plot registration to be used in such cases to do so would raise a number of practical difficulties for the parties and the Keeper which do not exist for leases and assignations of leases.

To rely on voluntary registration in the same way as is envisaged should the Sasine Register be closed to standard securities is more complicated and less practical. It could also lead to less transparency; if the debtor had to voluntarily register his or her property before being able to register a discharge it may be that such deeds would simply not be registered. Registration would only be necessary at the next transfer of the property or if a fresh standard security was required. Care would also need to be exercised to ensure such a provision would not cut across other policy initiatives or the ability of, for instance, local authorities who may wish to register a charge over a property. Consequently closing the Sasine Register to other deed types would require to be supported by the immediate Keeper induced-registration (KIR) of the property that is to be subject to the deed. The Keeper's view[70] is that closing the Sasine Register to other deed types is

70 Registers of Scotland, *Completion of the Land Register Public Consultation* (n 12) para 27.

best left until the volume of remaining properties is of a manageable scale to allow for a prior KIR; indeed it if KIR is to be aggressively used it may be that this provision will never be used as it may have the effect of running counter to a planned programme of KIR.

The crucial point is that the 2012 Act provides for the practical closure of the Sasine Register to an increasing range of deed types at some future point; a necessary pre-requisite for completion of the Land Register though not in itself actually delivering completion. For that to happen, there requires to be a subsequent transaction affecting a property held on title deeds in the Sasine Register in order to trigger registration in the Land Register. For most properties, there will eventually be a transaction but the point at which that transaction occurs could be well in to the future. Additionally, there will remain a percentage of properties that remain off the Land Register radar. If completion is to happen in a timescale other than that determined by the natural pace of the property market, the remaining unregistered properties need to be identified and brought on to the Land Register. Identification of land not on the Land Register is straightforward. If it has not been mapped and accorded a title number under the 1979 Act (cadastral unit number under the 2012 Act) then quite simply it has not been registered.

In order that this land can then be registered, the 2012 Act gives the Keeper the power to undertake KIR.[71] This power, active from the designated day, allows the Keeper "to register an unregistered plot of land or part of that lot." No application for registration is required and nor is the involvement or consent of the owner required though the Keeper must notify the owner upon completion of registration. So is KIR the answer to the question of whether or not completion is feasible?

It is unquestionably a large part of the answer. It cannot assist with those properties whose titles are not on the Sasine Register but, in principle, it can aid identification of those properties as they will be the gap areas left in a registration county once KIR has been completed. But just how practical is KIR? The SLC are relatively positive about it:[72]

> The draft Bill accordingly makes provision for the final completion of the Register. The Keeper would simply be empowered to register any unregistered property. In practice, the Keeper would usually have enough

71 2012 Act s 29.

72 Scottish Law Commission, Report on *Land Registration* (n 11) vol 1 para 33.49.

> information to make up the title sheet – information about boundaries, information about the identity of the owner, and information about any subordinate rights to be entered in the C and D sections as encumbrances or in the A section as pertinents. After all, when a title is registered in the Land Register, it is not (with very rare exceptions) moving out of the private realm. Title is already in another of the Keeper's registers – the Register of Sasines.

There are two key phrases in this statement: "final completion" and "usually have enough information." With a ten-year completion target, KIR will have to be used extensively. The completion consultation document envisages that through market growth, use of increased triggers, and the commitment to register public land, some 88% of Scotland's property will be registered by end 2024.[73] By the Keeper's reckoning, that leaves some 275,000 potential property titles (though some titles will inevitably include multiple properties) that require to be brought on to the register by voluntary registration or KIR. Even if the appetite for voluntary registration grows to levels experienced in England and Wales at the height of their marketing campaign, some 150,000 or more potential titles will require to be tackled under KIR. Consequently the use of KIR will not be limited to completing the final parts of the cadastral map jigsaw; it will require to play a much more extensive role.

The critical question is whether or not the KIR powers lend themselves to be used in such an extensive manner. The answer will largely be determined by the information available to the Keeper. The extent to which the Keeper will have enough information, and what can be done when she does not, was the focus of the KIR section in the completion consultation document. For urban residential properties stemming from common routes of title, the Keeper is more likely to have sufficient information as she has already carried out pre-registration title examination and, for a large number of these properties, has pre-mapped them. Fortunately, in terms of absolute numbers, these properties will form the majority of the titles that KIR will seek to register. The completion consultation document notes that there are 700,000 such property titles.[74] This does not mean that KIR will be straightforward but the challenges ought to be limited to issues other than mapping. Rural and commercial properties will be less straightforward, as indeed will be titles to minerals and other separate tenements of land, and

73 Registers of Scotland, *Completion of the Land Register Public Consultation* (n 12) para 19.
74 Ibid para 18.

will present a range of issues, not least the challenge of identification and mapping on to the cadastral map.

The challenge with KIR stems in large part from the absence of any active transaction and the associated involvement of legal professionals tasked with examining title, obtaining pre-registration reports, interacting with the parties and being clear as to what is to be presented for registration. The completion consultation document highlights areas around identification of the legal boundaries, establishing who the owner is and clarifying the encumbrances that affect a property, but also acknowledges that other legal and practical issues will undoubtedly emerge.

For a map-based Land Register, identifying and plotting the legal boundaries of a property on to the cadastral map is essential. Identification is the starting point for any KIR and will be the determining factor in assessing the ability of KIR to enable completion. The 2012 Act acknowledges that under KIR, the Keeper may not always be able accurately to identify the legal boundaries.[75] This alludes to the challenge of Sasine deeds, particularly older deeds and deeds relating to properties in rural areas where descriptions can be as general as "all and whole the farm and lands of hightae." Such a description would not meet the Keeper's deed plan criteria and so, in 2012 Act parlance, the conditions of registration would not be met. Yet the expectation is that KIR will overcome such technical difficulties. When the Land Register nears final completion, the challenge may be less as the entries already on the Land Register may offer a sufficient guide to the legal boundaries of the remaining unregistered properties. Where the volume of properties to be dealt with by KIR is large, the help offered by existing Land Register entries is less useful. The Keeper will have access to a range of old county series maps and more up-to-date Ordnance maps as well as any neighbouring registrations to assist in the mapping but this may not be sufficient in all cases to enable the boundaries to be plotted with absolute certainty.

The reality is that general descriptions could lead to the Keeper under- or over-mapping the extent of the property. If the extent is under-mapped, the proprietor will become aware when the Keeper notifies them with details of the registration, as is required. If the extent is over-mapped, the 2012 Act provides a general exception to the Keeper's warranty the effect of which is that the "over-registration" is not warranted. The owner or a

75 2012 Act s 74(3)(a)(ah).

third party with title and interest would be able to apply for rectification. If it is under-mapped, the registered proprietor will not have lost their land. It will remain in the Sasine Register and the assumption is that they would seek to rectify their title to include the omitted land. A technical solution is one thing but if such problems were to become commonplace there is a risk that KIR could be brought in to question. The same argument applies to the solution the 2012 Act offers in relation to problems identifying the proprietor;[76] these provisions resolve practical problems but there is as yet no clarity on the extent to which they would need to be used.

Notwithstanding that the 2012 Act seeks to provide statutory solutions for certain issues, the Keeper is mindful of the impact of the application of those solutions on those who own the properties in question. The challenge for the Keeper is to ensure KIR works in practice, to be transparent as to its use and ensure that its widespread adoption does not undermine the credibility or integrity of the Land Register. The completion consultation document emphasised that considerable more analysis and public discussion is required around the use of KIR. The Keeper proposes a series of pilot exercises to inform KIR, followed by a further public consultation focusing on the options for using KIR to enable completion. The proposed pilots will, in part, inform whether or not the 2012 Act provides a sufficiently flexible and robust basis for accommodating all possible title scenarios. (It is possible that the pilots will highlight issues that may benefit from a legislative solution.) At present it is not practical to draw firm conclusions other than to acknowledge that the ten-year completion target will require the extensive use of KIR.

(4) Will completion happen in ten years?

It is clear the road to completion will be well advanced. Market activity, the commitment to register public land, the proposed closure of the Sasine Register to other deed types and the continuing use of voluntary registration will all contribute to advancing completion. As indicated previously, the Keeper estimates that this would result in some 88% of property titles being registered. Indeed, the more active the property market, the less challenging and costly the task of completion. A return to the boom years of the mid 2000s, where the annual intake of first registration applications exceeded 50,000 per annum, would have a marked impact on the ease of completion

76 2012 Act s30(5).

and would reduce the dependency on both voluntary registration and KIR. However, achieving absolute completion, in the sense that every area of land or separate tenement of land, be it large or small, is on the Land Register with an identified owner is unlikely. There are a number of areas of challenge.

The main area falls around the many political considerations that have to be overcome. This essay does not focus on them; it acknowledges that there are cost issues for public bodies, resource allocation considerations for Scottish Ministers, the need for the legal marketplace to grow and accommodate the demand for legal resource, the need for continued political commitment and, of course, the flexibility of RoS to manage an unprecedented growth in applications. In many ways, these will be the determining factors but they are beyond the scope of an essay that is focused on whether or not the technical tools exist to enable completion within the ten-year target.

A key challenge will be those properties that are not held on titles recorded in the Sasine Register. These are largely unquantifiable. The ones that are known can be targeted for voluntary registration or could potentially form the subject matter of a KIR, based on working in tandem with the owner to register the land. Inevitably, many of these areas will only come to light as the Land Register nears completion. Strategies for dealing with those areas will need to be formulated and one senses that the matter may end up being the subject of further public consultation.

Linked to this are those areas of ground that unwittingly remain on titles recorded in the Sasine Register. As discussed previously, the 1979 Act encouraged this behaviour. Identifying these title issues will similarly only be practical once completion nears but resolving them may prove time consuming and resource intensive. On a pure cost versus benefit ratio, consideration will have to be given as to whether or not the cause of transparency is sufficiently aided by resolving the ownership question for these areas. A variation of this challenge relates to mineral titles. There are very few mineral titles in the Land Register. The majority of entries for property on the Land Register will note that the minerals have been reserved but will offer little guidance on where title rests. In some cases, the mineral title will rest on deeds recorded in the Sasine Register, though some will not, but identifying title will not necessarily be straightforward.

The use of voluntary registration needs to become much more frequent than is the case currently and needs to extend beyond public bodies. The

HMLR experience suggests that there is a market for voluntary registration; the challenge is to tap that market. The benefits of registration can be extolled, support from RoS can be offered and for some this will be sufficient. The Keeper is already reporting an upsurge of interest and joint initiatives based around the use of voluntary registration is progressing with a number of landowners and other bodies with significant landholdings. Somewhat perversely, one factor that may dissuade some property owners is that of KIR. Quite simply, KIR is free, voluntary registration is not. The risk the Keeper has to manage is that some property owners who are the subject of a voluntary registration campaign (large landowners for instance) may opt to do nothing in the knowledge that within a ten-year timeframe their property will have to be picked up under KIR. The less interest in voluntary registration the greater the scale of the KIR exercise the Keeper will be faced with. That of course will place pressure on the ten-year timeframe.

Linked to the above is the question of land owned by UK public bodies, such as the Ministry of Defence. These landholdings are not insignificant: the Secretary of State for Defence alone owns an estimated 2% of Scotland's land mass.[77] The commitment to register all public land within five years was first made against the backdrop of the independence referendum. Had the outcome of that referendum reflected Scottish Ministers' desires for an independent Scotland, then at some point in the near future all land owned by UK public bodies would have transferred and come within the orbit of Scottish Ministers. That is no longer the case and so presents a challenge for completion; Scottish Ministers can but encourage their UK counterparts to voluntarily register. If they choose not to then the remaining option is KIR. (That approach can of course create a tension with Scottish public bodies, particularly local authorities, who are being asked to progress registration of their landholdings through voluntary registration, which unlike KIR attracts a registration fee.)

The manner in which KIR can deliver completion is an unknown. In the same way that a series of policies and work practices were developed by the Keeper to support the 1979 Act, a similar approach will be required for KIR. The Keeper's recommendation in the completion consultation document that a series of pilot exercises be run to gain greater understanding of the range of practical and legal issues to be addressed is an acknowledgment of that. Only once the pilots have concluded and been analysed and the

77 Ministry of Defence, *Defence Infrastructure Organisation Estate Information* (2014).

findings and options for progressing KIR shared in a public consultation will it be possible to draw any definitive conclusions as to the use of KIR and the priority it should be given in delivering completion. It is, however, already clear that in offering solutions to some of the most pressing challenges the Keeper will encounter, the 2012 Act did envisage that KIR titles will not necessarily have the look and feel or the legal equivalence of other registered titles. Just how different they may be is yet to be seen but in an acceptance of that may lie the answer to completion.

E. Conclusion

Completion of the Land Register is now high on the political agenda. The continuing focus of the current Scottish Government on land reform matters has ensured a greater awareness amongst community groups, public and private bodies, professional organisations, land charities and citizens as to the information currently available on land ownership in Scotland and the central role of the Land Register in providing that information. This focus is timely, coming as it does on the heels of the implementation of the 2012 Act: legislation that has at its heart the completion of the Land Register.

Setting a ten-year target has brought an immediate focus on the completion provisions in the 2012 Act. They offer a significant improvement on the triggers for registration contained in the 1979 Act and compare favourably with the legislative framework for progressing completion that HMLR operates with. The 2012 Act provides a strategy: progressive closure of the Sasine Register to an increasing range of deeds, continued encouragement for voluntary registration, and the rolling introduction of KIR as operational counties near completion. The SLC's suggested timeframe for implementation of that strategy was not 10 years: they envisaged a longer time-scale.[78] Notwithstanding the timescale for delivering the strategy has shortened, the strategy that underpins the 2012 Act remains largely appropriate.

Achievement of the target will depend, in large part, on continuing political will; political support will be necessary if the legal powers in the 2012 Act are to be used to full effect. If the political desire to see completion continues, and signs are positive given the cross-party support for the completion provisions in the then Land Registration etc (Scotland) Bill,

78 Scottish Law Commission, Report on *Land Registration* (n 11) vol 1 paras 33.65-33.67.

then year-on-year progress to meeting the target will be evidenced. The powers to close the Sasine Register to deed types and those relating to KIR will be instrumental in delivering near completion. Further analysis on and options for the widespread use of KIR will be forthcoming from the Keeper. The Keeper is confident KIR can be used to drive completion but assessment of that confidence must await publication of the planned public consultation on its use.

With continuing political support completion will be well advanced by 2024 and indeed it may, at a practical level, be considered achieved. Inevitably, there will be areas of land for which no title can be readily traced and also areas where there is doubt as to where title rests. There may also be some registrations, particularly of bodies with extensive and complex landholdings where parts of that portfolio are still a work in progress. But come 2024 the completion landscape will have changed and the focus will have moved from enabling completion to ensuring Scotland maximises the social and economic benefits of a complete or near complete Land Register.

3

The Use of Praedial Servitudes to Benefit Land outside the Dominant Tenement

Professor Roderick R M Paisley

Throughout my entire legal career I have had the pleasure of discussing property law with my good friend Robert Rennie. Having learned much in the process, I hope that I have contributed at least a little. Such discussions were of particular value where the issue was one upon which only brief comment was available in the published legal literature. One of the issues that cropped up in our conversations is the subject matter of this essay. We both recognised that it was a topic requiring some detailed research. Having now had the opportunity to carry out that research I have pleasure in dedicating this essay to Robert as a token of my esteem.

A. Introduction

The rule now known to Scottish property lawyers as "the *Irvine Knitters* rule"[1] limits the use of praedial servitude rights.[2] It does so by linking

1 *Irvine Knitters Ltd v North Ayrshire Cooperative Society Ltd* 1978 SC 109. For material in the National Archives of Scotland see CS258/1976/11833.

2 Praedial (otherwise predial) servitudes benefit a plot of land known as the dominant tenement or benefited property. They are to be distinguished from personal servitudes which benefit a legal person. Both types of servitudes burden a plot of land known as the servient tenement or burdened property. However, given that they lack a dominant tenement, the *Irvine Knitters* rule has no application to personal servitudes or similar rights: *Monkland and Kirkintulloch Railway Company v Dixon* (1842) 1 Bell's App Cas 347 at 360 per the Lord Ordinary (Jeffrey).

exercise of the particular servitude to the purposes of the relevant dominant tenement (otherwise known as "the benefited property"). All other exercise is regarded as in excess of the proper use of the servitude and can be interdicted at the instance of the servient proprietor (otherwise known as "the burdened proprietor"). The rule may be classified as one of the three legally implied servitude conditions.[3] The effect of the rule is that the dominant tenement is fixed in geographic extent at the time of creation of the particular servitude and, apart from very specific statutory exceptions that have no general relevance,[4] does not expand to incorporate other land when the dominant proprietor acquires that other land even if that additional land is used together with the original dominant tenement to enable the carrying out of a single business or the construction of a single development project. What is required in such a situation of expansion is usually some variation of the existing servitude or the obtaining of a new, more expansive, servitude.[5] The issue therefore comes into sharp focus where potential development sites are being assembled from various constituent parts.

Although now widely known by the name of the pursuers in the particular case, *Irvine Knitters Ltd*,[6] and albeit the case was decided by the

---

3 D J Cusine and R R M Paisley, *Servitudes and Rights of Way* (1998) paras 12.164-12.179. The other two legally implied servitude conditions are that the servitude will be exercised (a) *civiliter*, i.e. in a reasonable manner and (b) so that it does not exceed the acceptable burden on the servient tenement. The dispute in *Irvine Knitters* was sparked by construction traffic on the servient tenement going to the redevelopment on the dominant tenement and *prima facie* engaged both of these. However, their application requires and assessment of the impact of conduct whereas the limitation of the servitude to the benefit of the purposes of the dominant tenement involves an examination of title and is often perceived as holding out a clearer way to stop the unacceptable behaviour of the dominant proprietor. The thrust of this essay is that matters are perhaps not so cut and dried as that.

4 See e.g. the limited number of government backed projects where the Scottish Parliament disapplied the *Irvine Knitters* to assist the development: Forth Crossing Act 2011 s 27; Airdrie-Bathgate Railway and Linked Improvements Act 2007 ss 37 and 54; Edinburgh Airport Rail Link Act 2007 s 55; Glasgow Airport Rail Link Act 2007 s 42; Waverley Railway (Scotland) Act 2006 s 44.

5 The legally implied servitude condition, being a negative in nature, cannot be varied or discharged by reference to the Lands Tribunal in terms of the Title Conditions (Scotland) Act 2003 ss 90 and 122(1) definition of "title condition," para (c).

6 The Irvine Knitters Limited, Company Number SC026008, was incorporated on 31 December 1947 but is now dissolved, having been taken over in 1968 by Courtaulds plc. The archives of the company are privately held and enquiries may be made to the National Archives (England), Archives Sector Development under reference NRA29343 Courtaulds plc and reference GB/NNAF/C102224 (former ISAAR ref GB/NNAF/B3426). See also B G Rudd, *Courtaulds and the Hosiery and Knitwear Industry* (2014) 68, 77-78, 126-28, 134-35 and 158.

First Division of the Court of Session in 1978, the rule is long established,[7] having its origins in the writings of various Roman jurists collected in the *Digest* of Justinian.[8] It is clear the Scottish rule did not appear out of nowhere. The prior Scottish authorities cited by Lord President Emslie in *Irvine Knitters* comprise two Nineteenth Century cases, *Scott v Bogle*[9] and *Anstruther v Caird*.[10] Despite the existence of these earlier authorities there is no record of the rule being known in Scotland as the *Scott* or *Anstruther* rule. Other, even older, Scottish authorities illustrating the rule also exist but are not now cited in modern practice having been eclipsed by the decision in *Irvine Knitters*.[11] The most recent Scottish restatement of the *Irvine Knitters* rule is found in *Alvis v Harrison*[12] (a Scottish appeal to the House of Lords) in the opinion of Lord Jauncey. He stated:[13]

> A servitude right of access inures to the benefit of the dominant tenement and no other. Thus it cannot be communicated for the benefit of other tenements contiguous thereto (*Scott v Bogle*). In *Irvine Knitters Ltd v North Ayrshire Co-operative Society Ltd* the Lord President ... said: "What they [the dominant proprietors] may not do, however, is to use the way, or permit its use by others, to obtain access to subjects other than the dominant tenement, whether or not they happen to be heritable proprietors of those others subjects. They may not, in short, increase the scope of the right of access, and in particular they may not use the way for the purpose of securing access for persons or goods to subjects contiguous to the dominant tenement by using the dominant tenement merely as a bridge between the end of the lane and the non dominant subjects."... The underlying reason for restricting the

---

7 It is described as "well known" in *Hay v Hay or Robertson* (1845) 17 Sc J 186 at 187 per the Lord Ordinary (Cuninghame).

8 D 8.3.29 (Paul); D 8.3.33 (Africanus).

9 1809, 15 FC 397. The case is named as *Bogle v Bogle* in Hume, *Lectures*, vol 3 (Stair Society No 15) 281.

10 (1862) 24 D 149. For material in the National Archives of Scotland, see reference RHP40965 containing a plan of part of lands concerned.

11 See e.g. *Brown v Kinloch*, 20 Dec 1775, M 14542, with a relevant plan in the National Archives of Scotland at reference RHP4008; *Stewart v Caithness: Stewart v Smart* (1788) Hume 731 with material in the National Archives at reference CS271/34657; *Scoullar (otherwise Brownlee) v Robertson* (1829) 7 S 344, with material in the National Archives at reference CS46/1830/3/4.

12 1991 *SLT* 64. For material in the National Archives of Scotland, see references CS258/1989/2650A and CS258/1992/4088.

13 1991 *SLT* 64 at 68. The law as stated in the latter part of the quotation is incorrect. The use of a servitude of access to benefit land outwith the dominant tenement breaches the *Irvine Knitters* rule even though such use reduces the burden of traffic passing on the servient tenement: Cusine and Paisley, *Servitudes and Rights of Way* (n 3) para 12.158. Material is available in the House of Lords archives under references HL/PO/JO/10/11/2590 and HL/PO/JU/4/3/1681.

> benefit of a servitude right of access to the dominant tenement alone is that to use it for the benefit of a second or third tenement is likely to generate more traffic and so increase the burden.

Not only in *Alvis v Harrison* but also in *Irvine Knitters*[14] has the substantial identity of English and Scots law on this point been emphasised. So too, in reported English cases, has Scottish authority been used to illustrate the application of the analogous common law principle.[15] As a result, with their usual caution, Scottish lawyers may look to English law, and also to Common law jurisdictions based on English authorities, to ascertain the likely position of Scots law.

It should be noted that almost all the reported cases relate to servitudes of access. The rule equally applies to egress (i.e. coming out of a property).[16] Moreover, it applies to all servitudes including servitudes involving transport of material extracted or abstracted from lands adjacent to the dominant tenement whether by means of a road or other service media. For example, in one Scottish case a party was not allowed to use a drain benefiting one field for another field owned by him nor to eject water from extra fields onto the original dominant tenement for onward drainage via the servitude of drain.[17] One of the reasons for the concentration of cases on access may be that such activity is usually obvious and thus discoverable in comparison with the leading of a drain to additional property which may be underground and substantially obscured from view.

The *Irvine Knitters* rule relates to the dominant proprietor taking unfair advantage of a servitude to the disadvantage of the servient proprietor. The rule permits the servient proprietor to restrain the dominant proprietor from doing so and, as such, imposes a negative restraint on the latter. Although the quotation from Lord Jauncey, above, indicates the dominant proprietor must not "permit" third parties using the servitude to pass to lands outwith the dominant tenement, it is hard to see how this can apply in such a way. The rule does not impose any positive obligation on the dominant proprietor. For example, there is no implied obligation on the

14 *Irvine Knitters Ltd v North Ayrshire Co-operative Society Ltd* 1978 SC 109 at 117 per Lord President Emslie and 121 per Lord Cameron.

15 See e.g. *Giles v Tarry* [2012] EWCA Civ 837 at para 41 per Lewison LJ; *Peacock v Custins* [2002] 1 WLR 1815 at para 19 per Schiemann LJ.

16 As is demonstrated by the English case of *Williams v James* (1867) LR 2 CP 577.

17 *Magistrates of Dunbar v Sawers* (1829) 7 S 672. For assorted relevant material in the National Archives of Scotland see the references CS235/D/27/2, CS271/55016, CS311/11, GD314/63 and GD314/64. See also *Scoullar (otherwise Brownlee) v Robertson* (1829) 7 S 344.

dominant proprietor to fence off the dominant tenement so that the taking of access into adjacent land from the dominant tenement is impossible. In Scotland such a positive obligation could be imposed by a real burden or possibly by a servitude condition. Such a provision is not unknown in practice[18] but appears to be rare. In one modern English case[19] it was observed that it is acceptable for a dominant proprietor, a farmer, to transport his sheep up an easement of access over the servient tenement onto the dominant tenement so that they might graze on the dominant tenement and, having grazed on that tenement, if the sheep spread out onto the adjacent land outwith the dominant tenement, the servient proprietor could have no objection. Although no time period as regards the sheep grazing on the dominant tenement was judicially specified, one would expect this observation would relate to a situation in which the sheep are allowed to move naturally as they graze. A different situation might arise if the dominant farmer used devices giving encouragement to the sheep to move quickly from the dominant tenement onto the adjacent land such as the storage on the adjacent land of particularly attractive food for the sheep. This sort of nutritional inducement to directed movement of the livestock may well be restricted by the negative restraint imposed by the *Irvine Knitters* rule. Difficult cases may arise if a shop has been built on a composite site comprising and extending beyond the dominant tenement in a servitude of access. It is undecided what sort of devices, presumably employed as part of what is now termed "the overall retail experience," would be regarded as unacceptable inducements to the potential customers to move from the dominant tenement into the remainder of the shop.

B. Minerals Rights

The Scottish case law decided in relation to the *Irvine Knitters* rule invariably relates to the use of the surface of land on both the servient and dominant tenements. However, given Professor Rennie's longstanding interest in

---

18 In *Magistrates of Dunbar v Sawers* (1829) 7 S 672, the magistrates granted a servitude of drainage. There was an express reservation of the magistrates (who were the servient proprietors) as a counter stipulation to the servitude of the right to enter the dominant tenement and put up works to ensure that the dominant proprietor did not use drain for adjacent land. The exact nature of that reservation is unclear. It may have been a real burden or a servitude condition.

19 *Giles v Tarry* [2012] EWCA Civ 837.

minerals rights and areas below the surface of land,[20] a brief comment on that particular matter is required.

Minerals rights are regarded in Scotland as capable of being conveyed as geographic separate tenements (i.e. slices of land) and there is no reason in principle why the *Irvine Knitters* rule should not apply to minerals rights just as it applies to slices of land such as storeys of property above first floor level, airspace above land[21] or land at ground level. Some Scottish cases[22] have been decided in which one of the parties has attempted to apply the *Irvine Knitters* rule so as to limit the other party's activity (usually access) in what the first party believed was his own land. However, this body of Scottish case law relating to minerals has typically dodged the application of the *Irvine Knitters* rule by deciding that the rule did not apply because the area where the activity was carried out was also owned as a property right by the owner of the minerals. Put another way, it was decided that the area in question was not owned by the party objecting to the activity and was not subject only to a servitude in favour of the minerals proprietor. These cases relate to the proper construction of the wording employed in particular grants or reservations of minerals. They in no way suggest that the *Irvine Knitters* rule does not apply to servitudes benefiting minerals held as a property right.

Two early English cases confirm that the analogous English rule does indeed apply to such minerals held as property rights.[23] Both of these cases were considered and distinguished in a Scottish case[24] but only on the basis that the Scottish court was not dealing with a servitude benefiting a

---

20 R Rennie, *Minerals and the Law of Scotland* (2001).

21 In this regard see the terms of the Tenements (Scotland) Act 2004 s 2(7). It is unstated whether this section carries with it a servitude of access to obtain access to the additional triangular area of airspace but, it is submitted, such a servitude is likely to be implied by statutory expansion of the dominant tenement of any servitude benefiting the sector including the roof failing which the taking of access to the triangular area may breach the *Irvine Knitters* rule.

22 See e.g. *Duke of Hamilton v Graham* (1871) 9 M (HL) 98; *W Davidson v Duke of Hamilton and W Walker* (1822) 1 S 411; *Turner (Tait's Trustee) v Ballandene and Husband* (1832) 10 S 415 at 418 per Lord Craigie.

23 *Dand v Kingscote* (1840) 6 M & W 174, 151 ER 370; *Durham and Sunderland Rail Co v Walker* [1842] 2 QB 940.

24 *Hamilton v Graham* (1871) 9 M (HL) 98. The rule in *Irvine Knitters* would also be inapplicable if the access were taken over an area held in common property by the owner of the benefited property: *Gavin v Junor* 2009 *SLT* (Sh Ct) 158; *MacKay v Gaylor* 2014 *SLT* (Sh Ct) 131. An issue of construction sometimes arises as to whether a right expressed in loose terms is a servitude of access or a right of common property: *Willemse v French* 2011 SC 576.

property right. It seems clear that the *Irvine Knitters* rule would be applied in a Scottish case to a servitude benefiting minerals held as a property right if the issue ever came up for decision in a pure and unavoidable form. That did occur in the two English cases just noticed. At that time the minerals working and processing appear to have been a relatively simple affair of the minerals being dug out by miners at a particular coal or mineral face in manageable amounts and immediately loaded into bogies. The material was then transported across the dominant tenement and onto the servient tenement. There was no issue of a manufacturing complex or any processing of the minerals within the dominant tenement. This is an issue that will be considered later in this essay.

C. Qualified Nature of the Rule

Absolute though the rule in *Irvine Knitters* appears to be at first blush, further examination shows that this is not so nor is it applied in a wholly inflexible way. Common law jurisdictions such as England, certain Canadian Provinces and some Australian States have attempted to mitigate the rigours of their own native version of the *Irvine Knitters* rule by developing a number of judicially created qualifications to permit extension of an easement of access to benefit additional land in several situations. These are not yet fully worked out in reported Scottish case law but, in principle, they all appear compatible with Scots law. These will be set out below as the first and second exceptions. In addition, there are a couple of exceptions that are better established in "native" Scottish authority. These are set out below as the third and fourth exceptions.

The qualifications permit the servitude to be used to benefit land outwith the dominant tenement where one or more of the following exceptions apply. In very brief summary they are:

(i) First exception – ancillary use.

(ii) Second exception – anticipated additional land.

(iii) Third exception – personal bar.

(iv) Fourth exception – separate journeys.

These will be examined in turn.

(1) The first exception

This applies where the use of the additional land outside the dominant tenement is ancillary to a permissible use of the dominant tenement.

The main body of case law illustrating this exception relates to English easements of access.[25] This indicates that access will be allowed to and from relatively small areas of land adjacent to the dominant tenement where access to such areas is required for the proper enjoyment of the dominant tenement. A similar notion of a servitude benefiting the dominant tenement being capable of facilitating access to an adjacent area of land where the use of that area is ancillary to the dominant tenement is seen in only one Scottish case.[26] In that Scottish case a stable originally built on the dominant tenement had been redeveloped and a new stable serving the house on the dominant tenement had been built so that it was located on a small plot of land adjacent to the dominant tenement. In a decision that has never properly been reported, the Sheriff took the view:[27]

> I am disposed to think that the subjects benefited in this case was [sic] still the same, the stable being really an adjunct to the dwellinghouse.

This case was appealed to the Court of Session and the Sheriff's interlocutor reversed in part but the judgement is not reported.[28] Albeit the records that remain are unclear, the Court of Session appears to have restricted the dominant proprietor's access to his house only and to have excluded access to the stable.[29] By reference to authority, therefore, one cannot therefore

25 The English cases comprise *National Trust v White* [1987] 1 WLR 907; *Macepark (Wittlebury) Ltd v Sargeant* [2003] 1 WLR 2284; *Das v Linden Mews Ltd* [2002] 2 EGLR 76; *Peacock v Custins* [2002] 1 WLR 1815; *Massey v Boulden* [2003] 1 WLR 1792; *Martin Wilkins and Wendy Wilkins v Thomas William Lewis* [2005] EWHC 1710 (Ch).

26 *Blair v Strachan*, 20 Jun 1889, Sheriff Guthrie Smith. See *Aberdeen Weekly Journal*, 25 Jun 1889. There is other material relevant to the case in the *Aberdeen Journal*, 13 Mar 1889 at 7; *Aberdeen Evening Express* 13 Mar 1889 at 3. The property was at 124 Hadden Street, Woodside, Aberdeen.

27 The use of "was" in the quoted text follows from the odd Scottish conveyancing convention that regards "the subjects" as singular.

28 There was further litigation on a matter of obstruction of the same servitude of access reported as *Blair v Strachan* (1894) 21 R 661. For material in the National Archives of Scotland relative to both actions see CS46/1890/6/56 and CS46/1894/6/65.

29 See the note of the terms of the interlocutor in that appeal at (1894) 31 SLR 548 at 549. There is similar authority in Canada excluding the possibility of taking access via an easement of access to a plot adjacent to the dominant tenement even though the use of that plot benefited the dominant tenement: *Gordon v Regan* (1985) 15 DLR (4th) 641 at paras 28-37 per Griffiths J.

argue with any assurance that the "ancillary use" exception has been judicially recognised as part of Scots law.

However, albeit seemingly rejected in this one Scottish case, there still appears to be room for development of the exception in cases with more suitable circumstances. What then might those circumstances be and how can one circumscribe them? Clearly this exception relating to "ancillary use" cannot be used to undermine the entire *Irvine Knitters* rule although it has been applied enthusiastically in some English cases. For example, in one case[30] where an easement of way benefitted a cottage it was held the easement could be used even where the cottage was extended with two rooms on adjacent land not part of the dominant tenement. By contrast, in a case decided only two years later,[31] it was held inadmissible to take access over an easement of way to some 800 acres of farm land outwith the dominant tenement which itself consisted of about 1,200 acres of agricultural land. Albeit some of the decisions are somewhat difficult to reconcile,[32] for this exception to the *Irvine Knitters* rule to operate, it remains the case that there must be some element of the use of the adjoining land being "ancillary" to the use of the dominant tenement. Consequently, a dominant proprietor cannot take access to adjacent land of whatever extent and whatever the slimness of the connection with the proper use of the dominant tenement. Furthermore, the use of the adjacent land must be ancillary to some use of the dominant tenement that was not expressly excluded by the terms of the servitude itself. For example, where a servitude of access is granted to a plot of land expressly on the basis that it may be used as an access to a house but not as an access to a vehicle garage, the owner of the house on the dominant tenement cannot build a garage on the adjacent land and claim to take access to the garage over the servitude route on the basis that the use of the garage is ancillary to the house.

A clear example of ancillary use as an exception to the *Irvine Knitters* rule that is recognised daily in Scotland is a servitude of access over a lane leading to a house on the dominant tenement that is also benefited by a servitude of drain and septic tank over a field in the ownership of a third party. If the owner of the house wishes to repair the drain and septic tank it is manifestly clear that he, together with his contractors and employees,

30 *Massey v Boulden* [2002] EWCA Civ 1634, [2003] 2 All ER 87.

31 *Martin Wilkins and Wendy Wilkins v Thomas William Lewis* [2005] EWHC 1710 (Ch).

32 As noted in *Macepark (Wittlebury) Ltd v Sargeant* [2003] 1 WLR 2284 by Gabriel Moss QC, who attempted to provide some guidance as to the meaning of "ancillary."

may take access from the public road, up the servitude lane, across his own property and into the land of the third party located outside the dominant tenement in the access servitude. It does not matter at all that the servitude of drainage and septic tank is first acquired long after the creation of the servitude of access and was not clearly envisaged by the parties to that original servitude of access. So too, can the owner of a dominant tenement use a servitude of way to take access to his property and then proceed to leave his property by another servitude of way leading over an entirely different servient tenement. Both such examples of ancillary use, however, could be regarded as being in excess of the servitude of access if the terms of the grant or reservation of that servitude of access expressly prohibit such use. That, however, would not be a breach of the *Irvine Knitters* rule but a transgression of an express servitude condition restricting the purpose of the servitude.

Another example would be where a person purchases a field with a servitude of access out to the public road along a private lane. The dominant field benefits from rights of lateral support, most likely in the form of servitudes or rights of common interest, owed to it by adjacent land in the ownership of third parties. The dominant proprietor may acquire rights of access to the adjacent land to carry out works to enhance that lateral support. The owner of the dominant tenement, together with his contractors and employees, may use the servitude of access and pass across his own property into the land of the third party to carry out the works to enhance lateral support. Again, this ancillary use could be excluded by express provision in the terms of the servitude of access.

So too, one may consider part of an underground tunnel used for passage based on a servitude of access where the next part of the same tunnel is also used for passage but this time based on a property right held by the person taking passage. The servitude of access over the first part of the tunnel may be regarded as benefiting, *inter alia*, the second part of the tunnel. It may happen that the owner of the second part of the tunnel may require to drive large pins into the roof and walls of that part of the tunnel to stop that roof and those walls falling in. Those pins will penetrate into the surrounding strata which are outside the dominant tenement and are owned by a third party.[33] So too, if the pins are insufficient, may the owner of the second part of the tunnel require to excavate part of the surrounding

33 For this a servitude *tigni inmittendi* would be needed.

rock outside the dominant tenement to stop the rock falling into the part of the tunnel comprising the dominant tenement. Additional rights from the third party may require to be obtained. In both of these cases, however, additional rights do not have to be acquired by the owner of the second part of the tunnel from the owner of the first part of the tunnel (the servient tenement) to enter or use the land of the latter. The owner of the second part of the tunnel may use the existing servitude of access over the first part of the tunnel to go into the dominant tenement and then enter the lands of the third party to carry out these works as they are ancillary to, and necessary for, the proper use of the dominant tenement comprising the second part of the tunnel.

A further example may be seen where a servitude of access benefits a dominant tenement consisting of a quarry. If the quarry is dug out of the ground so that it forms an open basin, the quarry walls cannot safely be dug in such a way that would leave a cliff face existing at ninety degrees to the remaining surrounding surface of the land. Instead, for safety sake, the walls of the quarry must be stepped at an angle so that there is a reduced danger of collapse or rockfall. If the stepping takes place entirely within the dominant tenement so that the top of the stepping, which is at the level of the surface of the land, is located inside or on the very boundary line this will inevitably result in a measure of rock within the dominant tenement remaining unexploited. This could be avoided if the dominant proprietor stepped the sides of the quarry by digging out some of the minerals on the neighbouring land owned by a third party leaving the bottom of the stepping on the boundary line between the dominant tenement and the third party land. Of course, the dominant proprietor would require to obtain rights from the third party to encroach in this way into the neighbouring land. However, as regards the servitude of access into the quarry, the stepping of the sides of the quarry may be regarded as ancillary to the originally envisaged and proper use of the dominant tenement to the extent that such digging and stepping is required to extract all of the minerals from the dominant tenement.

In all of the examples indicated above, the additional rights in the land adjacent to the dominant tenement may be obtained by means of a positive servitude benefiting the same dominant tenement served by the servitude of access. On one view, the very form of the additional rights as servitudes could be argued as fitting well with the "ancillary" use exception as a positive servitude, by definition, is ancillary to the relevant dominant tenement. The positive servitude over the adjacent land may exist only if it confers a benefit on the land which is also the dominant tenement in the servitude of access. However, it would be too much to suggest that the servient tenement in any positive servitude benefiting land which is also the dominant tenement in a servitude of access can be accessed by that servitude of access. Consider, for instance, a servitude of access benefiting a farm extending to 100 hectares. If the owner of the farm subsequently obtains a grant of a servitude of pasturage over 10,000 hectares of adjacent hill pasture benefiting the farm, it seems somewhat extravagant to suggest that he may use the existing servitude to take access to the extensive hill pasture. It seems likely that the "ancillary" use exception to the *Irvine Knitters* rule will be more tightly drawn but it is not at all clear upon what basis that will be done. Perhaps recourse could be had to an element of "reasonable foreseeability." That, however, is to speculate far beyond any decided authority.

Lastly, one should notice that other doctrines may assist the law to overcome some of the conceptual limitations and uncertainties of the "ancillary" use exception to the *Irvine Knitters* rule. Where the owner of the servient tenement in a proposed route of passage grants a servitude of access to a 100 hectare farm which is then already benefited by a servitude of pasturage over the adjacent 10,000 hectares of hill grazing, the access in favour of the farm is clearly a positive servitude. The access to the hill grazing cannot be a servitude unless separately granted in favour of the owner of the hill grazing over which the servitude of pasturage is exercised. If constituted in this way the owner of the hill grazing can then communicate the benefit of enjoyment of his servitude of access to the dominant proprietor in the servitude of pasturage as the latter has a lawful right to be on the dominant tenement in that servitude. Such a method of creation, however, requires the co-operation of the owner of the hill grazing and he is entitled to refuse to accept the benefit of a servitude of access. Alternatively, the party owning the servient tenement in the proposed servitude of access to the farm may simultaneously grant two rights. First, a servitude of access to that farm and, secondly, a right of access which, although not a separate servitude in its own right, is a right ancillary to the servitude of pasturage over the hill grazing.[34] There is no requirement, either at the time of grant of the ancillary access right

34 The possibility of the implied grant of such ancillary rights was recognised in *Moncrieff v Jamieson* 2008 SC (HL) 1. It is *a fortiori* the case that such rights may be granted expressly.

or at any time thereafter, that the servient tenement in the servitude of pasturage must be owned by the same person who owns the land subject to the right of access ancillary to that servitude of pasturage. So too there is no requirement that the servient tenement in the servitude of pasturage and the land subject to the ancillary right of access be contiguous and not separated by the dominant tenement in the servitude of access. This double grant is useful in two situations. First, where the grant of access is made when the farm is already benefited by the servitude of hill grazing. Second, where the owner of the route in the proposed servitude of access is also the owner of the hill grazing.

(2) The second exception

The second exception exists where, although there is no express provision to that effect,[35] it is clear by reasonably implication from the terms of the deed or the surrounding circumstances that it was always intended by both parties to the servitude that the dominant tenement would be extended to incorporate the additional land or, at least, this possibility was contemplated and left open by both parties to the servitude when the servitude was created.

The authority for this rule is contained in a number of English[36] and Australian cases.[37] For example, if a servitude is expressly created in favour of the front door and entrance hall of a house, it is reasonable to accept that the servitude benefits the entire house as the front door and access hall are merely means of access to the house itself. Another example is where the deed itself defines as the dominant tenement "Plot A" but contemplates access to Plot B even though the definition of the dominant tenement does not expressly extend to it. Involved in this exception are elements of the function of the dominant tenement and the adjacent land. The exception could be regarded as relating to situations in which it is reasonably

35 Express provision would expressly bring the additional land within the dominant tenement and thus access to that additional land would comply with the *Irvine Knitters* rule. However, there are difficulties in the drafting and registering of deeds with such express provision: Cusine and Paisley, *Servitudes and Rights of Way* (n 3) paras 2.41-2.43; Title Conditions (Scotland) Act 2003 s 75.

36 See e.g. *Thorpe v Brumfitt* (1872-73) LR 8 Ch App 650; *Callard v Beeney* [1930] 1 KB 353.

37 See e.g. *Shean Pty Ltd v Owners of Corinne Court* [2001] WASCA 311; *Owners Corporation – Strata Plan no 8450 v Owners Corporation – Strata Plan No 54547* [2002] NSWSC 780; *Perpetual Trustee Company Limited v Westfield Management Ltd* [2006] NSWCA 337; *Westfield Management Ltd v Perpetual Trustee Co Ltd* [2007] 233 CLR 528.

foreseeable that the dominant tenement, by design or natural topography, is to perform function ancillary to the adjacent land. It perhaps must perform a role benefiting the adjacent land similar to that performed by the servient tenement in relation to the dominant tenement. This seems to be the case in servitudes of access where the dominant tenement's only function is as a route of access to the adjacent property. If such be the case, when one considers the benefit to the adjacent land, the dominant tenement in the servitude of access operates functionally as part of a servient tenement. If indeed that is so, the elements of this function or design must exist as at the date of the grant or reservation of the servitude of access so that they are reasonably evident to the parties to that juristic act. Years after the grant of a servitude of access the dominant proprietor cannot so design a house so that the sole means of entry is located on Plot A and the remainder of the property on Plot B.

The argument is perhaps easiest to make where the servitude is one of drain or other service media. Consider the case where the servitude is phrased that a property owner is entitled to join a particular drain on his property into the main drain on the servient property and thereafter use it. It seems to be overly strict to argue that the dominant tenement is only the particular drain within the property owner's land. It seems manifestly obvious that it would always have been intended that this particular drain should be connected to a house or other structure on the land to which it provides a benefit and that that house or structure would be comprised within the dominant tenement for the servitude of drainage. Again, it is the function of the drain that strongly suggests the existence of a more extensive dominant tenement.

(3) The third exception

This applies where the owner of the servient tenement personally bars himself as regards objection to an extension of the benefit of the servitude to adjoining land. This is truly not a special exception to the *Irvine Knitters* rule but an application of a general principle. The basis of this line of authority is perhaps to be seen in Roman Dutch and Roman law. The Roman Dutch writer Johannes Voet (1647-1713) illustrates this by reference to a servitude of leading water:[38]

38 Voet, *Pandects*, 8 4 13.

Et aquae ductum habens, inde rursus aquam alteri nequit praedio concedere, nisi id nominatim pacto praeter ordinariam servitutum naturam actum sit. Nec ad alium fundum proprium postea forte acquisitum ducere: imo, ne ad aliam quidem eiusdem fundi partem, quam ad quam servitus ab initio acquisita fuit.	And one who has a right of water-leading cannot in turn grant water out of it to another tenement, unless that has been specially arranged by agreement apart from the ordinary nature of servitudes. Nor can he lead to another farm of his own which perhaps he has later acquired. Nay he cannot do so even to another part of the same farm than that for which the servitude was originally acquired.[1]

This, in turn, is derived from the writings of the Roman jurists Pomponius and Africanus collected in the *Digest* of Justinian.[39] They wrote respectively as follows:

Ex meo aquae ductu Labeo scribit cuilibet posse me vicino commodare: Proculus contra, ut ne in meam partem fundi aliam, quam ad quam servitus adquisita sit, uti ea possit. Proculi sententia verior est.	Labeo states that if I have a right to channel water, I can oblige any neighbour I chose with the use of the watercourse. Proculus, on the other hand, holds that I cannot even use it for the benefit of any part of my estate other than that for which the servitude was acquired.
Per plurium praedia aquam ducis quoquo modo imposita servitute: nisi pactum vel stipulatio etiam de hoc subsecuta est, neque eorum cuiuis neque alii vicino poteris haustum ex rivo cedere: pacto enim vel stipulatio intervenientibus et hoc concedi solet, ...	You are channelling water across the estates of a number of owners by virtue of a servitude, however created. You cannot grant the right to draw water from the channel to any of these owners whom you chose or to another neighbouring proprietor, unless a pact or stipulation was added to this effect. Such a right is normally granted by the addition of a pact or stipulation....

39 D 8.3.24 (Pomponius) and D 8.3.33 (Africanus).

This reference to a special arrangement in the passage from Voet, quoted above, was considered in the South African Courts as having the potential to permit the recognition of a new servitude in addition to the primary servitude.[40] In the case in hand that was regarded as an additional personal servitude but, on different facts, could potentially be a praedial servitude benefitting the additional land. Scots law has some difficulty in recognising that servitudes are created by personal bar alone.[41] The better analysis appears to be that the doctrine precludes the Erskine, John of Carnock enforcement of the *Irvine Knitters* rule by the person concerned, the present servient proprietor, but that this bar remains personal and would not bind his singular successors. They, of course, could bar themselves by their own acts. This personal bar preventing the servient proprietor's objection to an extension of the use of the servitude to benefit land adjacent to the dominant tenement has been recently applied in the Scottish case.[42] A broadly similar principle is known in England[43] albeit in the most recent case relating to the matter sufficient facts were not proved to apply the doctrine.[44]

To give rise to personal bar the actings of the dominant proprietor must be known to the servient proprietor or at least reasonably ascertainable by him. Similar actings, even if unknown to the servient proprietor, if not hidden could be regarded as being "open" as that term is recognised in the context of the Scottish doctrine of positive prescription and may, in due course of time give rise to a prescriptive servitude in respect of which

40 *Van der Merwe v Wiese* 1948 (4) SA 8 (C) at 14 per Fagan J and discussed in R J P Jordan, "Praedial servitudes: the imposition of positive duties upon the servient owner" (1958) 75 SALJ 181 at 186.

41 See Cusine and Paisley, *Servitudes and Rights of Way* (n 3) 377-85, para 11.37-11.46; E C Reid and J Blackie, *Personal Bar* (2006) paras 6.56 and 6.63; *Moncrieff v Jamieson* 2005 1 SC 281 at paras 25-29 per Lord Marnoch and paras 80-86 per Lord Hamilton; *Moncrieff v Jamieson* 2007 SC (HL) 1 at para 46 per Lord Scott of Foscote; *Robson v Chalmers Property Investment Co Ltd* 2008 *SLT* 1069; *George Jobson Forbes Fyvie v J Ross Morrison and Yvonne Morrison*, Arbroath Sheriff Court, case ref A155/98, decision of Sheriff Principal R A Dunlop QC and decision of the Sheriff on 10 Dec 1999. For more general application see *MacGregor v Balfour* (1899) 2 F 345 per Lord President Balfour at 352; *Munro v Jervey* (1821) 1 S 161; cf *Winans v Lord Tweedmouth* (1888) 15 R 540.

42 *Ben Henderson and Mrs M A (otherwise Rita) Henderson and Michael John Walker and Mrs Gail Mather Walker and Andrew Connor and Linda Connor v William Irvine and Mrs Gillian Irvine*, Alloa Sheriff Court, case ref A314/08 (hearing 20 Apr 2010), note of Sheriff D N Mackie. See K G C Reid and G L Gretton, *Conveyancing 2010* (2011) 13.

43 *Price and another v Nunn* [2013] EWCA Civ 1002.

44 At para 32.

the dominant tenement comprises an area outwith the dominant tenement in the original servitude.[45] The principle in all of this is clear. The servient proprietor, by doing nothing to prevent excessive use of a servitude, could contribute to the eventual creation of a second real right of servitude that entitles the dominant proprietor use the route of the original servitude to benefit an area outwith the dominant tenement in that original servitude.

(4) The fourth exception

This exception may be best illustrated in a servitude of access. It applies where the activity on the additional land does not lead to a direct and single journey from that land across the dominant tenement and down the servitude road but there are actually two journeys interspersed by an intervening legitimate act of "processing," "storage" or something similar.

This exception is truly a way of saying that the basic rule in *Irvine Knitters* is not engaged at all. Put another way, there is no breach of the *Irvine Knitters* rule where someone using the servitude to access the dominant tenement does so in connection with a legitimate and genuine purpose on that dominant tenement before passing through to the additional land and there are substantially two separate journeys. This applies equally in reverse when someone leaves the adjoining land via the dominant tenement and then passes out to the public road over the servient tenement. There is no need in this case to show the use of the adjoining land is "ancillary" to the proper use of the dominant tenement. There is no need to show that the access to adjacent land was envisaged when the servitude was originally constituted. There is no need to show that the servient proprietor is personally barred from objecting. This is an entirely different exception with a different justification. All that needs to be shown is that the journey to/from the adjoining land from/to the dominant tenement is genuinely separate from a genuine journey to/from the dominant tenement over the servitude access. To explain why this is so requires a detailed examination of the general *Irvine Knitters* rule.

---

45 Prescription and Limitation (Scotland) Act 1973 s 3(2); See also the observations in the English case of *Smiths v Muller and Fowlers* [2008] EWCA Civ 1425 at para 10 per Rimer LJ; *CDC2020 Plc v Ferreira* [2005] EWCA Civ 611 per Lloyd LJ at para 21; *Mills v Silver* [1991] Ch 271.

D. The Formulation of the General *Irvine Knitters* Rule with Specific Reference to the Fourth Exception

In the context of a servitude of access it is a convenient shorthand to express the *Irvine Knitters* rule to the effect that a servitude of access is to be used only for the purpose of taking access to the dominant tenement. However, this abbreviation does tend to mislead somewhat. The rule is not that the servitude of access can be used only to take access to the dominant tenement but that the servitude of access may be used only for the legitimate and genuine purposes of the dominant tenement. It is worth confirming that this formulation relating to the purposes of the dominant tenement is indeed the position of both Scots and English law. In one of the leading English cases[46] the various judges emphasised the easement of access could be used for the reasonable and honest use of the dominant tenement, a formulation which can be construed to open the door to consideration of the purposes of the dominant tenement. In *Irvine Knitters* the wording used was even more explicit in this regard in that Lord President Emslie spoke of the link of the servitude to the genuine "purposes of the dominant tenement."[47] This distinction between the servitude linked not to the dominant tenement but the purposes of the dominant tenement is subtle but very important. The distinction may immediately be illustrated by reference to simple examples with the underlying principle then being drawn out.

(1) Examples

A rule which limits the exercise of a servitude of way to the geographic bounds of the dominant tenement is a rule that seeks a red line to be drawn round a dominant tenement and this is to be regarded as the *ne plus ultra* of anyone properly using the servitude. It would preclude anyone using the servitude of access to access the dominant tenement and then moving outside the boundary to conduct a simple operation such as painting the outside face of the fence on the boundaries of the dominant tenement. It would preclude the taking of access into the dominant tenement by means of a servitude of way and leaving the dominant tenement by means of a second servitude of way as the *solum* of the second servitude would be

46 *Williams v James* (1867) LR 2 CP 577 at 580-81 per Bovill CJ, at 581-82 per Willes J and at 583 per Montague Smith J.

47 1978 SC 109 at 119.

outside the dominant tenement. It would preclude the receipt of water in a plot of land by means of a contract or lease or other right enabling aqueduct into the dominant tenement and then the transport of that same water in tankers down a servitude road where the dominant tenement in that servitude road comprised the plot of land but not the source of the water. It would prevent a plot of land being used as a distribution centre for goods that need to be carted to other lands operated as part of the same business group. None of these examples fall foul of the Scottish rule that is to the effect that a servitude must be used for the legitimate and genuine purposes of the dominant tenement.

In addition to these examples some further applications have been judicially noticed. If the rule were to the effect that the servitude may be used only to gain access to the dominant tenement (and not for the legitimate and genuine purposes of the dominant tenement) then the dominant proprietor taking access to the dominant tenement via the access servitude would have to retrace his steps if he wished to proceed to anywhere else. He clearly does not have to do so because this is not the rule. In the Canadian case of *Miller v Tipling*, Mulock CJ, sitting in the Ontario Court of Appeal, stated the matter thus:[48]

> The law is well established that a right-of-way appurtenant to a particular close must not be used colourably or for the real purpose of reaching a different close. This does not mean that where the way has been used in accordance with the terms of the grant for the benefit of the land to which it is appurtenant, the party having thus used it must retrace his steps. Having lawfully reached the dominant tenement, he may proceed therefrom to adjoining premises to which the way is not appurtenant; but, if his object is merely to pass over the dominant tenement in order to reach the other premises, that would be an unlawful user of the way...

One consequence of what is observed in this *dictum* is this. Having used the servitude and having reached the dominant tenement the dominant proprietor (and anyone else entitled to use the servitude as his invitee) is not wholly precluded from passing onto adjacent lands even if these adjacent lands are outside the dominant tenement. The point was re-emphasised in another Canadian case in which a passage from Gale on *Easements* was quoted. This is *Gamble v Birch Island Estates Ltd*, decided in the Ontario High Court.[49]

48 (1918) 43 DLR 469 at para 31.
49 (1970) 13 DLR (3d) 657 at para 23 per Stark J.

It now remains to consider whether the law will permit the extension of the user of the right of way to additional property acquired by the grantee or its successors in title. This branch of the law appears to be well established. In *Gale on Easements*, 13th ed. (1959), p. 265, one finds this language:

> "If a right of way be granted for the enjoyment of close A, the grantee, because he owns or acquires close B, cannot use the way in substance for passing over close A to close B. Romer L.J., *Harris v. Flower & Sons* (1905) 74 L.J.Ch. 127. It need hardly be said that the mere fact that the grantee uses the way to enter close A does not make close B incapable of access from A; the question must always be whether the ostensible use of the way for the purposes of the dominant tenement is genuine or colourable."

This is slightly reworded in later editions as may be illustrated by the nineteenth edition of Gale on *Easements* published in 2012:[50]

> "It does not, of course, follow that the mere fact that the grantee uses the way to enter close A makes close B incapable of access from close A. The question must always be whether the ostensible use of the way for the purposes of the dominant tenement is genuine or colourable: "the true point to be considered ... should seem to be, *quo animo* the party went to the close; whether really and *bona fide* to do business there, or merely in his way to some more distant place."

The quotation within this passage from the sixteenth edition of Gale is from the seventeenth-century English case of *Lawton v Ward*.[51] This indicates the longstanding nature of this form of the rule related to the legitimate purposes of the dominant tenement. In Scotland we are not dealing with a variant of or exception to the rule established for the first time in *Irvine Knitters* but with the true nature of the rule itself.

It is clear that a dominant proprietor may not use the servitude of access to the dominant tenement merely for the purpose of taking access to lands outwith the dominant tenement. A number of Australian,[52] English[53]

---

50 Para 9.56. This same passage also appears in earlier editions such as the 16th (1997) at para 9.31.

51 (1697) 1 Ld Raym 75 at 76 note (a); 91 ER 946 at 947.

52 See e.g. *Westfield Management Ltd v Perpetual Trustee Co Ltd* [2007] 233 CLR 528.

53 See e.g. *Skull v Glenister* (1864) 16 CBNS 81; 143 ER 1055; *Finch v Great Western R Co* (1879) 5 Ex D 254; *Harris v Flower & Sons Limited* [1904] WN 106; *Ackroyd v Smith* (1850) 10 CB 164, 138 ER 68.

Canadian[54] and South African[55] cases illustrate this. It is little surprise that Scots law is to similar effect.[56] The rule may now be regarded as well established and is expressed in the phrase – the dominant tenement may not be used as a "bridge." A clear cut case is where the dominant proprietor uses the servitude merely for the purpose of taking access to property outwith the dominant tenement and the servitude is used merely for the "colourable" purpose of taking access to those premises.[57] Such a taking of access to property outwith the dominant tenement without any reference to the use of the dominant tenement itself is not part of the legitimate purposes of the dominant tenement.

(2) "Legitimate and genuine purpose"

What then distinguishes the "legitimate and genuine" purposes of the dominant tenement from a mere "colourable purpose"? This is a simple question with a multifaceted answer. The following discussion may be helpful in making the distinction.

(3) Single journeys

Single unbroken journeys, particularly if repeated, are likely to fall foul of the *Irvine Knitters* rule and be regarded as using the dominant tenement as a "bridge." If the taking of access involves a single, unbroken journey over the servient tenement through the dominant tenement to the land outside the dominant tenement that is likely to be regarded as an improper use of the servitude. This would apply *mutatis mutandis* to egress out to the public road from land outwith the dominant tenement.

---

54 See e.g. *Telfer v Jacobs* (1888) 16 OR 35; *Purdom v Robinson*, [1899] 30 Can SCR 64 at 71 per Sir Henry Strong CJ; *Friedman v Murray* [1953] 3 DLR 313; *Pearsall v Power Supermarkets* [1957] 8 DLR (2d) 270; *Gordon v Regan* (1985) 15 DLR (4th) 641 at paras 28-37 per Griffiths J; *Eastern Contractors v Gamble* (1970) 13 DLR (3d) 657; *Graham v Kucera* 2009 BCSC 1508.

55 See e.g. *Berdur Properties (Pty) Ltd v 76 Commercial Road (Pty) Ltd* 1998 (4) SA 62 (D) examined in R R M Paisley, "The demon drink and the straight and narrow way: the expansion and limitation of praedial servitudes," in H Mostert and M J de Waal (eds), *Essays in Honour of CG van der Merwe* (2011) 193.

56 There is a discussion of the authorities in Cusine and Paisley, *Servitudes and Rights of Way* (n 3), paras 12.64 *et seq*.

57 See, once again, the Canadian case of *Miller v Tipling* (1918) 43 DLR 469 at para 31 per Mulock CJ.

However, this is not an absolute rule because, quite apart from the ancillary uses examples noticed above, it may be possible to construct an argument that there may be instances where a journey to a point outwith the dominant tenement could be regarded as genuinely for the purposes of the dominant tenement itself. For example, if a dominant proprietor is approached by a neighbour who requests a one off permission to use the servitude access and then to cross the dominant tenement to carry out some small task on the neighbouring property, it would appear to be good neighbourliness on the part of the dominant proprietor to allow such a journey. It seems at least arguable that such a good neighbourly act would be within the genuine purpose of the use of the dominant tenement and would not be regarded as using the dominant tenement as a bridge. However, such acts may require to be relatively small and this particular example does appear to stretch the point a little. The better view seems to be that such access may simply constitute a *de minimis* breach which is not truly an exception but is simply not worth litigating. It is most unlikely that this neighbourly behaviour example could be extrapolated to allow a journey for major engineering or building works (even on a one off basis) on the adjacent land or activities such as the widespread planting of trees on, or removal of trees from, the adjacent land if that was not also related to the legitimate and genuine purposes of the dominant tenement. On balance, it seems best to seek to justify single journeys to a point outwith the dominant tenement by reference to the "ancillary use" exception.

(4) Separate journeys

Separate journeys (a) over the servient tenement to the dominant tenement and (b) from the dominant tenement to the adjacent land comply with the *Irvine Knitters* rule in that they do not use the dominant tenement as a "bridge." Where the dominant proprietor takes access over the servitude road into the dominant tenement for legitimate and genuine purposes within the dominant tenement, this, if there were to be nothing else, clearly complies with the rule. If he should then make an entirely separate journey from the dominant tenement into the adjacent land, this will comply with the rule because he is not in any way exercising the servitude in respect of this second journey. So too if he returns to the dominant tenement and then makes a separate journey out through the servient tenement this is not in any way an exercise of the servitude and will not breach the *Irvine v Knitters* rule. The key issue is that the journey to the dominant tenement over the servient tenement and the journey from the dominant tenement to the servient tenement are "separate." It is not enough to preclude the journeys from being separate to show that the second journey into the adjacent lands could be made only after making the first journey. So too it is not enough to preclude the journeys from being regarded as separate to show the dominant proprietor has put himself into the position to make the second journey by making the first.

(5) How to distinguish separate journeys

The separate nature of the journeys (a) across the servient tenement to the dominant tenement ("the first journey") and (b) from the dominant tenement to adjacent land ("the second journey") can be observed from certain circumstances. It is important to note that none of the factors identified below will be determinative in its own right. They will all be assessed together to determine whether the servitude is being exercised for the genuine purposes of the dominant tenement.

(6) A gap in time between journeys

A gap in time between the various journeys assists in showing they are separate and thereby in complying with the *Irvine Knitters* rule. Let us look at an extreme case which illustrates the matter beyond all doubt and then move onto more usual situations. In the extreme case a person who has entered the dominant tenement a year ago may leave that dominant tenement and pass into adjacent land as he pleases. The gap of a year is more than sufficient to show the second journey has no connection with the first. More usual day to day cases involves a lesser period of time but this does not preclude a shorter period being a sufficient gap between the journeys. If a lorry or van leaves the public road, using the servitude of access to cross the servient land and enters a factory on the dominant tenement and stops there for a legitimate reason, that amounts to a genuine self-contained journey to the dominant tenement over the servitude road. If, later in the same day, for some legitimate reason that lorry or van then moves to another part of the factory complex on land adjacent to the dominant tenement that may be regarded as a separate self-contained journey from the dominant tenement to adjacent land and not an abuse of the servitude of access to the dominant tenement because it does not involve any exercise of the servitude. The fact that there is a gap in time between the two journeys assists in demonstrating the separate and legitimate nature of the journeys.

Certainly, it may be that the longer this intervening time gap is, the easier it may be to demonstrate two separate journeys. For example, in one nineteenth century English case, *Williams v James*,[58] the period of time between moving hay from adjacent fields onto the dominant tenement and the transport of the hay down the servient road was rather vaguely stated as the period between summer and September.[59] That might have been as little as a few weeks but also it could have been a month or so. The period was a factor in determining that the dominant proprietor's use of the easement of access to the dominant tenement was consistent with the proper exercise of that right. Another example of a time period of what is probably about a week or a fortnight may be observed in a Scottish case.[60] The exact time period is uncertain but, as will become clear from the *dictum* quoted below, may be calculated with reasonable certainty by reference to the time between repeat municipal bin collections. In the Scottish litigation in question the Lands Tribunal considered an expressly constituted servitude of passage in the following terms:

> ...a right of access over the footpath lying to the side and rear of the adjoining subjects known as number Six Maxwell Crescent, aforesaid which footpath is shown delineated and hatched in black on the plan Declaring that the right of access hereby granted is for the purpose of gaining access to and egress from the rear garden ground pertaining to the subjects disponed and for no other purpose whatsoever...

In their comments the Lands Tribunal observed:[61]

> We do not accept that the use of a wheelie bin is an improper use of the right of access. Use of a garden for storage of a wheelie bin must now be accepted as a reasonable garden use. That the refuse in the wheelie bin may come from the house rather than the garden does not affect the means for access and egress to and from the garden by someone using a wheelie bin.

In the *Irvine Knitters* case itself, a small shop on the original dominant tenement (84-90 High Street) and property on additional adjacent land on either side of the original dominant tenement were demolished and rebuilt

58 (1867) LR 2 CP 577.

59 Ibid.

60 *Forrester & Fleetham v Sharp*, 6 Mar 2001, unreported, LTS/LO/2000/45.

61 Page 5 of the written decision.

as a single larger shop on a composite site (78-106 High Street) including the original dominant tenement and the additional land.[62] It was during the construction phase that the servient proprietors first raised objections to construction traffic using the servitude over their land. Presumably the route of access had been a quiet back lane and then, without their agreement, it became an access to a construction site and was traversed by lorries carrying materials and equipment. One wonders if a degree of sensitivity and diplomacy on the part of the dominant proprietors or their contractors might have avoided any problem. However, that was not to be. What then followed was a little surprising, at least at first blush. Instead of litigating the matter on the basis of *inciviliter* use (the first legally implied servitude condition) or by reference to an asserted unwarranted increase in the burden on the servient tenement (the second legally implied servitude condition), the servient proprietors took a different approach. They argued that the proposed access to the new shop would breach the third legally implied servitude condition in that the dominant proprietor sought to take access to land outwith the dominant tenement. This approach had tactical advantages in that it avoided a difficult examination of matters of fact and law regarding the conduct of the dominant proprietors (or their contractors) within the servient tenement and concentrated attention on interpretation of titles where one might anticipate an answer might be more clear-cut particularly where a plan is attached to the title deeds. It also allowed the servient proprietors to seek the remedy of interdict even after the construction traffic had ceased and enabled them to object to the future commercial use of the composite shop. So, the commercial pressure could be maintained on the dominant proprietors even if they were to rush through the construction phase and claim the offending conduct had already ceased.

Consequently, it was not until the development was complete that litigation actually started as regards the proper use of the existing servitude of passage. That servitude was exercisable over a private lane and originally gave access only to the rear of the original shop on the dominant tenement but not to the property on the additional adjacent land on either side. Lord President Emslie and Lord Cameron considered that the dominant proprietor could comply with the rule limiting the exercise of the servitude to original dominant tenement by converting the part of

62 *Irvine Knitters Ltd v North Ayrshire Co-operative Society Ltd* 1978 SC 109.

the new shop within the footprint of the old shop into a distribution centre. Lord President Emslie observed:[63]

> ... the access may unquestionably be used for all purposes to which the [dominant proprietors] choose to devote the dominant tenement and it is easy to figure that some rearrangement of the [dominant proprietors'] use of their new building, even if they choose to devote that part of it built on the dominant tenement exclusively to the function of a genuine distribution centre or store in connection with all their retail enterprises, will result in their being able to use the right of access for purposes which can be identified as the purposes of the dominant tenement. That a proprietor may use his dominant subjects for a genuine purpose which serves the interests of his business enterprise, as a whole, carried on in those subjects and elsewhere, cannot be doubted and the case of *Williams v James* is a good example of circumstances in which a proprietor's use of a right of access to one of three fields on which he grew hay all of which he stacked on the dominant field, was held to be unexceptionable.

Lord Cameron set out a similar view, albeit his observations as regards distribution appear to me more limited to distribution not to all other retail outlets but to distribution within the greater retail outlet on the composite site:[64]

> I do not doubt that if the [dominant proprietors] decided to designate and to use the whole of the subjects 84-90 High Street as a store or distribution centre for the whole of their supermarket compound within the range of 78-106 High Street, they could legitimately do so, but equally I am of opinion that if they were to claim a right to import through the access or accesses giving on to 84-90, goods of any kind which immediately were delivered or transported to other parts of 78-106 High Street then they were acting beyond the legal limits of the right of way in favour of the subjects identified as 84-90 High Street. The proof appears to me to yield an inference beyond doubt that this is precisely what the [dominant proprietors] have been doing to a material degree. What the [dominant proprietors] are not entitled, in my opinion, to claim a right to do in virtue of this servitude right, is to use the subjects Nos. 84-90 as a "bridge" over which passengers or goods can pass as of right to the subjects Nos. 78-82. That the [dominant proprietors] might legitimately "ferry" such goods once properly received by this right of access into the subjects Nos. 84-90, used as a storage and distribution centre, by way of the public highway to other subjects in the same ownership is a very separate issue, and one in which other considerations might operate and I expressly reserve my opinion on that matter.

63 At 119.
64 At 122.

There probably is an element of time delay suggested in these judicial references to the legitimate use of the dominant tenement as a storage or distribution centre in the context of a single retail unit straddling the dominant tenement and adjoining land. The process of storage or distribution usually takes some time. However, it would be fair to say that one would not expect material to rest in a store for months or even for weeks. It is worth remembering that the entire premises in *Irvine Knitters* were developed as a supermarket. It is reasonable to assume that perishables and fresh food would be delivered. It is equally reasonable to assume that when delivered to a distribution centre within the dominant tenement it would be a legitimate use of the dominant tenement to distribute this sort of material within a very short period of time, certainly within the same day, probably within hours if not minutes of its delivery to the distribution centre.

Albeit Lord Cameron observed that materials could not be "immediately" delivered from the storage centre forming the dominant tenement to other parts of the building outside that tenement, the gap in time to constitute legitimate "storage" or "distribution" may be very short – possibly extending to a few minutes in appropriate commercial cases. One might surmise that the courts might be tempted to allow a party conducting a genuine business on the dominant tenement the opportunity to make a genuine business choice as to how long this period should be. If good commercial practice indicates that the storage period should be a certain period of time, it is to be doubted if the courts will take the view that this is wrong and impose some arbitrary period divorced from commercial reality. For example, it seems unlikely that the Courts would require fresh milk to be stored for days in order to qualify as the legitimate and genuine use of the area to which the milk was delivered as a storage facility. Similarly, where stone is extracted from a quarry face on the land outwith a dominant tenement and conveyed to places within the dominant tenement for processing and storage, it seems unlikely that the courts would require that process to be extended to some arbitrary minimum of time so that it might be regarded as sufficiently stored or processed to form part of the legitimate purposes of the dominant tenement. The important issue is that the material has gone through a genuine commercial process within the dominant tenement. Although foreseeability is not required, this seems all the more acceptable where the process is one which was within the contemplation of the parties when the servitude right of access and egress to and from that dominant tenement was granted.

Indeed, it may be possible with regard to some journeys, that a gap in time is not essential to show that they are separate. A gap in time is just one factor in the identification of a gap between two legitimate journeys. For example, if a postman enters a factory on the dominant tenement via the servitude road and hands in a letter at the factory office, an employee in the office who picks up the same letter may wish to deliver it immediately to the addressee in another part of the factory complex which is located outside the dominant tenement. On the face of it there appear to be two separate legitimate journeys. The first enables access to the dominant tenement via the servient tenement. The second is undertaken as part of the purposes of the dominant tenement.

(7) Different transport for the two journeys

A factor in showing the distinction between the two journeys may be the method of transport. Where different vehicles are used for the two journeys this may assist in showing the journeys are separate and thus in complying with the *Irvine Knitters* rule. This is particularly so where the vehicles carrying out the second journey never enter the servient tenement but are specialised vehicles adapted for the second journey. The access over the servient tenement to the dominant tenement is a general access for all purposes but the access taken to the adjacent land from the dominant tenement is for certain defined, limited purposes. For example, let us consider a dominant tenement operated as a quarry and containing rock crushing machinery, quarry offices and a weighbridge. Assume that the source of the rock is outside the dominant tenement and the dominant tenement is accessed via a single servitude of access from the main public road. If workmen employed at the quarry travel along the public road and up the servitude road and arrive in their own private cars they may park them in a safe area within the quarry (the dominant tenement). Following modern work practices, we may assume, typically, they will then dismount from their vehicles and sign into work in some way and not use their private cars until they leave at the end of the day. That entry into the quarry on the dominant tenement represents a single journey. It is separate and distinct from any journeys they might make within the quarry. Even if these same employees drive quarry trucks, vans or lorries back and forth all day between the dominant tenement and the rock face within the adjoining land, this is arguably not a misuse of the servitude of access. These journeys made during the working day are all separate journeys between the dominant tenement and the adjacent land and the workmen do not use the servitude route at all. These journeys are all legitimate uses of the dominant tenement. Even if the initial journey of the employee in the morning and his last journey at night both require him or her to cross the servient tenement, and even though this initial and last journey is carried out to enable the workmen to carry out their jobs (which necessarily involves repeatedly passing into land adjacent to the dominant tenement), arguably this would not be a misuse of the servitude of access. In addition, the position appears to be no different even if a workman had a role in the quarry that required him to spend most of his working day at the quarry face in the adjacent land. His private car, presumably, is parked at a safe place in the quarry (the dominant tenement).

This applies *mutatis mutandis* to journeys out of the adjacent land and into the dominant tenement. For example, where material is ferried into the dominant tenement from the quarry face on the adjacent land by special vehicles (such as large quarry trucks unsuited or un-licenced for the public road) and deposited in the dominant tenement and, at some later stage, is taken out of the quarry on the dominant tenement over the servitude in different vehicles licenced for public road use, this will be a factor in demonstrating two separate journeys.

An example in a domestic setting could be as follows. A house with attendant garage is built on a dominant tenement benefited by a vehicular servitude of access. A part of the garden to the house, comprising the lawn, is held on a separate title not benefited by the servitude of access. If the owner of the house comes home from work in her car she will park it in the garage. After entering the house to change clothing she may take a mower from the same garage and proceed to the lawn to cut the grass. The second journey to the lawn outside the dominant tenement is made on foot. An additional factor favourable to regarding this journey as separate from the one taken over the servient tenement is the fact that the second journey is not taken every time the first journey is completed. Normally, a person does not mow his or her lawn every evening in the year. In this regard it is possible to argue there is a distinction with the quarry example given above. It may be a factor adverse to showing the journey to the quarry face is indeed separate journey if the workmen invariably make the second journey every time they complete the first journey.

(8) Nature of the activity between the journeys

The *dicta* quoted above from the *Irvine Knitters* case contemplated involved storage and distribution on the dominant tenement. It is important to note that this is not a closed list of the activities that may be taken into account in determining if there are two separate journeys. These two activities identified in *Irvine Knitters* are largely "passive" in their nature, albeit distribution infers the activity of sorting and taking away. If such passive activities are sufficient to distinguish one journey from another, it seems likely that a more "active" manufacturing process between journeys would lead to a stronger case.

At the lower end of the spectrum of "active" behaviour one could cite the instance of employees reporting for work at a site hut on the dominant tenement and then passing to a point of work on the adjacent land outwith the dominant tenement whether that land is owned or leased by the employer. The fact that signs are placed on the dominant tenement which expressly require such reporting of employees and members of the public could be argued to indicate, in a modest way, the policy of complying with a two separate journey requirement. Further across the spectrum one may refer to a process of manufacture of some sort on the dominant tenement which is a much more active "activity." For example, where a source of sand or particular clay in an adjacent field facilitates a cement making business on a dominant tenement, the servitude of egress from that dominant tenement may be used to ferry out the finished product of cement even though it contains sand that had its origins in the land outwith the dominant tenement. This seems to hold good whether the sand is dug out of the adjacent land by vehicular diggers driven by men or by some sort or automated machine with conveyor belts. A multitude of other variants, of even more intense activity and duration, can be imagined.

(9) No artificial expedients to mark a distinction

It is clear that the Courts will be alert to artificial expedients intended to exaggerate a distinction between the two journeys. Such artificial expedients will be discounted entirely. This approach is clear from the highly significant nineteenth century English case of *Williams v James*[65] *which was relied on in Irvine Knitters*. This English case involved the owner of the *solum* of the route of an easement of access seeking a declaration for

65 (1867) LR 2 CP 577.

trespass to land. The easement benefited a field known as the Nine acre field. The owner of that field also owned two adjoining fields known as Parrott's land. Those two fields had no easement over the plaintiff's land. In the summer of 1866 the tenant of all three fields mowed all three fields and stacked the hay on the Nine acre field. In September the tenant sold the hay to the defendant who extracted it via the route of the easement. The jury found that the stacking of the hay was done "honestly."[66] All the judges opining considered this significant. Bovill, C.J. indicated that there must be a *bona fide* and not a mere colourable use of the right of way.[67] The stacking of the hay was in the ordinary and reasonable uses of the dominant tenement and therefore complied with this. So too was carriage of the hay out within the "ordinary and reasonable" uses of the servitude itself. Similar sentiments were expressed by Montague Smith J[68] and Willes J. The latter of these judges expressed himself as follows:[69]

> The finding of the jury was, that the land was used honestly, and not in order to get a right of way further on. This is equivalent to finding that the stacking of hay on the Nine acre field was in the reasonable and ordinary use of it as a field; and also that the carting was from the Nine acre field and not from Parrott's land.

There was no issue of using the ground as a distribution centre to commercial retail centres in this English case although, it seems reasonable to surmise that the hay would be used on other farms or perhaps even sold at market.

In the passage of his opinion in *Irvine Knitters* quoted earlier, Lord Cameron expressly reserved his view as to whether goods could be taken over the servient tenement by means of the servitude into the part of the new shop located on the dominant tenement, then immediately out onto the public road and then directly into the remainder of the shop outside the dominant tenement. If this indeed were to be possible it would amount to a neat trick in the particular location of the shop to enable circumvention of the *Irvine Knitters* rule. The very same device came up for consideration in a more recent English case involving an agricultural operation.[70] A farmer owned two separate but adjacent fields only the first of which was benefited by an easement of access. The first field also benefited from a gate leading directly out to the public highway. The easement could not be used by the

66 At 577.
67 At 580.
68 At 582-83.
69 At 582.
70 *Giles v Tarry* [2012] EWCA Civ 837.

famer to bring his sheep directly to the second field. So, to circumvent this limitation, he led them over the easement of access into the first field and out onto the public road. Following a brief pause on the public road, he led them back into the dominant tenement and across into the adjacent land. In the Court of Appeal it was held this was an artificial device or expedient and the farmer, in substance and intention, was using the easement to access property outwith the dominant tenement.[71] From this it is clear that in applying the *Irvine Knitters* rule that the law will give no regard to commercially pointless and self cancelling manoeuvres intended to give an impression that there are two separate journeys.

(10) Servitude conditions in the servitude excluding the activity

In some situations the servient proprietor may be able to preclude the activity which the dominant proprietor wishes to carry out on the dominant tenement to justify the distinction between the first and second journeys. For example, if a servitude of access is granted with the express servitude condition that the servitude will not be used to facilitate storage or a distribution centre on the dominant tenement, the servient proprietor will be entitled to seek interdict of any traffic purporting to use the servitude where that traffic is bringing material into the dominant tenement for storage or distribution even to adjacent property owned by the dominant proprietor. An example of this occurred in a recent English case.[72] In that case the storage of agricultural materials on the dominant tenement where those materials had been grown outside the dominant tenement was held to be in breach of the title conditions (imposing a servitude condition) requiring it to be used for the business of running an agricultural and forestry estate.[73] Consequently, it was not permissible to seek to use the easement to facilitate such storage.

E. Conclusion

In all of the above it is important to recognise that the potential existence of various exceptions does not empty the *Irvine Knitters* rule against use of the dominant tenement as a bridge of all substance. There remain

71 At paras 10-23 per Norris J.

72 *Wilkins and Wilkins v Lewis* [2005] EWHC 1710 (Ch).

73 See *Wilkins* at paras 31 and 37 et seq, especially at 50.

cases, chiefly involving a building or a business in a building straddling the dominant tenement and adjacent land, where it does operate – indeed this is illustrated by the actual decision in *Irvine Knitters*.[74] However, the various exceptions outlined above are yet to be fully judicially explored and developed. If this is done the rigid use of the rule to cause injustice will be avoided and Scottish property law will operate better for both the dominant and servient proprietors.

74 See also the South African case of *Berdur Properties (Pty) Ltd v 76 Commercial Road (Pty) Ltd* 1998 (4) SA 62 (D).

4

Primary Clients, Secondary Clients, Surrogate Clients and Non-Clients – The Expanding Duty of Care of Scottish Solicitors

Kenneth Swinton

Until the publication by Professor Rennie of his monograph *Solicitors' Negligence*[1] in 1997 there was no coherent treatment of the liability of Scottish solicitors for their negligent acts or omissions. Thereafter Professor Rennie published a volume of opinions on professional negligence[2] and has published a stream of articles which relate to the professional practice of conveyancing. He has continued to make himself available for opinion work as well as appearing as an expert witness in many cases. Law and practice has continued to develop over the last two decades and this chapter considers how factors have developed which may have expanded the duty of care over this period without seeking to provide a comprehensive update of Professor Rennie's work.

1 R Rennie, *Solicitors' Negligence* (1997).
2 R Rennie, *Opinions on Professional Negligence in Conveyancing – The Opinions of Professor Robert Rennie* (2004).

A. Introduction

The fundamental duties of a Scottish solicitor have not changed over the years. However they have been subject to formal elaboration and expansion in Codes of Conduct, Standards of Conduct and Standards of Service. A solicitor is expected to place the interests of the client above her own,[3] to avoid conflicts of interest[4] and to respect the confidentiality of a client's business.[5] It is trite law that a solicitor owes those duties to a client but does not owe duties to third parties, in general. Where a solicitor acts for more than one party then she may do so only where there is no conflict or at least there is only a potential conflict of interests[6] but not an actual conflict.[7] Where confidential information is obtained from one client and it becomes of value to another client then a conflict will occur. The dilemma is whether to breach confidence and make a disclosure or to maintain the confidence and risk a subsequent claim for negligence or negligent misrepresentation.[8] There is only one course of action which is to resign the agency for one or both parties.[9]

The primary duty of a solicitor is to the client and is based on the law of agency. While the term professional negligence is commonly used this is not based on delictual liability but a breach of contract. Where a claim is made by a third party it must be based on delict. This is problematic as pure economic loss cannot be recovered in delict although it is available in cases based on negligent misstatement.[10]

Over the last two decades, a uniform series of basic contractual obligations owed by solicitors to lenders has resulted from the introduction of the Council of Mortgage Lenders Scottish Solicitors' Handbook,[11] This

---

3 Law Society of Scotland Practice Rules 2011, r B1.4.

4 2011 Rules, r B1.7; Charter of Core Principles of the European Legal Profession and Code of Conduct for European Lawyers (2008) principle C, Code 3.2.

5 2011 Rules, r B1.6; Charter of Core Principles of the European Legal Profession and Code of Conduct for European Lawyers (2008) principle B, Code 2.3.

6 2011 Rules, r B1.7.2.

7 Ibid, r B1.7.1.

8 *Bank of East Asia Ltd v Shepherd & Wedderburn* 1995 *SLT* 1074; *Frank Houlgate Investment Co Ltd v Biggart Baillie LLP* [2014] CSIH 79; *Marks & Spencer Group Plc v Freshfields Bruckhaus Deringer* [2004] EWCA Civ 741, [2004] 1 WLR 2331; *Prince Jefri Bolkiah v KPMG* [1999] 2 AC 222; *Bristol & West Building Society v Aitken Nairn* 1999 SC 678;*Clark Boyce v Mouat* [1994] 1 AC 428; *Leeds & Holbeck Building Society v Alex Morrison* 2001 SCLR 41.

9 See A Paterson and B Ritchie *Law, Practice and Conduct for Solicitors* (2006), Ch 7 for a discussion.

10 Rennie, *Negligence* (n 1), para 2.01 and the authorities cited there.

11 Available at http://www.cml.org.uk/cml/handbook/scotland

covers solicitors acting in the constitution of securities for lenders in relation to residential mortgages, both for purchase and re-mortgage purposes as well as many buy to let commercial loans. The existence of clear standard obligations has led to the growth of situations where solicitors have been found wanting in failing to either (a) recognise the existence of an actual conflict of interests between a purchaser client and lender client or (b) obtain the purchasing client's authority to make disclosures to the lender. Smith and Barton[12] writing in 1995 devote a whole chapter to disciplinary proceedings relating to conflicts of interest. None of the cases digested refer to conflicts between purchaser and lender. The Scottish Solicitors Discipline Tribunal has in recent years considered what appears to be a steady stream of cases where solicitors appear to have regarded their purchasing clients as the primary clients and the disclosure to the lenders of surrounding circumstances as of secondary importance.

Furthermore the Money Laundering Regulations 1993[13] imposed new obligations on solicitors to identify their clients. Those duties had not had a significant impact on practice when *Solicitors' Negligence* was published. In the intervening years the obligations in relation to prevention of money laundering have expanded considerably,[14] imposing increasingly onerous duties on solicitors to identify the clients, the source of funds and the wealth of the clients from which these funds are obtained. The intention is to prevent the legal profession and the financial system becoming conduits which assist criminals in concealing or converting the proceeds of their unlawful activities. Furthermore solicitors fall within the regulated sector and are obliged to make authorised disclosures of suspicious activity to the relevant authority under pain of criminal prosecution[15] or regulatory sanctions.[16] This has led to attempts founded on failures in a criminal or regulatory sense as evidence of a contractual or delictual failure on solicitors acting for private clients with a view to imposing civil liability, even where separate agents are instructed by the borrower and lender.[17]

12 I Smith and J Barton, *Procedures and Decisions of the Scottish Solicitors Discipline Tribunal* (1995).

13 Money Laundering Regulation 1993, SI 1993/1933.

14 Currently represented by the Money Laundering Regulations 2007, SI 2007/2157 and the Proceeds of Crime Act 2002, particularly Part 7 Money Laundering.

15 Proceeds of Crime Act 2002, s330.

16 Money Laundering Regulations 1993, SI 1993/1933, reg 42.

17 *Cheshire Mortgage Corporation Ltd v Grandison* [2012] CSIH 66; 2013 SC 160; *Frank Houlgate Investment Co Ltd v Biggart Baillie LLP* [2014] CSIH 79, where there was a finding against the solicitors on other grounds.

Such a possibility in the context of inadequate professional service claims has been recognised by Professor Rennie.[18] In this way, the Law Society of Scotland investigating conduct complaints or the Scottish Legal Services Commission investigating service complaints may in fact operate as a surrogate for the client in providing a basis for a negligence claim.

The consolidated Practice Rules[19] require that a solicitor should provide in writing details of the work to be undertaken at the earliest opportunity.[20] A solicitor should accordingly be aware of who their client is. Such terms of engagement will generally not only specify what work is to be done but what is not to be done. Thus it should prevent the subsequent expansion through leakage into other areas or others who might potentially later claim client status.

B. The Move to Written Terms of Business

The relationship between solicitor and client is one of agency,[21] which makes entirely appropriate the term "law agent."[22] As noted, above lenders instructing solicitors in residential lending work will impose their terms for business through the CML Handbook. It would however be unusual for consumers to impose written terms. Writing in 1996, Professor Rennie stated:[23]

> The basic duty of care owed by a solicitor is to his or her client. Similarly any specific contractual obligations are, generally speaking, owed to the client who instructs the legal task concerned.

The corollary to this simple truth is that no duty of care is owed to others in pursuit of the interests of the client. Professor Rennie noted then that the contract between solicitor and client is rarely in writing.[24] The converse is now the case as a result of the imposition of a practice rule. The terms of business on which the client instructs the agent must be set out in writing

18 Rennie, *Negligence* (n 1), para 11.03.
19 Law Society of Scotland Practice Rules 2011, r B4.1-4.2.
20 This is subject to certain exceptions which are not discussed here.
21 Rennie, *Negligence* (n 1), para 3.02.
22 Law Agents (Scotland) Act 1873; J H Begg, *A Treatise on the Law of Scotland Relating to Law Agents* (1873); The Scottish Law Agents Society was incorporated by Royal Charter in 1884, all indicating this then universal usage.
23 Rennie, *Negligence* (n 1), para 4.01.
24 Ibid para 3.02.

at the earliest practical opportunity.[25] There should be no doubt as to the identity of the client, therefore, in contemporary practice. Nor should there be doubt as to the nature of the work for which the solicitor has been instructed. The terms of business should set out the extent of the services to be provided and the estimated fees and outlays.[26] Setting out the scope of the engagement offers comfort to the solicitor which can prevent subsequent claims arising out of "mission creep" to other areas which were beyond the initial instructions. For example, when instructed in relation to the sale of an investment property, a solicitor may undertake the conveyancing work and exclude liability for advice in relation to taxation.[27]

There might be a temptation to include in the written terms of engagement some restriction of liability on the part of the solicitor. Such attempted limitations of liability are unlikely to be effective. Firstly, solicitors are under the general obligation to act in the best interests of clients and not to allow personal interests to affect advice to or actings on behalf of clients.[28] Secondly, under the Unfair Contract Terms Act 1977, any exclusion of liability for loss or other damage through negligence can only be given effect where it satisfies a reasonableness test.[29] In *Killick v PricewaterhouseCoopers [No1]*[30] the defendant accountants argued unsuccessfully before Neuberger, J (as he then was) that the cap on liability of £10m imposed in their terms of business was reasonable. On this basis, it is submitted that exclusions or limitations of liability in terms of business are unlikely to meet the threshold required to establish reasonableness. Furthermore, where the client is a consumer, the Unfair Terms in Consumer Contract Regulations will apply[31] provided the contract is in standard terms – in other words, where the consumer has no opportunity to individually negotiate it. If an imbalance in parties' rights and obligations to the detriment of the consumer arises from the terms of the contract it is to be regarded as *prima facie* unfair. Where, for example, a term excludes or limits liability in the event of total or partial non-performance or inadequate performance of a

25 Law Society of Scotland Practice Rules 2011. r B4.2.
26 Ibid.
27 In *Stevens v Hewats* [2013] CSOH 61; 2013 *SLT* 763 the agents in question had been instructed to prepare a gift of heritable property. Had the terms of engagement specifically excluded the provision of advice in relation to inheritance tax then, arguably, there would have been no basis of action.
28 Law Society of Scotland Practice Rules 2011, r B1.4.1 and B1.4.2.
29 Unfair Contract Terms Act 1977, s 2.
30 [2001] PNLR 1.
31 Unfair Terms in Consumer Contract Regulations 1999, SI 1999/2083.

contract for services, this is like to fall within the ambit of unfairness.[32] In this context, a limitation of liability clause has been held to contravene the Regulations.[33] Where the client is a commercial entity the economic balance may favour the client. The CML Handbook[34] adopts the common law standard[35] in respect of the duty of care owed by the solicitor to the lender and then imposes a series of specific and more onerous duties.[36] These may in turn be supplemented by individual lenders' own requirements and the possibility exists of transaction-specific further instructions issued with the loan papers. There is no opportunity for the solicitor to include a term which might limit her liability to the lender.

As well as providing clearer guidance to clients through having written terms of business the use of such terms should allow solicitors to avoid claims where the alleged want of due care and skills relates to a matter which is ancillary to the business undertaken – such as advice regarding surveys[37] or finance[38] in relation to a purchase. Of course those terms of engagement might seek to restrict liability to third parties. Whether this would be effective would depend on whether such a limitation of liability was reasonable.[39]

C. Identification of the Client

As noted in the previous section, the change brought about through professional practice rules requiring written terms of business has brought clarity in identifying to whom the legal services are delivered and who will be responsible for payment. However that is not quite the same thing as identification of the person who provides the instructions. Are the instructions those of the person who presents herself as the client to the

---

32 1999 Regulations, art 5 and schedule para 1 (b).

33 *West v Ian Finlay and Associates* [2014] EWCA Civ 316, in relation to the terms of business of a firm of architects.

34 CML Handbook (n 11).

35 Ibid para 1.4.

36 For example in terms of para 5.9.1, the solicitor must ask a purchasing client if the balance of the price is being provided without resort to other lending and where there is other lending to disclose this to the instructing lender. This is the case whether or not that loan is to be secured on the property and has no impact of the validity or ranking of the security.

37 Rennie, *Opinions* (n 2), p 436.

38 Ibid p 438.

39 Unfair Contract Terms Act 1977, s2; *Hedley Byrne v Heller and Partners* [1964] AC 465; [1963] 1 All ER 575; *Caparo Industries v Dickman* [1990] 2 AC 605; [1990] 1 All ER 568.

solicitor or who she represents she is? There has been no change in the underlying common law in relation to agency. However the imposition of duties in relation to anti-money laundering processes has clouded this issue. The first Money Laundering Regulations[40] in the UK came into force on 1st April 1994. Solicitors fell within the regulated sector for the purposes of the Regulations and were obliged to identify clients. A major exemption permitted solicitors to excuse existing clients from the requirements to produce documentary evidence of identity. Given the novelty of the obligations and the noted exemption it is unsurprising that Professor Rennie did not require to address these issues in 1996.

The relationship between solicitor and client is one principally governed by the law of agency. Where the solicitor is acting for a disclosed principal then the solicitor will not, in general, become personally liable to third parties.[41] The position is less straightforward where the principal turns out to be a fraudster, impersonating another. In such a situation there is scope to argue for the solicitor to incur personal liability on the basis she had no instructions from the appropriate party. Laura Macgregor suggests that where the agent has been neither fraudulent nor negligent in misrepresenting his authority, the only possible action which the third party has against the agent is the contractual action of breach of warranty of authority.[42] She indicates that the theoretical basis of the action is difficult to discover,[43] but adopts the approach taken by Gloag,[44] who refers to the principle as arising out of the contract between the third party and the agent. In this context, however, there is no effective contract between the agent and the third party. In *Scott v J. B. Livingston & Nicol*[45] Lord Coulsfield states that the normal rule is that the agent is liable in delict on the basis of breach of warranty of authority.[46] This is borne out by the earlier case of *Anderson v John Croall & Sons Ltd*[47] which is generally taken as the standard authority for this proposition in Scotland.

---

40 Money Laundering Regulations 1993, SI 1993/1933.

41 W M Gloag and R C Henderson *The Law of Scotland*, 13th edn, by H Macqueen et al (2012) para 19.27 and the authorities referred to therein.

42 L Macgregor, "Agency," in *The Laws of Scotland: Stair Memorial Encyclopaedia*, Reissue (2002) para 168.

43 Ibid.

44 W M Gloag, *Law of Contract*, 2nd edn (1929) p 155.

45 1990 *SLT* 305.

46 *Scott* (n 45) at 307.

47 (1903) 11 *SLT* 163; see also *Salvesen & Co v Rederi AB Nordstjernan* (1903) 6 F 64 9 (which was partially reversed in the House of Lords on other grounds (1905) 7 F (HL) 101; (1905) 13 *SLT* 20.

The point was raised in sharp focus in the recent case of *Cheshire Mortgage Corporation v Grandison*.[48] Lenders who were separately represented raised actions against firms of solicitors who had acted apparently for the owners of properties who raised funds from the pursuers secured over the properties. Some time after the recording of the relevant standard securities it became apparent that the persons who had instructed the solicitors in relation to representing their interests in the constitution of the securities had impersonated the true owners of the properties. The securities, based on forged signatures and false identities were worthless. The lenders sued on the basis of breach of warranty of authority.[49]

Evidence was led as to the steps taken by the agents in question to identify the persons who presented themselves as the clients.[50] In neither the Outer House nor Inner House judgments is any reference made to the purposes for which identification was being sought. The items sought would of course be familiar to anyone dealing with the anti-money laundering requirements in contemporary practice. A professional operating within the regulated sector, such as a solicitor, is obliged to carry out customer due diligence.[51] This requires sufficient proof of identity on the basis of documents obtained from reliable and independent sources.[52] The 1993 Regulations themselves do not specify what these might be. However guidance from the Joint Money Laundering Steering Group[53] is regarded as authoritative[54] and requires two forms of check – the first to identify the person and the second to tie that person to the address provided. A failure by a regulated professional to comply with these requirements is a criminal offence.[55] Furthermore it is a regulatory requirement for solicitors to comply with this regime[56] in all cases whether or not the business falls with the statutory money laundering definitions. It is surprising that there is no mention in the case of basis on which the solicitors in question collected

---

48 [2012] CSIH 66; 2013 SC 160.

49 Further claims were made based on the letters of obligation which had been issued by the "borrowers" agent. These were disposed of on the basis that a letter of obligation was granted as an ancillary obligation to those which were established in the principal contract. Where that principal contract had been reduced then the ancillary obligations must also fall: *Mason v AR Robertson and Black* 1993 *SLT* 773.

50 *Cheshire Mortgage Corporation* (n 48) at para 11.

51 Money Laundering Regulations 2007, SI 2007/ 2157, reg 7.

52 2007 Regulations, reg 5.

53 Available at http://www.jmlsg.org.uk/industry-guidance/article/guidance

54 It must now be approved by HM Treasury.

55 2007 Regulations, reg 45.

56 Law Society of Scotland Practice Rules 2011, r B6.23.1.

these data or whether they met the statutory and regulatory requirements. It is submitted that compliance with those standards will satisfy the common law requirement of absence of knowledge or lack of negligence necessary to make a breach of warranty of authority entirely innocent. In order for there to be a successful prosecution then a criminal standard of proof would be required. The Scottish Solicitors Discipline Tribunal also applies a criminal standard in relation to evidence. In the context of a civil action for breach of warranty of authority presumably the agent would have to address having taken reasonable steps only. In the instant case it is apparent that the identification requirements did comply with the anti-money laundering regime in place at the time.[57] What is equally clear is that while the practices of the solicitors in question met the standards in place in 2004 when the frauds occurred, the need for ongoing monitoring on a risk-based approach required under the 2007 Regulations ought to have raised suspicions about the written requests to transmit funds electronically to third parties. Once funds had been transmitted to the agent acting for the borrowers they become the property of the borrowers.[58] Arguably the solicitor would not come any duty to the lender to disclose suspicions at this point unless the security was in an "all sums due and to be become due" format. However, she must make a suspicious activity to report to the National Crime Agency.[59] Nonetheless the compliance with the statutory and regulatory requirements and the ability of an authorised person to rely on identification carried out by another such authorised person[60]were referred to in the *Cheshire Mortgage Corporation* case.[61] It was not accepted that there had been any such reliance as the business had already been introduced to the lender prior to the involvement of the solicitor for the "borrower."[62] As the court noted:[63]

57 *Frank Houlgate Ltd v Biggart Baillie* [2009] CSOH 165; 2010 *SLT* 527. Lord Drummond Young's opinion at para 25 dismissed claims based on the Money Laundering Regulations 2003 which have now been replaced by the 2007 Regulations.

58 *R v Preddy* [1996] AC 815; [1996] 3 WLR 255; [1996] 3 All ER 481; *R v Waya* [2012] UKSC 51; [2013] 1 AC 294; [2012] 3 WLR 1188; [2013] 1 All ER 889.

59 Proceeds of Crime Act 2002 part VII. See n 105 in relation to the timing of the duty.

60 See currently Money Laundering Regulations 2007, SI 2007/ 2157, reg 17.

61 Outer House judgment [2011] CSOH 157; 2012 *SLT* 672 at para 16 being referred to as 'KYC rules.' See further K Swinton, "The Potential for civil liability arising from failures in client identification requirements under the Money Laundering Regulations" (2011) 79 SLG 97.

62 Nor for that matter had the solicitor confirmed in writing that he consented to his identification being relied on as required by the Regulations.

63 *Cheshire Mortgage Corporation Ltd v Grandison* [2012] CSIH 66; 2013 SC 160 at para 32 per

> All that the agent is warranting is that he has a client and that client has given him authority to act. It would be quite unreasonable and inappropriate to extend this to an implied warranty that his client has a certain attribute or attributes.

While there may be circumstances where the solicitor does warrant some attribute in relation to the client which can be relied on by third parties then that will amount to a representation and will bring matters with the principle articulated in *Hedley Bryne & Co Ltd v Heller & Partners*[64] as refined in *Caparo Industries v Dickman*.[65] There may be situations where the client's identity is correctly ascertained by the solicitor but an important attribute becomes a matter of contention. In *Frank Houlgate v Biggart Baillie*[66] solicitors acted for a party who was exactly who he claimed to be. However he represented that he owned an estate which was owned by another unrelated person with a similar name. The solicitors acted on behalf of the fraudster who borrowed money on the security of the property with other agents acting for the lenders. The action was framed in part on the basis of breach of warranty of authority. For the reasons discussed above it was held there was no warranty on the part of the agents for the fraudster that he was the registered proprietor of the subjects.[67] However the solicitors were subsequently found liable on other grounds. After the security had been registered the fraud came to light and the fraudster admitted to his solicitor that the fraud had been committed. He asked for time to put matters right and repay the loan. However the fraudster used the breathing space to top up the sums advanced. The solicitor failed to withdraw from acting, advise the agents acting for the lender or make a suspicious activity report at this point under the Proceeds of Crime Act 2002.[68] It was held that the solicitor ought to have resigned the agency and disclosed the fraud to the solicitors acting for the lender, the perception in the mind of the solicitor that he was bound by client confidentiality being entirely misplaced.[69] The policy argument on which the decision is based is clear:[70]

L Clarke, delivering the opinion of the Court.

64 [1964] AC 465; [1963] 1 All ER 575.

65 [1990] 2 AC 605; [1990] 1 All ER 568. See further Rennie, *Negligence* (n 1), para 4.03 et seq.

66 [2009] CSOH 165; 2010 *SLT* 527.

67 *Frank Houlgate* (n 66) at para 28 (opinion of Lord Drummond Young).

68 *Frank Houlgate Investment Co Ltd v Biggart Baillie* LLP [2014] CSIH 79; 2014 *SLT* 1001 paragraph 9.

69 The solicitor in question was censured for his conduct and fined the maximum £10000: *Mair* [2009] SSDT 1463.

70 *Frank Houlgate* (n 68) at para 34 (opinion of Lord Menzies).

> Society expects high standards from a Scottish solicitor. Perhaps first and foremost, a solicitor is expected to have the highest standards of honesty. She is an officer of the court, and owes obligations to the client, to the court, to fellow members of the profession, and to the general public.

The legal basis on which to hang that policy provided divided opinions. In the Inner House, Lord Menzies held that once the solicitor became aware of the fraud and failed to take steps to dissociate himself from it be became an accessory to the fraud.[71] There was, in effect, a continuing implied representation to the solicitor for the lender that he is not aware of any fundamental dishonesty or fraud which might make the security transaction worthless.[72] This line of reasoning is supported by the three Lords Ordinary who gave opinions at earlier stages of the proceedings[73] and Lord McEwan sitting in the Inner House.[74] It must be taken as settling the law. Lord Malcolm however dissented from this analysis – in his view there was no need to invoke the concept of accessory to the fraud. Rather, he held that once the fraud became known the solicitor came under a freestanding duty to take reasonable care to prevent further foreseeable losses flowing from the fraudulent transaction which he had unwittingly facilitated.[75] This may be sufficient to dispose of the case in question, but had the security granted been for a fixed amount rather than 'all sums due or to become due', then this suggests that no such duty would have arisen. On the other hand if the test is accessory to the fraud then in the fixed security example the solicitor would still come under a duty of disclosure. It would be odd if the resulting obligation on the solicitor depended solely on whether the security covered further advances or not. Accordingly the analysis of all the other senators who have given opinions is preferable to that of Lord Malcolm.

D. The Primary Client and the Secondary Client

Where the same solicitor acts for both the lender and the borrower each is owed a duty of care by the solicitor. This causes no issues where the interests of the lender and borrower coincide – most obviously in ensuring

71 Ibid at para 45.
72 Ibid at para 43.
73 *Frank Houlgate Investment Co Ltd v Biggart Baillie* LLP [2009] CSOH 165; 2010 *SLT* 527 at para 21 (Lord Drummond Young); 2011 CSOH 160; 2012 *SLT* 256 at para 33 (Lord Glennie); [2013] CSOH 80; 2013 *SLT* 993 at para 43 (Lord Hodge).
74 *Frank Houlgate* (n 68) at para 89.
75 Ibid at para 81.

there is a good and marketable title.[76] However the Practice Rules distinguish the situation where there is potential for conflict from that where there is actual conflict. In the former situation, the rules provide a series of limited exceptions.[77] However, the primary rule must be adhered to where an actual conflict arises. In *Midland Bank plc v Cameron, Thom, Peterkin & Duncans*[78] solicitors had made representations to the lender as to the borrowing client's means. This was inaccurate and the lenders sought to hold the agents liable. Lord Jauncey in finding for the defenders established a four part test: (a) there must be an assumption of responsibility; (b) the solicitor must represent to the other party that he has the necessary skill in relation to the representation; (c) the other party must rely on the representation and; (d) the solicitor must be aware that the third party would rely on the representation. This is a straightforward restatement of the principle in *Hedley Byrne*. Lord Jauncey expressed the view that where the solicitor is engaged to prepare the security by a lender the decision to lend has already been taken and there are no other duties incumbent on the solicitor.[79] The decision in *Midland Bank* has been followed in the Irish Supreme Court case of *Doran v Delaney*[80] and has never been expressly overruled in this jurisdiction, however Rennie doubted it would be followed today.[81] That must be correct – in the post-*Caparo* era cases such as *White v Jones,*[82] *Robertson v Watt & Co*[83] and *Holmes v Bank of Scotland,*[84] step (b) in particular was absent.

Rennie, in considering the attitudes which prevailed at the time of *Midland Bank*, expressed the view that at the time the solicitor treated the purchasing/borrowing client as primary and the lending client was accorded a secondary status.[85] If that ever was true, the CML Handbook, applying to residential transactions, makes explicit the obligations on a solicitor to make disclosures. The decision to lend is now subject to revision right up until release of funds. Notwithstanding the contractual equal status of

76 Law Society of Scotland Practice Rules 2011, r B1.7.1 and B2.1.2: "You shall not act for two or more parties whose interests conflict."

77 See 2011 Rules, r B1.2 generally.

78 1988 *SLT* 611.

79 *Midland Bank* (n 78) at 618.

80 [1998] IESC 66.

81 Rennie, *Negligence* (n 1) para 5.01.

82 [1995] 2 AC 207; [1995] 1 All ER 691.

83 2nd Div, 4 July 1995, unreported.

84 2002 *SLT* 544.

85 Rennie, *Negligence* (n 1) para 5.01.

both borrowing and lending clients it will be seen below that the primary/secondary approach has not entirely died out. Two issues in the Handbook require special attention. Solicitors are obliged to report cash incentives[86] and situations where they will not have control over the whole purchase price[87] on the one hand and on the other surrounding circumstances such as the property having changed hands in the six months prior to the current transaction.[88] These provisions are designed to prevent lenders becoming victims of mortgage fraud by the ramping up of the purchase price and circulation of deposits. Some instances have involved a combination of all three techniques.

E. The Regulator as a Surrogate for Client Claims

The Law Society has taken disciplinary action *ex proprio motu*[89] in a number of cases where the lender has not raised any complaint. Over the last six years, fifteen such surrogate claims have come before the Scottish Solicitors Discipline Tribunal. In these cases, with the exception of *Baillie,* no disclosure as required in the CML Handbook was made to the respective lenders at the time of making a report on title and requesting the funds. In *Baillie,* disclosures were made in bald terms that the property had not been owned by the seller in the present transaction. The Tribunal were critical of the solicitor in meeting the literal obligations specified in the Handbook[90] but failing to provide information that the settlement of the current and prior transactions were simultaneous, thus failing to meet the common law duties which are preserved by the Handbook.[91] On the basis of these decisions it would appear that there still remain a number of solicitors who are prepared to treat the interests of a lending client as secondary to those of a private purchaser.

86 CML Handbook (n 11), para 6.4.4.

87 Ibid, 6.4.5.

88 Ibid, 5.1.1.

89 *Pervez* [No5] 2008 SSDT 1427; *Dunbar* [No1] 2011 SSDT 1540; *Davidson* 2011 SSDT 1557; *Campbell* 2012 SSDT 1585; *Coogans* [No2] 2012 SSDT 1580; *Kerr* 2012 SSDT 1587; *Joss* 2012 SSDT 1603; *Lints* [No1] 2013 SSDT 1607; *Campbell* 2013 SSDT 1613; *MacDonald* 2013 SSDT 1618; *Aikman* 2013 1629; *Tulips* [2013] SSDT 1631; *Haywood* [2014] SSDT 1645; *Baillie* [2014] SSDT; *Muir* [2014] SSDT; K Swinton, "Compliance with CML Handbook" (2012) 80 SLG 92; K Swinton, "SSDT and CML Handbook Breaches" (2014) 82 SLG 21.

90 CML Handbook (n 11), para 5.1.1.

91 Ibid, para 1.4.

Where subsequent disclosures were made by the solicitors concerned, the funds had already been advanced and the securities registered. It was too late for the lenders to reconsider the underwriting of the loans. The prompt for the late disclosures appears to have been the Society, following on routine Accounts Rules[92] inspections of the respective firms. By taking these matters to the Tribunal it is argued that the Society has become a surrogate client – it appears that the Society has moved away from inspections for mere compliance with the Accounts Rules to a quality inspection of the work undertaken by solicitors at least in respect of secured lending work. Disciplinary penalties sanctioned by the Tribunal do not amount to findings of negligence. It may be that lenders involved in all the cases which have come before the Tribunal have not experienced defaults and have not had cause to call up the respective securities. Even if they had, it would only be in the event that they suffered a shortfall on the realisation of the security subjects that any claim for negligence would lie against the solicitor. Nonetheless it would be a powerful argument should such a claim arise that the Tribunal had regarded the solicitor's conduct to amount to a serious and reprehensible breach of the standards required of a solicitor.[93] The surrogate claimant, the Society, thus paves the way for the natural claimant should a loss subsequently be incurred.

The counter argument is that the Society has not expanded its role at all. The original purpose of Accounts Rules inspections was to assure the Society, representing the broader profession, that the Guarantee Fund is not put at risk.[94] The Fund is available to compensate persons who in the opinion of the Council suffer pecuniary loss by reason of dishonesty on the part of any solicitor.[95] However the role of inspection has now broadened to include a supervisory remit under the Money Laundering Regulations.[96] The typical situation where the Guarantee Fund is invoked is that where the solicitor has misappropriated funds under her control but it is not restricted to such situations. For example where a solicitor conveyed a property not to the original purchaser but to an innocent third party by fraudulently altering a signed deed in the event of that party suffering loss then the third party may have a claim on the Fund[97] Similarly, conduct which is contrary to

---

92 Law Society of Scotland Practice Rules 2011, r B6.18.2.
93 *Sharp v Council of Law Society of Scotland* 1984 SC 129, 1984 *SLT* 313.
94 Law Society of Scotland Practice Rules 2011 B6.18.3.
95 Solicitors (Scotland) Act 1980, s43.
96 Law Society of Scotland Practice Rules 2011, r B6.18.3.
97 *Pocock's Trustee v Skene Investments* [2012] CSIH 61; *Russell Taylor* [2004] SSDT 1148.

the express terms of Practice Rules may give rise to a claim but not where the party seeking to found on that conduct was aware of the terms of the Rules breach.[98] However in the cases before the Tribunal discussed above, the lender and purchaser were both represented by the same agent and duties are owed to both parties so there is direct representation. In *Target Holdings Ltd v Redferns*[99] it was held that the solicitor was under a duty in a back to back situation, as occurred in the recent Discipline Tribunal cases, at common law to disclose to the lender the nature of the back to back transaction.[100] In such circumstances lenders typically argue that had a partial disclosure or in some cases full disclosure of the facts been made then the decision to lend would have been rescinded and therefore but for the failure to disclose relevant information no loss would have been incurred.[101]

Quick successive sales of property are a means of inflating the price of property which can be used to induce lenders to advance more money on property than might otherwise be the case. This is a recognised typology of money laundering.[102] Of course, if the solicitor is aware of such a situation he is obliged under the common law principles[103] including accessory to fraud to make a disclosure to the lender.[104] Furthermore, once the mortgage

98 See *Billig v Council of the Law Society of Scotland* [2006] CSOH 148, 2007 SC 32. The appellant who had lent money to a client of a solicitor sought to found on personal guarantees issued by the solicitor which were prohibited by the Accounts Rules then in operation. He was aware as a result of legal advice received that the solicitor was not in a position to grant those guarantees but proceeded on the mistaken belief that he might successfully look to the Fund to make good the losses as the conduct of the solicitor must have been dishonest. It was held that it was reasonable to exercise discretion in such circumstances to refuse payment.

99 [1996] AC 421.

100 See Rennie, *Negligence* (n 1), para 5.04 for a detailed discussion of the decision in the Court of Appeal. By the time the case came to be discussed by the House of Lords it proceeded on a presumed set of facts where the solicitors were assumed to have advanced the funds ahead of obtaining a valid security which was later registered. It was held on the basis of breach of trust that this should be calculated on a basis of the actual loss attributable directly to the breach.

101 *AIB Group (UK) Plc v Mark Redler & Co Solicitors* [2014] UKSC 58, reaffirming the decision in *Target* should be narrowly interpreted. As Rennie has noted *Negligence* (n 1) para 5.05 English law is rendered more complex by discussions of breach of trust in addition to contractual and tortious liability. See also Lord Toulson's opinion at paragraph 1 in *AIB Group*.

102 Financial Action Task Force, Report on *Money Laundering and Terrorist Financing: Vulnerabilities of Legal Professionals* (June 2013) p 46 Technique: Transferring Value – Back to Back or ABC Sales.

103 CML Handbook (n 11), para 1.4.

104 *Frank Houlgate Investment Co Ltd v Biggart Baillie LLP* [2014] CSIH 79. In *Cheshire*

funds have been received and used in conjunction with any deposit to acquire the property, at that point the proceeds of crime are being converted into another form which then itself represents the proceeds of crime.[105] This and only this triggers the requirement to make a suspicious activity report to the National Crime Agency.[106] Once the transaction is tainted by fraud then negligence claims will follow and will be irresistible.[107]

F. Third Party Claims

Begg notes:[108]

> Law Agents are under no obligation to attend to the interests of any persons except their own clients. To third parties they owe no duty but the negative one of abstaining from the commission of actual wrong.

Professor Rennie was able to restate this proposition from Begg when writing in 1996. The position in Scotland was that a solicitor was not liable in negligence to third parties.[109] The leading authority, as at the time of Begg's work, was *Robertson v Fleming*.[110] Professor Rennie predicted that the position adopted by the House of Lords in *Robertson* was liable to be reversed should the House be called to determine a similar point in the future. The House had recently considered matters in England in *White v Jones*[111] in relation to the liability of solicitors to disappointed beneficiaries. Lord Goff[112] referred to dicta in *Robertson*,[113] where the Lord Chancellor had stated that an entitlement to claim by disappointed beneficiaries did not form part of the law of Scotland nor of England. Lord Goff noted that this dicta, strictly speaking, did not form part of the *ratio* of the case. In *Robertson* the solicitor concerned had failed to create an effective security over a long

Mortgage Corporation (n 48) the solicitor had no knowledge, suspicion or grounds on which to suspect that there was a case of identity fraud.

105 Proceeds of Crime Act 2002 s340. Law Society [of England and Wales] *Anti-money Laundering Practice Note* (October 2013), para 11.4.4 – Lender issues. The SSDT has wrongly stated there to be a duty to make a SAR at a much earlier stage in a number of the cases cited above, for example, *Baillie* (n 89) at 58-59.

106 Proceeds of Crime Act 2002 s330.

107 *Frank Houlgate Investment Co Ltd v Biggart Baillie LLP* [2014] CSIH 79.

108 Begg, *Treatise* (n 22), ch 21, para 1.

109 Rennie, *Negligence* (n 1), para 4.01.

110 (1861) 23D (HL) 8; (1861) 4 Macq 167.

111 *White v Jones* [1995] 2 AC 207; [1995] 1 All ER 691.

112 *White* (n 111) at 258.

113 Ibid at 177.

lease. When the intended security holder died a claim was made by his beneficiaries which claim was ultimately unsuccessful. On that basis the comments were merely *obiter* and Lord Goff's analysis must be correct. The House of Lords by a majority of three to two in *White* held that a solicitor assumed a special duty towards potential beneficiaries and if that duty was breached then liability would follow. Such a duty could be by omission and not only negligent acts of commission.[114] The House found that it was a case akin to transferred loss,[115] where the beneficiary had a loss and no claim in contract and the deceased had a claim but no loss, and that it was fair just and reasonable in all the circumstances to hold the solicitor liable which was an incremental approach.[116]

While *White* may have set a new course in England, *Robertson* was a Scottish case, hence Professor Rennie's views that this still represented the law in Scotland but that it would be unlikely to remain good law should a Scottish case be taken to their Lordships' House. However, their Lordship's intervention did not prove necessary. As recently as 1990, *Robertson* had been seen as binding and determinative of the issue by Lord Weir in *Weir v J M Hodge & Son*.[117] However *Holmes v Bank of Scotland*[118] saw Lord Kingarth sitting in the Outer House depart from the line of authorities starting with *Robertson*. The reason for so doing was an unremarked upon and unreported Inner House decision from 1995[119] decided shortly after *White* and therefore binding upon him. For his part, Lord Kingarth saw no reason why *White* should not be followed in Scotland, notwithstanding the strong dissents therein from Lord Jauncey and Lord Mustill.[120]

That the deceased had a claim but no loss and the disappointed beneficiaries did is borne out by *Matthews v Hunter & Robertson Ltd*.[121] The executor brought a claim against the solicitors alleging that they had failed to effectively revoke a survivorship destination. The executor is said to be *eadam personam cum defuncto* and if the deceased had no loss to his estate at the moment prior to his death then the estate suffered no loss either. It was held by Lord Brodie that the additional *Caparo* limb of the test, that it

114 *Hedley Byrne & Co Ltd v Heller & Partners Ltd* [1964] AC 465; [1963] 2 All ER 575; *Henderson v. Merrett Syndicates Ltd*. [1995] 2 AC 14 5, 182, *per* Lord Goff.

115 *White* (n 111) at 265 (Lord Goff).

116 Ibid at 270 citing *Caparo Industies plc v Dickman* [1990] 2 AC 605 (Lord Brown Wilkinson).

117 1990 *SLT* 266.

118 2002 *SLT* 544.

119 *Robertson v Watt & Co*, 2nd Div, 4 July 1995, unreported.

120 *Holmes v Bank of Scotland* 2002 *SLT* 544 para 19.

121 [2008] CSOH 88; 2008 *SLT* 634.

was fair, just and reasonable in the circumstances, would not be satisfied in this situation. The principle of assumption of duty has been held to extend potentially to recipients of lifetime gifts. There is a fine distinction between the sort of negligent omission as in *White* or *Holmes* and a situation where there is advice tendered negligently to a client who then acts on that advice and the resulting will or conveyance which in its own terms is perfectly in order does not produce the desired effect. In *Fraser v McArthur Stewart*,[122] which related to the ineffective legacy of a croft based on negligent advice, it was held by Lord Brailsfield that *White* was not directly in point and that the facts were distinguishable. As a result the advice and the effects of the advice were severable and there was no assumption of duty on which the disappointed beneficiaries might found. In *Stevens v Hewats*[123] on the other hand the solicitors were instructed to convey a house and associated lands by way of gift. The disponer continued to reside in the property notwithstanding the gift. Some eight years later it was discovered that the conveyance was ineffective and a new conveyance was registered. At this time consideration was also given to the gifts with reservation rules for inheritance tax and a lease drawn up at market rent whereby the donor paid rent to the donee. Unfortunately the donor did not survive the necessary seven years. Claims were made both by the executors and the donee, in relation to the additional inheritance tax which was payable. The registering of a disposition on behalf of the donee has contractual aspects of the duty of care, as noted by Lord Tyre[124] but the assertion was made by the claimants that general tax planning advice was or ought to have been provided. Lord Tyre was of the view that a stateable case had been made out on the basis of the decision in *White* but that the issue required proof.[125] In the parallel action by the executors, Lord Tyre held on the same basis as *Matthews* that no claim lay against the solicitors.[126] To date *Stevens* is the only example of the *White* principle being applied in a conveyancing context in a reported case in Scotland. It is however clear that Lord Goff's incremental approach to the extension of liability expressed in *White* is exactly that and the application of the principle of assumption of risk is capable of adaptation to a number of different situations. The law will continue to develop.

122 [2008] CSOH 159; 2009 *SLT* 31.
123 [2013] CSOH 61; 2013 *SLT* 763.
124 *Stevens* (n 123) at para 13.
125 Ibid at 16.
126 *Milligan's Executors v Hewats* [2013] CSOH 60; 2013 *SLT* 758.

G. Third Party Claims for Inadequate Professional Service

Inadequate professional service is now defined as "professional services provided by a practitioner in connection with any matter in which the practitioner has been instructed by a client [which] were inadequate."[127] These provisions replace earlier provisions[128] which defined such services as not of the quality which could reasonably be expected of a competent solicitor. The relationship of inadequate professional service with negligence has been a source of uncertainty since the provisions were first enacted. Professor Rennie expressed the opinion that inadequate professional service is possible without negligence but whether the converse is true remains contentious in relation to the earlier provisions.[129] Paterson and Ritchie are of the opinion that the two often overlap.[130] In terms of section 11 of the 2007 Act the Scottish Legal Complaints Commission must, in considering what is fair and reasonable in all the circumstances, take into account the law, professional rules standards and guidance and any relevant codes of practice. When the provisions were being debated before the Scottish Parliament, the minister considered that there would be serious problems with requiring the Commission to separate negligence aspects from wider aspects of inadequate professional services.[131] So overlap is the order of the day and there is no comprehensive definition of inadequate professional services. Given the compensation levels are up to £20,000 and the Commission has a number of other tools such as ordering other steps to rectify the inadequate service this is a significant remedy for those affected by inadequate professional service.[132] Furthermore there is no need to prove loss as exists in the law of negligence.[133] Such services according to the definition must relate to a matter instructed by a client there is no requirement for the person affected to be the client.

The test for service complaints is that the Commission must be satisfied that the complainer has an interest to enforce. Paterson and Ritchie suggest that the category has the potential to be broad and is capable of including

127 Legal Profession and Legal Aid (Scotland) Act 2007, s2(1)(b).
128 Solicitors (Scotland) Act 1980 s65(1).
129 Rennie, *Negligence* (n 1), para 11.06.
130 Paterson and Ritchie, *Law, Practice and Conduct* (n 9), para 1.04.
131 SP Committee Official Report, 23rd Meeting (Session 2), September 26, 2006.
132 Legal Profession and Legal Aid (Scotland) Act 2007, s10.
133 Rennie, *Negligence* (n 1), para 11.05.

beneficiaries (and presumably disappointed beneficiaries) in an executry, opponents in a court case or perhaps where the agent for one side delays a conveyancing matter to the prejudice of the other.[134] The Commission's ability to accept third party complaints is now circumscribed by the decision in *Council of the Law Society of Scotland v Scottish Legal Complaints Commission*.[135] A complaint was accepted in relation to a conduct matter but the principle is equally applicable to service complaints where the person making the complaint had received a letter from a firm of solicitors regarding an alleged trespass on their property on the basis of information supplied by the client. The Court held that a solicitor had a duty to represent her client and was entitled to rely on the information supplied. Furthermore a solicitor is not bound to respond to any complaint made by third parties.[136] In *Saville-Smith v Scottish Legal Complaints Commission*[137] the pursuer sought to complain against the solicitor acting for his former employer on the basis that the solicitor had both revised the letter of dismissal and had appeared in the subsequent Tribunal proceedings. This was rejected as frivolous – again illustrating a narrow approach to third party claims. While these cases may restrict the scope of complaints they do not entirely exclude it and a third party complaint by a disappointed beneficiary may be admitted with the possibility of compensation being paid to complainer in circumstances where negligence need not be proved or where there is no incidence between liability and the loss. For example, the fine distinction drawn in *Fraser* in relation to the advice and the subsequent ineffective legacy, might not trouble the Commission when considering what is fair and reasonable in all the circumstances.

H. Conclusions

The fundamental tenets of practice – fidelity, confidentiality and the avoidance of conflicts of interest – remain the same as they did two decades ago. Some measures of regulatory reform such as written terms of business

---

134 Ibid para 16.04.

135 [2010] CSIH 79; 2011 SC 94; 2011 *SLT* 31; for a similar cases see SLCC Annual Report 2011/12 case 4 letter to third party, SLCC Annual Report 2010/11 case 4 opponent's agent in court action.

136 Scottish Legal Complaints Commission, Third Party Complaints advice sheet available at http://www.scottishlegalcomplaints.org.uk/for-practitioners/guidance-advice/advice-and-information.aspx

137 [2012] CSIH 99.

may clarify the obligations undertaken by solicitors which will tend to reduce the scope for negligence and in a few restricted situations may permit the limitation of liability. On the other hand the increasing interest of the legislature in anti-money laundering measures and the reduction of financial crime have imposed duties on solicitors that have fundamentally affected practice, undermining the duty of confidentiality, as well as requiring regulatory bodies to expand the ambit of the supervision of the profession. Inevitably these duties have been seized upon by the victims of identity theft in conveyancing matters as enhancing the obligations of solicitors to third parties.

Lenders have organised themselves to require solicitors to act on their behalf subject to standard terms which are significantly more explicit than the common law standards which are preserved. The result of such explicit standards is that a 'tick-box' approach can be adopted in regulatory inspections to demonstrate compliance or otherwise with those standards without the need to explore the perimeters of common law duties which can, on occasions, appear hazy.

Finally the creation of a new simplified regime for service complaints with significantly increased limits of compensation opens the door to fairly sizeable negligence claims being dealt with as inadequate professional service claims without the need to prove loss and without the client being required to incur the potential costs involved in litigation.

There can be little doubt that the duty of care owed by solicitors to their clients and third parties has expanded since Professor Rennie wrote his authoritative work.

5

Two Questions in the Law of Leases

Lord Gill

A. Introduction

In his years as a practitioner and as holder of the Chair of Conveyancing at Glasgow University, Professor Robert Rennie has served his profession and his *alma mater* with distinction. His contribution to the development of our property law is fittingly recognised by the publication of this *Festschrift*. It is a privilege to contribute this essay in honour of my good and esteemed friend.

In this essay I consider the meaning and effect of the decision of the House of Lords in *Clydesdale Bank plc v Davidson*.[1] That decision raised two fundamental questions; namely, the nature of the rights of *pro indiviso* proprietors of heritable property and the nature of the tenant's right in a contract of lease. I put forward the following propositions, namely (1) that in modern Scots law, on entry or, in the case of a long lease, on registration, the tenant in every contract of lease has a right *in rem* in respect of the subjects of let; (2) that on the question of the validity of the lease in that case, the *Clydesdale Bank* case was correctly decided; (3) that the decision of the Scottish Land Court in *Serup v McCormack*,[2] being a logical extension of that decision, was correctly decided; and (4) that the *obiter dicta* of the judges in the *Clydesdale Bank* case to the effect that the invalid lease was a valid contract for occupation and management of the land were unsound.

1 1998 SC (HL) 51 ("the *Clydesdale Bank* case").
2 2012 SLCR 189.

B. The Nature of the Rights of a *Pro Indiviso* Proprietor

In *Magistrates of Banff v Ruthin Castle Ltd*[3] Lord Justice Clerk Cooper, as he then was, eruditely expounded the distinction in Scots law between joint ownership, being the class of right typified by the ownership of co-trustees, and ownership in common, being the right typified by the ownership of two or more persons in whom the right to a single subject has come to be vested, each being entitled by his separate act to dispose of his separate share. I am concerned in this article with owners in common in the sense in which Lord Justice Clerk Cooper used that expression.[4] There are three defining characteristics of the relationship that governs such owners.

(1) Unanimity

Since *pro indiviso* proprietors hold the property in common, there is deemed to be unititular possession among them, each having an equal share or such proportionate share as they may agree upon.[5] The universal rule of common ownership is that there must be unanimity in decision-making affecting the subjects. This principle is based on the Roman law.[6] Bell recognised that that was the law,[7] but he advocated a principle of majority-based decision making.[8] That idea failed to find favour in the courts. In the *Clydesdale Bank* case Lord Clyde described it as "somewhat delphic" and as being "unilluminated by authority."[9] But in the context of this essay that is a side issue, since Bell insisted that there had to be unanimity in the granting of leases.[10] That has been the consistent view of the courts. It is now beyond question that a single *pro indiviso* proprietor cannot grant a lease that would be binding on singular successors.[11] Each individual proprietor has an effective veto, unless by contract he renounces it, on any proposed act of management with which he disagrees.

3 1944 SC 36.
4 *Magistrates of Banff* (n 3) at p 68.
5 Cf K G C Reid, "Property," in *The Laws of Scotland: Stair Memorial Encyclopaedia* vol 18 (1993) paras 22-34.
6 J Inst 3.27.3; C 10.35.2.
7 Bell, *Principles* §1072.
8 Ibid §1077.
9 *Clydesdale Bank* (n 1) at 61.
10 Bell, *Principles* §1075.
11 *Campbell and Stewart v Campbell* Fac Coll 24 January 1809; *Morrison, Petr* (1857) 20 D 276; cf *Bell's Exrs v Inland Revenue* 1986 SC 252.

(2) Use

Each proprietor is entitled to make use of every inch of the property. Therefore, no single *pro indiviso* proprietor may take exclusive possession of any part of the property unless the others consent.[12] If the land is let, each proprietor is entitled to a share of the rents.[13] No individual proprietor may obtain an excessive benefit at the expense of the other proprietors without prior agreement.[14] If he does so, he must account to them for the ordinary profits accruing to him from the period of his possession.

Nevertheless, the proprietors may validly agree *inter se* that the subjects will be possessed by one or more of their number. It is then a matter for agreement on what terms the occupying proprietor will occupy the subjects.[15] In such a contract, it is open to the proprietors to agree that in return for having sole and exclusive possession, the occupying proprietor will make a compensatory payment to the others.[16]

(3) Division and sale

In a relationship of the kind considered in the *Clydesdale Bank* case each of the *pro indiviso* proprietors can rely on the rule *nemo in communione invitus detineri potest*, a rule said by Lord Jauncey to be justified by considerations of public policy. The dissatisfied proprietor has no right to evict a co-proprietor from the subjects. His only remedy is the drastic remedy of the action of division and sale, which is derived from the Roman *actio de communi dividundo*. The right of each proprietor to enforce this remedy is absolute.[17] In an action of division and sale the court may order that the subjects should be divided up rateably or, if that is impracticable, that they should be sold and the proceeds divided.[18]

12 *Bailey v Scott* (1860) 22 D 1105, Lord Benholme at 1109.
13 Erskine, *Principles* 3.3.56; Bell, *Principles* §1072.
14 *George Watson's Hospital Governors v Cormack* (1883) 11 R 320.
15 *Price v Watson* 1951 SC 359.
16 *Price* (n 15), Lord Keith at 366.
17 *Brock v Hamilton* (1857) 19 D 701 at 703; *Banff Magistrates v Ruthin Castle Ltd* 1944 SC 36, Lord Justice-Clerk Cooper at 68.
18 *Brock* (n 17) Lord Rutherford at 702-03.

C. The Decision in *Clydesdale Bank Plc v Davidson*

In the *Clydesdale Bank* case the central question for the House of Lords was whether *pro indiviso* proprietors could grant a valid lease to one of their number.

The appellant was one of three *pro indiviso* proprietors of a tract of agricultural land. All three entered into a contract that purported to be a lease by which the other two let the land to the appellant. A month later, all three granted a standard security in favour of the Bank over part of the property. Some years later, they granted a further standard security over the rest of the property. The standard securities were granted in consideration of loans to the appellant only. When the appellant defaulted, the Bank enforced the securities and raised an action of removing against him. The appellant defended the action on the plea that he had a protected agricultural tenancy.

A straightforward resolution of the case was set out by Lord Jauncey to the following effect. At the date of the purported lease the appellant enjoyed a real right in the subjects entitling him to possess them jointly with the other *pro indiviso* proprietors. The contract concluded on that date neither superseded nor altered that real right. It conferred on the appellant a personal right to enforce the obligation by his co-proprietors to refrain from exercising their rights to joint possession in return for the compensatory payments. When the contract ceased to have effect, the appellant's right to possession *qua* proprietor would continue unchanged but his co-proprietors would no longer be disabled from jointly exercising their possessory rights. The contract was not a lease.[19]

Lord Clyde and Lord Hope concurred in holding that on general principles of contract a body of *pro indiviso* proprietors cannot grant a valid lease to one of their number. In doing so they adopted the reasoning of Lord Justice Clerk Ross in the court below, which was based on the view that a party cannot be both creditor and debtor in the same obligation, and that the purported lease could not validly confer on the appellant the subordinate right *in rem* of tenancy in respect of land over which he enjoyed the pre-eminent right of ownership.

19 *Clydesdale Bank* (n 1) at 54.

D. *Serup v McCormack*

A similar issue has since been considered by the Scottish Land Court in *Serup v McCormack*.[20] In that case a tenant who had a valid lease of an agricultural holding became one of the *pro indiviso* proprietors of the subjects of let during the course of the lease. Some years later she conveyed her *pro indiviso* share to a partnership in which she was one of the partners. The Land Court's general conclusion was that on the tenant's becoming a *pro indiviso* proprietor, all of the considerations relied on by the Inner House and by the House of Lords in the *Clydesdale Bank* case applied. Therefore the lease then became invalid. Distinguishing the principle that applies in the case of a servitude[21] the Land Court held that when the former tenant thereafter divested herself of her *pro indiviso* share in the subjects, the lease was not thereby resuscitated.

On the first point, the Land Court was clearly right in interpreting the *Clydesdale Bank* decision as it did and in following it. The considerations that in the *Clydesdale Bank* case invalidated the lease at the outset had the same effect when they arose during its currency. In particular, on the tenant's acquiring *pro indiviso* ownership, the greater right of ownership absorbed and extinguished the lesser right of tenancy[22] and the now *pro indiviso* proprietor thereupon became immune from eviction at the hands of his fellow proprietors.[23] On the second point, the lease, when entered into, was a valid lease of an agricultural holding that conferred on the tenant security of tenure by statutory relocation on the expiry of the contractual term;[24] restricted the landlord's opportunities to serve notice to

20 2012 SLCR 189.

21 In relation to the distinction, the court said this: "We accept that there is a tract of authority which would support the view that a servitude should not be regarded as extinguished by operation of confusion except in the case of a sole proprietor coming into possession of both dominant and servient tenements in the same capacity. It may well be that, in relation to servitudes, the position is different where there are co-proprietors. But we are satisfied that nothing in the material relating to servitudes can prevail by analogy against the direct weight to be given to the views expressed in the context of leases in the *Clydesdale Bank* case." (*Serup v McCormack* (n 20) at para 44)

22 *Clydesdale Bank* (n 1) Lord Clyde at 61A-B.

23 *Price* (n 15).

24 Agricultural Holdings (Scotland) Act 1949 (the 1949 Act), s 3 (which applied at the date of the lease) and Agricultural Holdings (Scotland) Act 1991 (the 1991 Act, s 3) (which applied when the lease was extinguished).

quit;[25] and created the prospect that the tenancy could be continued under the same statutory provisions in the hands of an acquirer after the tenant's death.[26] These considerations plainly ruled out the idea that the tenancy was not extinguished but instead went into a state of suspended animation in which it would remain until the uncertain day when the tenant should cease to be a *pro indiviso* proprietor.

E. The Personal Right Theory

Catherine Bury and Douglas Bain have recently published a stimulating article in which they question the soundness of the *Clydesdale Bank* decision and advance a theory that a lease that does not confer a right *in rem* upon the tenant may nevertheless be validly constituted among *pro indiviso* proprietors.[27] They describe this as the "non-real personal lease."[28] They argue that since the House of Lords accepted in the *Clydesdale Bank* case that the contract was a valid contract between the proprietors for the occupation and management of the land by one of their number, that contract should have been recognised as in substance a personal lease. Such a lease qualifies as a lease to which the agricultural holdings legislation applies and should therefore have been held to confer the security of tenure that was unsuccessfully claimed by the appellant. I shall refer to this as "the alternative theory."

In briefest outline the conclusion of the alternative theory is that it is not necessarily a requirement for the protection of the Agricultural Holdings (Scotland) Act 1991 that the lease should confer a real right. Therefore, a contract of the kind considered by the House of Lords to be a valid occupation and management contract may qualify as a personal lease that is protected under the 1991 Act.

This theory therefore raises the two fundamental questions to which I have referred. On the first, the essential issues are whether, despite the Leases Act 1449, the common law personal lease survives in Scots law; and, if so, whether it can attract the protection of the agricultural holdings legislation. On the second question, the essential issue is whether, although the contract in the *Clydesdale Bank* case did not confer on the purported

25 1949 Act, ss 24-27;1991 Act, s 21.
26 Succession (Scotland) Act 1964, s 16.
27 C Bury and D Bain, "A, B and C to A, Revisited" 2013 *Juridical Review* 77.
28 Bury and Bain (n 27), 82-86.

tenant the right *in rem* of tenancy, since he already had a right *in rem* as a proprietor, the contract was nonetheless a valid contract the effect of which was to confer on the appellant a personal lease, and in consequence the protection of the agricultural holdings legislation. The success of the alternative theory depends on there being favourable answers to both questions.

F. The Nature of the Tenant's Right in the Contract of Lease

(1) The common law

The common law adopted the general principle of the Roman law that the right of the lessee in the contract *locatio conductio* was prestable against the lessor, but not against a subsequent owner. The *locus classicus* in Stair is as follows:[29]

> A tack of itself is no more than a personal contract of location, whereby land, or any other thing having profit or fruit, is set to the tacksman for enjoying the fruit or profit thereof, for a hire, which is called the tack-duty; which therefore did only oblige the setter and his heirs, to make it effectual to the tacksman, but did not introduce any real right, affecting the thing set, and carried therewith to singular successors; but so soon as the thing set ceased to be the setter's, the tack could only defend the tenant till the next term of removing.

At common law, therefore, the lessee had only a right of action against the lessor and his representatives to be maintained in possession for the duration of the lease. Since feudal law did not allow a right in land to be effectual against singular successors of the proprietor without sasine, the tenant had no protection against them and could be removed from the tenancy with ease.

In that state of the law, conveyancers attempted to secure the tenant's vulnerable position in relation to a singular successor of the landlord by drawing on the analogy of sasine and conferring on the tenant a simulated form of infeftment for the purpose of creating a real right. This procedure is described with derision by Paton and Cameron as a "specious form of

29 Stair, *Inst* 2.9.1-2; 1.15.4. The first edition is to similar effect cf Stair, *Inst* (1st ed) 1.29.1-2.

charter and sasine."[30] It was not, and could not be, a true infeftment since the tenant's right was that of temporary occupation only.[31]

(2) The emergence of the right in rem

The Leases Act 1449

The Leases Act 1449 was passed with the specific purpose of correcting the weakness in the law that left the agricultural tenant defenceless to removal by a singular successor of the landlord.

The Act, in the Glendook version quoted by Rankine,[32] provided as follows:[33]

> It is ordained for the safetie and favour of the puir people that labouris the ground, that they, and all utheris that hes taken or sall take landes in time to cum fra lordes, and hes termes and zeires thereof, that suppose the lordes sell or annaly that land or landes, the takers sall remaine with their tackes, unto the ischew of their termes, quhais handes that ever thay landes cum to for siklike maill as they tooke them for.

Although the Act was introduced at the instance of James II to remedy the injustice of the eviction of labourer tenants at the will of the landlord, its scope was not limited to the "puir people that labouris the ground." It extended to "all utheris."

---

30 G C H Paton and J G S Cameron, *The Law of Landlord and Tenant in Scotland* (1967) 3.

31 "Of old, it was usual to sanction the right of the tenant by infeftment, and by that means he held under the real right of infeftment what is now held by mere acquisition of the subject" (*Hamilton v Hamilton* (1845) 8 D 308, Lord Jeffrey at 312).

32 *A Treatise on the Law of Leases in Scotland*, 3rd edn (1916) 132.

33 Leases Act 1449. In *Mountain's Trs v Mountain* 2013 SC 202, the First Division preferred the text given in the Records of the Parliaments of Scotland to 1707, namely
"Item it is ordanit and statute that for the saueritie and favour of the pure pupil that laubouris the grunde that thai and al uthiris that has takyn or sal tak landis in tym to cum fra lordis and has termes and yeris tharof, that suppose the lordis sel or analy thai landis, that the takaris sall remain with thare takis one to the ische of thare termez quhais handis at evir thai landis cum to for sic lik male as thai tuk thaim of befor."
A modern version of the text is as follows:
"For the security and benefit of those who work upon the land, it is decreed that they and anyone else who have rented or who shall rent lands from landlords for a fixed term shall remain entitled under their leases until the ish [termination date] thereof, nowithstanding that their landlord has sold or alienated the land, and irrespective of the identity of the transferee of the land, for the same amount of rent as was initially agreed." (Hugo and Simpson, "Lease" in Zimmermann, Visser and Reid (eds), *Mixed Legal Systems in Comparative Perspective: Property and Obligations in Scotland and South Africa* (2005) 307.

In the *Ius Feudale*, Craig interprets the 1449 Act as having conferred on the tenant a real right:[34]

> Again, a covenant sometimes appears in a tack whereby the lessor undertakes that he will not remove the tenant from his holding. Such a covenant is however personal to the lessor who enters into it; and although the original grantor of the tack (being owner of the subject at the time he granted it) is bound by his obligation not to remove the tenant, the covenant loses its force on a change of ownership and cannot be enforced against a singular successor. As has been seen, the opposite rule applies to a tack covenanted to endure for a fixed term of years, for such a tack confers a real right on the tenant and affects the subject itself, especially when (as I have explained) possession has followed upon it.

Stair,[35] Erskine[36] and Bell[37] are to the same effect. Bankton is to similar effect;[38] but Kames adheres to the view that a tack is a mere personal right that was not made real by the 1449 Act.[39]

Mackenzie describes the effect of the Act in the following way:[40]

> Tacks which before this Act were only personal rights are by this Act made real rights ... Possession is the same thing to tacks that sasines are to alienations: and of old some tacks had sasines or instruments of possession: but neither was necessary nor is now usual. And the reason why they used sasines then, being to make the tack real, and to defend against singular successors; this was no more used after the Act of Parliament by which possession makes a tack a real right.

In consequence of the 1449 Act the practice of taking sasine on a lease fell into disuse in the 15th century. Mackenzie's confident interpretation of the Act goes to the heart of the matter.

The nineteenth century controversy

The words of Sir George Mackenzie are a useful preface to the controversy that preoccupied the Court of Session as to the effect of the 1449 Act on the nature of the tenant's right. In the early nineteenth century the nature of

34 *Ius Feudale*, 2.10.9 (trans Lord Clyde (1934)).
35 Stair, *Inst* (1st edn), 2.9.4 and 7.
36 Erskine, *Inst* 2.6.25.
37 Bell, *Principles* §1177.
38 Bankton, *Institute*, 2.9 (1752).
39 H H Kames, *Elucidations respecting the Common and Statute Law of Scotland* (1777) 8-9.
40 G Mackenzie, *The Works of that Eminent and Learned Lawyer, Sir George Mackenzie of Rosehaugh* (1716) vol 1, 188-89.

the tenant's right became the subject of judicial controversy in the context of commercial leases.[41] The controversy was precipitated by the attempt by conveyancers to secure a debt over the debtor's tenancy by having the debtor assign the tenancy to the creditor and by the creditor's granting a sub-tenancy to the debtor. If the debtor's tenancy conferred only a right *in personam* under such an arrangement, the assignation would effectively transfer the lease to the creditor upon intimation of it to the landlord; whereas if the tenancy conferred a right *in rem*, the creditor's right to the tenancy would be perfected only upon his taking possession.

At that stage, the preponderant view of the writers was that the 1449 Act conferred a real right of tenancy.[42] In a lecture prepared for delivery in 1821-1822 Baron Hume described the far-reaching effects of the statute. Having expounded the principle that the lease, in its native and proper character, is a matter of personal contract, he describes the lease as a sort of estate or real interest in the tenant. This, he says, is a new and foreign character bestowed by the 1449 Act and is the oldest ordinance to that purpose in the law of any country of Europe.[43]

Inglis v Paul

Inglis v Paul[44] brought the controversy into the open. In that case a sub-tenant assigned his sub-tenancy to a bank in security of a cash-credit. Two days later, the assignation was intimated to the principal tenant, but not to the sub-sub-tenant who occupied part of the subjects. The bank did not enter into possession. About two years later, the sub-tenant was sequestrated. The bank thereupon intimated the assignation to the tenants of the property and required that they should pay the rents to the bank. Thereafter the trustee was elected and was granted decree of adjudication. The resulting competition between the assignee of the sub-lease, who had failed to take possession of the subjects, and the sub-tenant's trustee in sequestration was considered by the whole court.

---

41 The principal cases on the point and the origins of the Registration of Leases (Scotland) Act 1857 were usefully reviewed by W Guy, "Registration of Leases" (1908-1909) 20 *Juridical Review* 234, 239.

42 J Balfour, *Practicks* (1754) 200; Craig, *Jus feudale* 2.10.2-10; Stair, *Inst* 2.9.2; Mackenzie, *Institutions* 2.6.5 and *Observations* 37; Erskine, *Inst* 2.6.23; Bankton, *Institute* 2.9.1; W Ross, *Lectures on the practice of law in Scotland* (1792) vol 2, 476; Bell, *Commentaries* 1.65.

43 G Campbell H Paton (ed), *Baron David Hume's Lectures 1786-1822: Volume IV* (1952) 73.

44 (1829) 7 S 469.

The view of Lord Justice Clerk Boyle and seven other judges on the point was as follows:[45]

> The rule of law is, that rights are completed by delivery. In feudal subjects, this is accomplished by sasine or symbolical delivery; and in subjects which do not admit of sasine, by giving natural or civil possession. Tacks, in one respect, are personal; and in another, real rights. In a question between the landlord and the tenant or his assignees, they are personal rights; therefore, in a competition between two *bona fide* and onerous assignees, the landlord is bound to prefer him who first intimates his assignation (which is the way of completing a personal right) and to put him in possession accordingly. But, in a question with the singular successors of the landlord and the tenant or his assignee, a tack is a real right by force of the statute of 1449; and therefore it is incomplete, unless possession, natural or civil, has been attained.

Lord Balgray agreed that the bank's case failed for want of possession. He accepted that until possession followed on the assignation of the lease, the title of the assignee was not secure; but he rejected the idea that the assignation was not perfected by intimation to the landlord, but only by possession. Assignation of the lease, although quite complete as to title, might be defeated and disappointed by allowing the cedent to remain in possession. The assignee thereby exposed his right to danger and risk. But in the view of Lord Balgray, the question was not what was necessary to complete the assignee's right to the tenancy. The decision depended on different principles. This was his view:[46]

> It was constantly to be kept in mind, that a lease by the law of Scotland was nothing but a personal right. It was a *bona fide* contract for the use of land or other subject, as laid down by the civil law. It was very true that the Scotch act 1449 bestowed, from public utility, a peculiar privilege on those who held leases of heritable subjects, that they should be protected in the possession of their subjects against all persons till the contract expired, if they were in the actual possession. This was an exception from the general rule, and a privilege bestowed; but it altered not the nature of the right. To say that a lease is a real right, is a most egregious mistake in point of law. No doubt it is effectual against singular successors, and it descends to heirs; but this arises from other extrinsic and adventitious circumstances, totally distinct from the true legal nature of the right. Being a personal right, a lease naturally becomes the subject of assignation; and that assignation is perfected by intimation to the landlord or author from whom it flows,

45 *Inglis* (n 44) at 473.
46 Ibid at 474.

> or acknowledgment by them, provided always he has originally bestowed the right of conveyance. Abstractly, therefore, the assignation of a lease is perfected, and must be perfected, by intimation to the landlord. It requires intimation to no other human being. So much is this the case, that suppose a number of intimations were made to a landlord, and it is required of him to give possession, he is bound to deliver it to the first intimated assignation. No authority can be pointed out in the law of Scotland to the contrary.

In this view Lord Balgray was supported by his First Division colleagues Lord Craigie and Lord Gillies, who expressly dissented from the majority view that the assignee acquired right to the tenancy of the subjects only by taking possession.[47]

Brock v Cabbell

A year later the point came up again in *Brock v Cabbell*[48] and was considered by a court of 15 judges including all 12 of the judges who had taken part in *Inglis v Paul*. The point arose in similar circumstances. The tenant granted an assignation of the tenancy in security to a bank. The assignation was intimated to the landlord. The bank thereupon sub-let the subjects to the former tenant who remained in possession and paid the rents. The bank at no time thereafter entered into possession. The competition was between the bank and the trustee in bankruptcy of the former tenant. In that context, the lease controversy inevitably returned.

The Lord President and five judges, four of whom had been in the majority in *Inglis v Paul*, gave the majority opinion. It begins in uncompromising terms:[49]

> It is a general rule in the law of Scotland, that possession, natural or civil, is necessary to complete the transference of a real right. A tack is a real right, by force of the statute 1449, in a question been assignees and adjudgers from the tenant; and to that case, therefore, the general rule applies. This is vouched by the concurrent authority of every institutional writer, and by an uninterrupted series of decisions for more than two centuries.

Lord Fullerton concluded that the lease became:[50]

> ... in virtue of the statute 1449 a real right, a character uniformly assigned to it by our institutional writers and confirmed by a series of decisions which it is impossible now to disturb.

47 *Inglis* (n 44) at 474.
48 (1830) 8 S 647.
49 *Brock* (n 48) at 652.
50 Ibid at 661.

The conclusion of the majority was that since the bank had never taken possession of the land after the assignation, the assignation/sub-tenancy arrangement was "a collusive device to create a latent security over a real right, without change of possession."[51]

Lord Gillies again allied himself with Lord Balgray, concurring in the result advocated by the majority but challenging the general propositions that I have quoted. Their position was succinctly expressed as follows:[52]

> We consider a lease to be a right of an anomalous nature. Its creation and its transmission are to be regulated as if it were, what it truly is, a personal right. We, therefore, cannot affirm that it is the law of Scotland that an assignation of a lease duly intimated is *per se* an imperfect right, unless followed by natural or civil possession.

The usually taciturn Lord Craigie delivered an erudite opinion, lengthy by the standards of the day, that has not attracted academic attention. In it the true point of division clearly emerges. The opinion gives us an insight into the mind of a conveyancer who, even four centuries after the 1449 Act, was still influenced by the spirit of the Roman law.

Lord Craigie's opening statement makes his position clear. He quotes the 1449 Act and immediately concludes from the wording of it as follows:[53]

> Thus it appears, 1. That, by the common law, the landlord or proprietor of lands could not effectually grant a lease to endure beyond the period of his right. 2. That the extension of the right of the tenant by positive statute, and in express deviation from the common law, is confined to the case of buyers or singular successors in the property of the lands.

He then makes the claim that that is how in practice the 1449 Act has been understood. He cites three cases in which the tenant's right does not prevail against third parties who acquire the landlord's interest; namely where the land falls into the hands of the superior by virtue of a feudal casualty; or in the case of a lease granted by a wadsetter when the right of reversion has been exercised; and in the case where the right of the lessor has been set aside. In all of these cases, he says, the current leases flowing from the landlord are of no effect for ensuring possession to the lessee.

At this point, Lord Craigie has to face the fact that nearly all of the writers take a different view. This is his untroubled response:[54]

---

51 *Brock* (n 48) at 653.
52 Ibid.
53 Ibid at 654.
54 Ibid.

> It is the more necessary to attend to this, because in many of the books of authority there are expressions from which it has been inferred, that, by the statute, leases had become real rights, and that they could not in any case be effectual to third parties, unless followed with natural and actual possession. The very opposite proposition, as it humbly appears to me, is the true one.

Lord Craigie then emphasises that, properly speaking, a lessee of lands has no right to the lands. He has only a right of possession. Therefore his possession must be governed by the properly attested agreements between those who have an interest in it.[55]

As matters stood after 1830, the clear division of opinion on the controversy had been resolved in favour of the strong majority view that the right of the lessee was a real right. In that respect, the court was at one with the writers. After *Brock v Cabbell* the real right theory was not to be challenged for nearly forty years.

By 1838, the Third Report of the Law Commissioners in Scotland, of whom George Joseph Bell was one, expressed the view that the law respecting the effect of the 1449 Act on the rights of singular successors in the land was well settled by the statute and by a long series of decisions making the possession of the tenant serve the purpose of sasine on the lease, to the effect of conferring a real right independently of any record.[56] The Law Commissioners recommended[57] that it should be possible for a tenant to create a security over his lease by an assignation that would be recorded in a public register, the register being a form of publication that would make the creditor's security effectual.[58] In due course the Registration of Leases (Scotland) Act 1857 provided that the registration of a long lease, would make the tenant's right valid against singular successors of the landlord,[59] the act of registration having the same effect as entry into possession had been held to have in the case law;[60] and that on being recorded the

55 We can leave the opinion at this point because his Lordship then turns to questions of assignation.

56 Third Report of the Commissioners, *Conveyancing* 13 January 1838 (HMSO: London) xl. The report also states in more general terms not limited to agricultural leases, that "in order to the constitution of a real right in land, or other heritable subject, whether absolute, conditional, irredeemable, or in security, the law requires symbolic delivery of possession, or sasine, as it was termed, of which the only evidence is an instrument prepared and authenticated by a notary-public."(ibid, xxiii)

57 Commissioners, *Conveyancing* (n 56), 52.

58 Ibid.

59 1857 Act, s 2.

60 Ibid, s 16.

assignation of the lease in security constituted a "real security" over the lease.[61]

In 1845 the real right issue arose obliquely in *Hamilton v Hamilton*[62] in relation to an agricultural lease that did not contain a conventional irritancy. The question was whether the landlord could nevertheless irritate the lease for the tenant's failure to implement certain obligations *ad factum praestandum*. In finding against the landlord on that point, two of the majority judges, Lord Mackenzie and Lord Jeffrey, expressly relied on the consideration that the tenant had acquired a real right by entering into possession of the land. They held that such a right could be terminated by irritancy only where the irritancy was expressly warranted by a statutory or a conventional provision.

In 1867 in *Campbell v McKinnon*[63] Lord Kinloch in the Outer House took the view that a lease conferred only a personal right. The Inner House overturned his judgment. In the leading opinion Lord Curriehill described the principle that possession under a lease conferred real rights on the tenant as "trite law."[64] The judgment of the Inner House was affirmed by the House of Lords,[65] where Lord Westbury said that the effect of the 1449 Act was that upon entry to the land the lessee's right became real.[66]

Only a year later, the question arose again in *Edmond v Reid*.[67] In that case an agricultural tenant was bound by a residence clause. She indicated her intention not to reside on the farm. There was no irritancy clause in the lease. The landlord concluded for declarator of the existence of the tenant's obligation to reside and, if the tenant should fail to reside, for decree that she had forfeited all right to possession of the farm.

The action was defended on the ground *inter alia* that the landlord was not entitled to a declarator of forfeiture since there was no irritancy clause to support it. In pursuing that defence, counsel relied on *Hamilton v Hamilton*[68] for the submission that "a lease was a real right. Non-residence did not create an irritancy, and there was no conventional irritancy."[69] On being pressed by the court to make her intentions clear, the tenant lodged a

61 1857 Act, s 4.
62 (1845) 8 D 308.
63 1867 5 M 636 at 644.
64 *Campbell* (n 63) at 649.
65 *sub nom Campbell v McLean* (1870) 8 M (HL) 40.
66 *Campbell* (n 63) at 46.
67 (1871) 9 M 782.
68 *Hamilton* (n 30).
69 *Edmond* (n 66) at 783

minute that was construed as a judicial declaration that she would not fulfil the residence condition.

In the leading opinion, Lord Justice Clerk Moncreiff took the line that the landlord was not seeking declarator of irritancy at all, because the conclusions were "entirely for the future" and related solely to the effect of a subsequent refusal by the tenant to fulfil the conditions of the lease. He then turned to the real right issue. He said that he did not question the "doctrine" in *Hamilton v Hamilton*[70] that a lease conferred a real right on the tenant; but in his view the lease was nevertheless a mutual contract and was subject to the principle that no-one could take the benefit of the lease and at the same time repudiate its conditions. He followed the decision in *Drummond*[71] where the court had held that although a residence clause was not fenced with a power of irritancy, the contract would necessarily come to an end if the tenant should put it out of his power to fulfil the conditions of the lease. On that point, the Lord Justice Clerk relied on *Hamilton v Hamilton* in holding that the tenant's declared inability or unwillingness to fulfil the lease constituted a renunciation.

The other three judges concurred in the result; but the submission for the tenant, and the Lord Justice Clerk's support for the decision in *Hamilton v Hamilton*, provoked Lord Cowan and Lord Neaves. While both were content to decide the case on the basis of the tenant's declared intention not to observe the residence clause, neither was prepared to accede to the real right theory. Lord Cowan put the matter as follows:[72]

> The argument of the defender was founded on a fallacy. He said a lease was a real right, and to be assimilated to a feu-right. That is not its nature. A contract of lease is a mutual contract, and although, under the statute 1449, with some of the privileges of a real right, it does not substantially differ from a mutual contract.

Lord Neaves' view was as follows:[73]

> The defenders' counsel was in error when he argued that a lease was the same in character as a feu-contract. It is no doubt an heritable contract, on account of its being for a tract of future time. That is a totally different matter from its being a real right.

70 *Hamilton* (n 31).
71 1806, Mor app Tack, No 6.
72 *Edmond* (n 67) at 785.
73 Ibid.

> The Act of 1449 was for the benefit of the poor people who laboured the ground. It prevented the vendees of the lessor from turning out the lessee. It declares the right followed by possession to have that effect, but that is not making it, properly speaking, a real right.

These *dicta* are the starting point for the alternative theory.

A decade later, in his *Lectures on Conveyancing*,[74] Montgomerie Bell concluded that leases at an early period were raised to the position of real rights, conferring a title of possession preferable to that of purchasers and creditors whose rights were subsequent to the date when possession was taken under the lease.[75]

(3) Twentieth century developments

The state of the law on the nature of the tenant's right in the early twentieth century is summarised in Rankine's conclusion that leases, originally and in their nature merely personal contracts, were in certain cases converted into real rights by the 1449 Act "as liberally construed by the Court."[76] That can fairly be said to be the starting point for the modern expositions of the law on the nature of the tenant's right.

The question arose again in 1949 in *Millar v McRobbie*.[77] In December 1947 the then proprietors of an arable farm granted the defender a 14-year lease with entry at Whitsunday 1948. The lease conditions provided for the customary sequence of handover arrangements by which the incoming tenant would have access to parts of the land from 1 March 1948 for the purpose of sowing and by which, in due course, the tenant would have access after his waygoing to reap his final crop. Thereafter the landlords sold the farm to the pursuer with entry at 29 February 1948. The defender duly took access to the land under green crop between late March and early May and during that period prepared and sowed the ground. The pursuer then had the defender interdicted from entering on the land on the plea that the lease was not binding on him as a singular successor of the landlords, the defender not having taken entry to the land in terms of the lease.

74 M Bell, *Lectures on Conveyancing*, 3rd edn, vol 2 (1882).
75 Bell, *Lectures* (n 74) 1197.
76 Rankine, *Leases*, 3rd edn (n 32) 132. This is the authoritative edition published in February 1916.
77 1949 SC 1.

In the appeal of the defender to the Inner House, counsel for the defender did not argue that his right *in personam* against the former proprietor was good against the singular successor. Instead, he argued that he had been in possession of part of the land from March onwards and that that limited possession was sufficient to confer on him the protection of the 1449 Act. The First Division refused the appeal by distinguishing between the possession that would have followed from entry at the specified date and the anticipatory or deferred occupation of certain parts of the land by which the agricultural cycle was maintained.[78]

The significance of this case is that it established that the theory that the tenant has a right *in rem*, and that the right is made effective by the taking of possession, was firmly part of the law of Scotland. That is clear in Lord President Cooper's opening statement:[79]

> It has been well settled for centuries that possession under a lease is the equivalent of sasine in relation to feudal property. Without possession the tenant is merely the personal creditor of the lessor. By entering into possession the lessee publishes to the world in general, and to singular successors in particular, the fact of his lease, and since the practice of taking sasine on a tack fell into disuse in the 15th century, no substitute has been recognised by our law for possession except registration of long leases under the Act of 1857.

In view of the classic statement of Lord Kinloch in *Wight v Earl of Hopetoun*[80] which was affirmed by the House of Lords,[81] that a lease of that kind ran from Whitsunday to Whitsunday, notwithstanding handover arrangements, the decision in *Millar v McRobbie* was inevitable. It is significant however that neither the arguments of counsel nor the opinions of the judges make any reference at all to the nineteenth century controversy.

The decision in the *Clydesdale Bank* case further affirmed that the tenant's entry into possession conferred the real right.[82]

---

78 Lord President Cooper at 6-8.

79 *Millar* (n 77) at 6.

80 (1863) 1 M 1074 at 1099.

81 *Wight v Earl of Hopetoun* (1864) 2 M (HL) 35.

82 In the most recent consideration of the 1449 Act and of s 85(1) of the 1991 Act, the First Division took that proposition for granted (*Mountain's Trs* v *Mountain* 2013 SC 202, Lord President Gill at para [10]).

G. Conclusions

(1) The personal right theory

Two influences underlay the minority view in this extended controversy. First, the Roman law in which a lease of land, as part of the wider contract of hire, conferred on the lessee only a right *in personam* against the lessor; and second, the strict feudal theory on which sasine endowed the proprietor with rights of ownership that were valid against all comers.

The essence of the argument for those judges who held to the personal right theory was simple. The tenant under the Roman contract *locatio conductio* had a right *in personam*, against the lessor only, to be maintained in possession. The purpose of the 1449 Act was to protect the tenant against removal by the landlord's singular successor. On that view, there was an interpretation of the 1449 Act that dealt with the perceived mischief in a perfectly intelligible way without the need to confect a right *in rem*; namely that the Act protected the tenant's right *in personam* by making it prestable against the singular successor. In this way the 1449 Act secured the tenant's position against the singular successor,[83] with minimal change to the existing law, while remaining true to its civilian roots.

To those who held the minority view, the analogy between the taking of sasine under a disposition and the taking of possession under a lease was at best an imperfect one. To them, the taking of possession was only the palest shadow of sasine. The idea that the mere taking of possession could confer a right *in rem* was heresy.

This line of argument came naturally to judges who were steeped in the principles of the Roman law and of feudal conveyancing. To them the taking of sasine was a significant juristic act by which the fullest rights of ownership were conferred and publicly acknowledged. The private act of taking possession under a private contract that endowed the lessee with, at most, subordinate and temporary rights in the subjects could not meaningfully be equiparated with sasine.

But this view failed to win the day. The liberal construction to which Rankine referred was favoured by most of the writers from earliest times and has had a secure place in the case law for the last two hundred

83 As Lord Neaves explicitly held (cf *Wilson v Mann* (1876) 3 R 527 at 532).

years. The *obiter dicta* of two judges in *Edmond v Reid* are the last judicial statements to have been made in support of the personal right theory. It is perhaps a criticism of the alternative theory that in wresting these *dicta* from that single case, Bury and Bain have failed to place their theory in its full historical context.

Over time, the 1449 Act has come to be accepted as (1) conferring a right *in rem* on the tenant in a contract that meets the requirements of a valid lease; and (2) applying to leases of subjects of all kinds.[84] Although the 1449 Act specifically refers to "lands," the courts have interpreted it as applying also to residential dwellings, minerals, quarries, ferries, harbours and salmon fishings.[85]

In their critique of the *Clydesdale Bank* case, Bury and Bain suggest that because the contract between the *pro indiviso* proprietors was held not to be a true lease, nevertheless because it regulated the terms upon which the defender would occupy and farm the subjects, it qualified as a personal lease and fell within the definition of "lease" in section 85(1) of the Agricultural Holdings (Scotland) Act 1991.

Even on the assumption that the contract in the *Clydesdale Bank* case was a valid contract between the *pro indiviso* proprietors for occupation and maintenance of the farm, there is, I think, a flaw in this line of argument. If I am right in my interpretation of the twentieth century authorities, it is beyond any reasonable challenge, in my view, that in the modern law of Scotland a contract of lease that meets the essential requirements that were agreed and re-stated in *Gray v Edinburgh University*[86] confers a right *in rem* on the tenant. On the other hand, if the contract fails to meet those requirements, it is not a lease at all.

The argument for the survival of the common law form of personal lease suggests that such a lease may attract the protection of various statutory regimes and, in particular, when it is a lease of agricultural land will be a "lease" within the definition of that term in section 85(1) of the Agricultural Holdings (Scotland) Act 1991.

For the reasons that I have given, I conclude that the common law personal lease is no longer part of the law of Scotland. But even if it were a

84 *Waddell v Brown* 1794 M 10309; *Campbell v Mc Kinnon* (1867) 5 M 636, Lord Deas at 651.

85 *Waddell* (n 84); *McArthur v Simpson* 1804 M 15181; *Pollock, Gilmour & Co v Harvey* (1828) 6 S 913; *Clerk v Farquharson* 1799 M 15225; *Lumsden v Stewart* (1843) 5 D 501; *Gentle v Henry* 1747 M 13804.

86 1962 SC 157.

valid form of lease, the question whether it fell with any particular statutory regime would depend on the relevant legislation. For example, it may be that under the Housing (Scotland) Acts a party may be deemed to be a tenant even if he holds under a form of tenure that is not a lease at all.[87] That however does not advance the argument.

On the assumption that a contract of the kind considered in the *Clydesdale Bank* case were to constitute a personal lease, such a lease would not necessarily come within the special definition of "lease" in section 85(1) of the Agricultural Holdings (Scotland) Act 1991.[88] *Ex hypothesi* a personal lease is good only against the lessor. It cannot therefore fit into the scheme of the 1991 Act where every lease to which the Act applies is subject to a statutory form of annual relocation[89] after the expiry of the contractual term and is good against any subsequent landlord of the holding. Moreover, the wideness of the definition of "landlord" in section 85(1) of the 1991 Act is such that the landlord may be a person who is not vested in the ownership of the land. The definitions of landlord and tenant in section 85(1) apply, of course, only for the purposes of the 1991 Act.

In any event, the results of the alternative theory would be incongruous. If a *pro indiviso* proprietor were to acquire a purported personal lease of agricultural land granted by his co-proprietors, his co-proprietors would not qualify as the "landlord" in terms of section 85(1) of the 1991 Act because under that definition all persons having a share in the title to the land constitute the landlord. Even if it were possible for the lease to be granted by the co-proprietors including himself, the lease would be unworkable. By reason of the rights of every individual *pro indiviso* proprietor that are inherent in his ownership, and by reason of the principle of unanimity to which I have referred, the appellant – on that hypothesis – could prevent *inter alia* the service upon him of any notice to quit under section 21 of the 1991 Act, any notice for a review of rent under section 13, any demand to remedy fixed equipment under section 22 and any application for a certificate of bad husbandry under section 28. That would be an unreasonable result.

---

87 As Bury and Bain (n 27) submit at their footnote 29 under reference to *Kinghorn v Glasgow DC* 1984 *SLT* (Lands Tr) 9; and *Andrew v North Lanarkshire Council* 2011 Lands Tribunal, available at http://www.lands-tribunal-scotland.org.uk/decisions/LTS.TR.2010.10.html

88 Or for that matter qualify as one of the limited duration tenancies introduced by the Agricultural Holdings (Scotland) Act 2003.

89 1991 Act, s 3.

One other aspect of the case for the alternative view is the suggestion that in the *Clydesdale Bank* case the House of Lords failed adequately to consider what constitutes one of the cardinal elements of a lease, namely a rent. The suggestion is that their Lordships took too narrow a view of rent as being a payment of money, there being wide definitions of rent given by the writers which comprehend a non-pecuniary consideration. This again seems not to advance the argument. No-one would dispute that the cardinal element of rent covers payment in money's worth; but the judges of the House of Lords were dealing with a contract which, whatever its substance or validity, purported to provide for payment of a money rent.

(2) The *pro indiviso* proprietor issue

The discussion as to the nature of the tenant's interest in a lease may in the event be futile if the contract in the *Clydesdale Bank* case was invalid on other grounds. To succeed in the alternative theory its proponents must still establish that a personal lease created by several *pro indiviso* proprietors in favour of one of their number is a valid contract. In my view, if the personal lease known to the Scottish common law had survived to the present day, the arrangement between the *pro indiviso* proprietors in the *Clydesdale Bank* case could not have been such a contract, for the good and sufficient reason that it is not possible for a party to be both creditor and debtor in a contract. The logic of this principle is recognised as a general principle of the law of contract.[90] In the specific case of leases the principle is established by a powerful tract of authority in cases such as *Price v Watson*[91] and *Kildrummy (Jersey) Limited v IRC*.[92] These authorities were reviewed and affirmed by the House of Lords in the *Clydesdale Bank* case.

Although the principle can be securely rested on logic, it is also justified by a consideration of the consequence identified in *Price v Watson*,[93] namely that the so-called tenant, as a *pro indiviso* proprietor, has rights of ownership over every inch of the subjects of let and would therefore be secure against eviction.[94]

In this discussion I am considering only the case where *pro indiviso* proprietors grant a purported lease to one of their number. In the *Clydesdale*

90 W M Gloag, *The Law of Contract*, 2nd edn (1929) 4; *Church of Scotland Endowment Committee v Provident Association of London Ltd* 1914 SC 165.

91 1951 SC 359. Cf also *Denholm's Trs v Denholm* 1984 SLT 319; *Bell's Exrs v Inland Revenue* 1986 SC 252; *Barclay v Penman* 1984 SLT 376.

92 1991 SC 1.

93 1951 SC 359.

94 Bell, *Principles* §1072; Erskine, *Principles* 2.6.53.

Bank case, in both the Inner House and the House of Lords, the court was referred to the Outer House decision in *Pinkerton v Pinkerton*.[95] That was an example of the converse case where an individual granted a lease to four joint tenants of whom he was one. Neither court found it necessary to consider the validity of such a contract. In my view, it is irrelevant to the present discussion; but it may be that the judgment of Lord Mackay of Clashfern in that case is not the last word on that subject.

Bury and Bain seek support for their argument in a statement of Lord Johnston in *Higgins v Assessor for Lanarkshire*,[96] a case where the *pro indiviso* proprietors let the subjects to one of their number, namely:[97]

> That [the tenant] could be ejected by his co-proprietors I have no doubt. *Qua* tenant, he could not avail himself of his rights as co-proprietor *pro indiviso* to resist removal at the instance of his co-proprietors ... that fact does not enable him to maintain himself in possession *qua* tenant till he is removed with his own consent.

Higgins v Assessor for Lanarkshire was a case about valuation for rating. The question was whether the rent passing under the lease was a true indicator of the annual value of the subjects on the statutory valuation hypothesis. For the answer to that question, it did not matter whether the lease was valid or not. The issue of the validity of the lease was not raised by either party to the appeal and none of the judges considered it. Lord Johnston's statement, which was plainly an *obiter dictum*, simply assumed the validity of the lease. That *dictum* was referred to in the *Clydesdale Bank* case both in the Inner House and in the House of Lords. Neither court considered it to have any persuasive value.

All of these points are raised to support the general contention that the House of Lords while ruling out the validity of the contract as a lease by *pro indiviso* proprietors to one of their number, nevertheless upheld the validity of it as an occupation and management contract and, by extension, a personal lease. This is the key element in the alternative theory; but it may be a step too far.

The House of Lords authoritatively confirmed the now uncontroversial point that the *pro indiviso* proprietors of land are entitled to agree among themselves that one of their number will have sole occupancy of the land and to agree on the terms and conditions on which he will occupy it. Such terms and conditions could include, for example, the payment by the

95 1986 *SLT* 672.

96 1911 SC 931.

97 *Higgins* (n 96) at 934.

occupying proprietor to the others of a sum reflecting their share of the rents that would have been received if the land had been let to a third party; or the payment of a sum representing a proportion of the net profits of the occupier's farming enterprise; and the payment by them to the occupier, at the termination of the contract, of their share of the value of the occupier's improvements.

In this way, the contract could achieve a similar result to that which would have applied if the land had been let to a third party. However, in such a contract, the parties would be, on one side, the occupier and, on the other side, the other *pro indiviso* proprietors. The contract in this case was between different parties, namely, on one side, all of the *pro indiviso* proprietors and, on the other, one of the three *qua* individual. The judges of the House of Lords regarded the purported lease document as being in itself a valid contract by which the *pro indiviso* proprietors regulated the occupation and management of the land. Those statements were plainly *obiter*. In my view, they are unsound. Since the contract was between all three proprietors and one of their number, it failed as a contract for occupation and management on the same logic on which it failed as a lease.

This objection could be dismissed as raising a mere matter of form. But the objection goes beyond that. The contract bore to be, and was intended to be, a lease. I cannot understand how, as the judges of the House of Lords seem to have implied, it fell to be read as being what it did not bear to be, and was not intended to be; namely, a contract between all three *pro indiviso* proprietors contracting as such *inter se*. It would seem to be an extraordinary interpretation of the purported lease that the parties to it, having reached *consensus* on the creation of a lease over the subjects, however mistakenly, should be held to have had the common intention of creating a contract of an entirely different kind.

Furthermore, if the purported lease could have been so regarded, I cannot see how intelligible terms could have been read into it. The contract was intended to make the appellant tenant of the land, and as such vested in the rights conferred by the contract and subject to the duties that it imposed; but subject also to the provisions of the 1991 Act and related statutes such as the Succession (Scotland) Act 1964. I fail to see how the contract could be read as having entirely different consequences for the appellant *qua* owner in occupation. On that view, therefore, I conclude that the appellant in the *Clydesdale Bank* case acquired neither a right *in rem* to occupy the land *qua* tenant, nor a right *in personam* to the exclusive occupation of it *qua* proprietor.

6

Conveyancing: A Bright Digital Future?

Professor Stewart Brymer

A. Introduction

We are all accustomed to how heritable property transactions work – and sometimes do not work. If we were creating a property transfer system from scratch today, what would it look like? Indeed, how might a conveyancing system operate in, say, 2050? Is it too fanciful to suggest that transactions will be carried out electronically from start to finish with electronic paperwork, electronic examination of title and a clean and accessible Land Register holding all information relative to land and property in Scotland with experienced property lawyers advising clients on the important aspects of the transaction assisted by trained legal executives? This essay aims to look at the conveyancing process as we know it with a view to assessing how close we are today to that vision becoming a reality.

B. Conveyancing Past and Present

Prior to the enactment of the Conveyancing and Feudal Reform (Scotland) Act 1970, the Land Tenure Reform (Scotland) Act 1974 and prior to the Land Registration (Scotland) Act 1979, there had been very little change in conveyancing law and practice. Indeed, the pace of change could be said to have been somewhat glacial. The combined effect of the aforementioned statutes was radical given the introduction of *inter alia* the Standard

Security; redemption of feu duty on sale; and registration of title. The first two statutes were the result of earlier analysis of Scots property law by the Reid, Henry and Halliday Reports.[1]

There was little further in the way of legislative intervention in the area of property law until 2000. That was not to say that the Scottish Law Commission was not busy however.[2] The result was the enactment of the Abolition of Feudal Tenure Etc. (Scotland) Act 2000; the Title Conditions (Scotland) Act 2003; and the Tenements (Scotland) Act 2004 which all came into force on the Appointed Day.[3] If there was ever a significant date in Scots property law, that was it. We are now some ten years on from the Appointed Day and the Scottish Law Commission has completed another highly regarded review of registration law and practice.[4] The 1979 Act has been criticised over the years, most notably when it was described as having, "all the intellectual sharpness of a mashed potato,"[5] but the fact of the matter is that the Act has worked and solicitors and the public generally have benefited from registration of title. The time was right for a complete overhaul of the system however. This resulted in the enactment of the Land Registration etc. (Scotland) Act 2012 ("the 2012 Act"), Part 10 of which[6] came into force on 11 May 2014 by virtue of The Electronic Documents (Scotland) Regulations 2014.[7] These Regulations were introduced under the 2012 Act, the balance of which came into force on 8 December 2014. The Regulations prescribe the requirements for electronic signatures that will allow documents covered by the Requirements of Writing (Scotland) Act 1995 ("the 1995 Act"), with the exception of Wills and other testamentary writings meantime, to be signed by applying a suitable electronic signature and thus be both legally valid and self-proving. This means that contracts

1 Registration of Title to Land (Cmnd 2032: 1963) ("Reid Committee Report"); Registration of Title to Land (Cmnd 4137: 1969) ("Henry Committee Report"); and Conveyancing Legislation and Practice (Cmnd 3118: 1968) ("Halliday Committee Report"). See also *Land Tenure in Scotland: A Plan for Reform* (Cmnd 4099: 1969) (the White paper) and *Land Tenure in Scotland: A Plan for Reform* (1972) (the Green paper).

2 Report on Abolition of the Feudal System (Scot Law Com Report n 168, 1999); Report on the Law of the Tenement (Scot Law Com Report n 162, 1998) and Report on the law of Real Burdens (Scot Law Com Report n 181, 2000).

3 28 November 2004.

4 Report on *Land Registration* (Volumes 1 and 2) (Scot Law Com Report n 222, 2010)

5 Discussion Paper on *Land Registration: Void and Voidable Titles* (Scot Law Com DP n 125, 2004) para 2.24.

6 s 96 to s 100.

7 See Registers of Scotland Electronic Documents (Scotland) Regulations Consultation Report.

for the sale, purchase and leasing of land and property can be completed electronically instead of in writing with a "wet" signature being applied thereto. For more on this, see below.

There has been considerable change in the practice of conveyancing during the past 45 years. There will be some who argue that these changes have not had any major effect on the practice of conveyancing and, in any event, that the profession has adapted to change and will continue to do so. That may well be the case. Nevertheless, in a lecture given in 1998, Professor Robert Rennie said: "Some conveyancing solicitors look back to the past with nostalgia and forward to the future with a degree of trepidation." It is suggested that the full implications of the 2000, 2003 and 2004 Acts have not yet been felt and, when combined with the enabling provisions of the 2012 Act, the changes to Property law and Conveyancing law and practice in particular will be significant. There are those who believe that any change is unwelcome. The combined effect of the pace of change in today's society and developments in IT over the past 30 years dictate against that view being an acceptable position however. The World Wide Web was only created in 1990[8] and look at the effect that that has had on our lives. Who would have predicted that? These developments are exponential and all-invasive in every aspect of our business and personal lives. Is there any reason why conveyancing should be immune from such changes? I suggest not.

In a thesis written in 1989, Ian Burdon, then with Registers of Scotland, concluded that:[9]

> The present millennium began with feudalism and reliance on the literacy of the clerical elite. The vision of the beginning of the next millennium is of an automated land registration system alongside a fully integrated digital information system, unencumbered by those administrative and bureaucratic structures which serve only to impede the public.

In the preface to our book entitled "Conveyancing in the Electronic Age,"[10] Robert Rennie and I stated that we hoped that there was considerable future potential for Scotland to develop land registration coverage with additional content that meets the needs of a much more informed and information-hungry society. That is precisely what is now happening with the 2012 Act and the Scottish Government's desire to see the whole

8 J Ryan, *A History of the Internet and the Digital Future* (2010) 107.

9 I Burdon, *Automated Registration of Title to Land: A report for the Government Study Fellowship* (1998).

10 R Rennie and S Brymer, *Conveyancing in the Electronic Age* (2008).

of Scotland on the Land Register during the course of the next 10 years.[11] That may be seen as an ambitious target by some,[12] but is there any reason why such an objective cannot be achieved? The political will exists and Registers of Scotland have shown how responsive they can be in embracing all the statutory obligations on them under the 2000 and 2003 Acts and also under the 2012 Act. The Keeper's challenges are considerable but there is an enthusiastic and well-informed team in Registers that is engaging with its stakeholders and can see the potential that exists. The benefits of the Land Register being completed are social and economic as well as political and it is appropriate that we consider the benefits that this may bring. Change is all around us and it is suggested that it is better being involved in the change process rather than being outside the tent looking in. Life without change would mean that there would never be any progress.

So, what are the changes introduced by Part 10 of the 2012 Act and how will those changes impact on conveyancing law and practice?

(1) 2012 Act ss 96-100 ("Part 10")

Credit for what has been a formidable piece of work in the shape of the 2012 Act must go to the Scottish Law Commission and to Professors George Gretton and Kenneth Reid in particular. The profession is indebted to these two individuals. They have played a pivotal role in reforming the Scots law of property over the past 35 years while, at the same time, retaining the underlying principles established over the last 400 years. Credit must also go to the Registers of Scotland and to the Scottish Government for having the vision to progress the statutory timetable through a period of economic uncertainty.

Part 10 makes changes to the 1995 Act so as to make digital execution equivalent to a traditional "wet" signature. In essence, it e-enables all the documents referred to in s 1(2)(a) of the 1995 Act. Digital signatures are, of themselves, not new of course as the profession has had experience of using the whe undertaking transactions involving Automated Registration of Title to Land ("ARTL").

---

11 Registers of Scotland, Completion of the Land Register, Public Consultation (2014) paras 8-15, available at http://www.scotland.gov.uk/Resource/0045/00451087.pdf and Report of the Land Reform Review Group: The Land of Scotland and the Common Good (2014) para 24 ff, available at http://www.scotland.gov.uk/Resource/0045/00451087.pdf

12 "Target Set to Register all of Scotland's Land" *Scottish Legal News*, 27 May 2014.

ARTL was introduced in 2006[13] when an Order made changes to the 1995 Act for the purposes of ARTL. The introduction of this change by secondary legislation under s 8 of the Electronic Communications Act 2000 came about following a Joint Opinion of the so-called Professorial Panel (Professors Brymer, Gretton, Paisley and Rennie – Professor Reid being excused given his then role with the Scottish Law Commission) which was delivered to the then Keeper of the Registers of Scotland ("RoS") in April 2003 and later published in the *Juridical Review*.[14] Digital execution under ARTL was a necessary first step. Originally, it was proposed that a digital signature would still require to be witnessed in order to be probative. The view of the Professorial Panel was that the conferring of probative status on an unwitnessed deed was beyond the scope of a Section 8 Order. However, there is no requirement on the Keeper to only accept probative deeds in respect of land registration applications. Accordingly, the unanimous view in the Joint Opinion was that the Keeper was perfectly entitled to accept a digitally executed deed without the need for that deed to be probative. Authentication by way of a digital signature which is validated by a third party gives the degree of security that is required for those placing reliance on such deeds.

The 1995 Act was suitably amended and in his annotations to the amended 1995 Act,[15] Professor Kenneth Reid indicated that in the case of electronic documents, the distinction between probative and non-probative deeds was abandoned. ARTL was subsequently introduced and is still in use today[16] – although not as widespread as originally envisaged. There are a number of reasons why this is the case, the principal and somewhat non-technical explanation being that its operation is somewhat "clunky" and in need of an overhaul. In truth, ARTL was not embraced fully by conveyancers and was not widely used in transactions other than remortgages, Improvement Grants and certain Charging Orders. Such an overhaul will be undertaken and an upgraded version of ARTL will be launched by RoS (Registers of Scotland) in due course. This is also permitted under Part 10. In the words of Gilbert, it is easy to "carp and criticise" about anything in life and developments in the law and practice are no exception.[17] In the case of ARTL, however, one would do well to reflect on just how ground-breaking

---

13 The Automated Registration of Title to Land (Electronic Communications) (Scotland) Order 2006 (SSI 2006/491) ("the 2006 Order").

14 2005 JR 201.

15 K Reid, *Requirements of Writing (Scotland) Act 1995* (1995).

16 Over 91,000 transactions to date (as of 31 October 2014).

17 *The Pirates of Penzance; or, The Slave of Duty.*

the system was and what other benefits it will bring when upgraded as part of the move towards Scotland having a fully digitised Land Register. Could ARTL have been introduced in a different manner? With the benefit of hindsight, this is undoubtedly the case. It is hoped that ARTL Mark 2 will be introduced and that practice will develop as a result of demand from the profession. That will occur once all the other building blocks for digital transactions are in place and we see that purchasers, sellers and lenders want to transact in this way. That will complete the change process which will begin after the Designated Day for the 2012 Act when a large number of services will be provided by RoS in an electronic manner.

(2) What is a Digital Signature?

The term "digital signature" is in many ways a convenient tag for the authentication of a document by electronic means. There are many variations including machines that allow a signature to be traced which then appears on a screen. Indeed, such systems could have been adapted for use in such a way that an electronic signed deed could have accompanied an ARTL application. That is not what would be regarded as a digital signature in a technological sense however. The crucial element is not the digital signature itself but the digital certificate which provides the security for the adhibition of the signature and which thus underpins same. In strict technological terms, the certificate is used to create the digital signature which is a product of the actual document and the digital certificate together. This detail is suitably encrypted and lies behind the signature.

In the ARTL system, the digital certificates comply with the X509 standard.[18] As a general rule, the longer the length of cryptographic keys, the stronger the encryption. For example, a 20BIT key is twice as strong as a 19BIT key and so on. A digital signature with a robust encryption such as the ARTL digital certificate is therefore very secure and one might remember that in the not so recent past, a digital certificate with a key length of over 56BITs was classed as a military weapon for export purposes and special licences were required. What is important is the strength of the digital certificate. In other words, not every digital signature can be used in the knowledge that it is secure. Put simply, a cheap digital signature obtained on the internet on a credit card payment is never likely to be acceptable for the processes envisaged by Part 10 because the digital

18 See J R Vacca, *Computer and Information Security Handbook* (2008) 436 ff.

certificate which is used to adhibit the digital signature is simply not secure enough. Any digital signature has to be one which is backed by a digital certificate trusted by people in a business and commercial context. It is not just the technological content that is important. Of particular importance for property lawyers given the uses to which a digital signature is to be put in conveyancing transactions is the identity check which is made by the provider of the digital certificate before that certificate is issued.

As mentioned above, in a very basic sense, an electronic signature could be simply a name at the end of an email or an image of a person's written signature added to an electronic document. Neither of these would meet the terms of the requirements set out in the Regulations. An advanced electronic signature is uniquely linked to the signatory and is capable of identifying the signatory. It is created using systems that the signatory can maintain under his/her sole control. This, by necessity, means that the digital signature will only be processed by a certification authority after robust security and ID checks are carried out. An advanced electronic signature will, however, require a certification authority[19] to have verified the identity of the individual using same however.

For an electronic signature to become an advanced electronic signature it must be:

(i) uniquely linked to the signatory;

(ii) capable of identifying the signatory;

(iii) created using means that the signatory can maintain under their sole control; and

(iv) linked to the data to which it relates so that any subsequent change of the data is detectable.

An advanced electronic signature has more significant value than an electronic signature: it guarantees the integrity of the text, as well as the authentication. The juridical value it has is for integrity: one is sure the text received is the same that was sent, and that no hacker has changed it.

The only practical way to meet these requirements is to use the technology called Public Key Infrastructure ("PKI"). PKI is the technology that provides a solution for secure electronic signatures. The key components are the digital certificates that form part of the signature. These allow for the validity of an electronic signature and the identity of the signatory to be

19 See below.

authenticated. The electronic signature and the digital certificate are both provided by the certification service provider. The electronic signature that incorporates the digital certificate is usually held on a chip embedded within a pin protected smart card that the signatory can maintain under their sole control or held remotely and securely by a third party.[20]

The authentication of a deed or a missive by a person using a digital signature operates within PKI. There are two mirror aspects of digital signatures. From the point of view of the party who holds the signature no-one else must be able to use it. However, from the point of view of the party who is to receive and rely on the document authenticated by a digital signature, there must be a method of verifying that the document has, indeed, been digitally signed. The technology is complicated as one might expect but it essentially operates on the basis of a private key and a public key. The private key is held by the holder of the digital signature and is not made known to the other party who is to receive the digitally signed document. The public key on the other hand is available to the recipient of the document and that party uses the public key to verify simply that the document in question has been authenticated by the digital signature. A PKI infrastructure employs advanced encryption techniques. It is obvious that there must be a closed, robust and secure environment in which solicitors can interact with each other and indeed, interact with the Land Register and other bodies with a view to processing electronic dealings free from any interference by any unauthorised outsiders. Referring once again to the ARTL system, the PKI created for the Land Register is a closed tactical public key infrastructure. This means that the digital certificates were/are issued to licensed ARTL users only and cannot be used for any purpose other than for the purposes of the ARTL system.

A significant step forward was made on 11 May 2014 when the Electronic Documents (Scotland) Regulations 2014 ("the 2014 Regulations") came into force. The Regulations are a small but very important step that will help facilitate conveyancing in Scotland to be carried out electronically. The 2014 Regulations were made under powers that were inserted into the 1995 Act by the 2012 Act. The 2014 Regulations allow legal documents that the 1995 Act specifies must be in writing (other than wills and other testamentary writings at present) to take an electronic form and be legally valid.

20 See below.

The 2014 Regulations provide that electronic versions of legal documents governed by the 1995 Act can be legally valid if they are signed by using what is termed an "advanced electronic signature." For a document to obtain the presumption that it is has been signed by the granter, and to become self-proving, it must be signed using an advanced electronic signature, and that signature must be certified using a "qualified certificate."

The terms "advanced electronic signature" and "qualified certificate" used in the 2014 Regulations are defined in the Electronic Signatures Regulations 2002 ("the 2002 Regulations"), a piece of Westminster legislation that adopted into UK law Directive 1999/93EC of the European Parliament and Council on a Community framework for electronic signatures.

Advanced electronic signatures are issued by what is termed a "certification authority." For an electronic document to become self-proving, the documents must be signed using an advanced electronic signature that is certified using a qualified certificate. The 2002 Regulations prescribe that a qualified certificate must contain:

(i) an indication that the certificate is issued as a qualified certificate;

(ii) the identification of the certification-service-provider and the State in which it is established;

(iii) the name of the signatory or a pseudonym, which shall be identified as such;

(iv) provision for a specific attribute of the signatory to be included if relevant, depending on the purpose for which the certificate is intended;

(v) signature-verification data which corresponds to signature-creation data under the control of the signatory;

(vi) an indication of the beginning and end of the period of validity of the certificate;

(vii) the identity code of the certificate;

(viii) the advanced electronic signature of the certification-service-provider issuing it;

(ix) limitations on the scope of use of the certificate, if applicable; and

(x) limits on the value of transactions for which the certificate can be used, if applicable.

The Law Society of Scotland is currently in the process of introducing an electronic practising certificate or Smartcard which will contain within it a secure digital signature that meets the requirements for an advanced electronic signature that is certified using a qualified certificate.[21] These Smartcards will give Scottish solicitors the ability to benefit from the 2014 Regulations and sign legal documents electronically. This is being achieved by way of a phased roll-out which commenced in Summer 2014.

Trust is a key element of every PKI infrastructure. Under the ARTL system, the procedure for obtaining a Digital Signature began with a personal visit by Land Register staff in order to validate the identities of those people who were to act as local registration authorities in face to face meetings. A similar certification process is being undertaken by the Law Society and that is exactly as it should be in order to ensure that public confidence in the system is maintained.

As far as general practice is concerned, it might well be prudent for solicitors to incorporate authority from clients in Terms of Business to the effect that the client authorises their solicitor to sign missives and any other permitted document, electronically on his/her behalf. No such authority is given under current practice when adjusting missives, of course, but it is good practice at the moment to seek authority from one's client before issuing an offer or formal missive. It therefore makes sense to add a simple provision to this effect in Terms of Business.

The full effects of the change to digital signatures will not be harnessed until a secure electronic document exchange facility is available. That has been talked about for some time. The reality, however, is that such document exchange facilities already exist. The stockbroking community, among others, is well versed at dealing in this way. This is a natural progression for conveyancing and the sale/purchase of heritable property generally. It is envisaged that this will be a secure online portal or platform on which solicitors can communicate in a secure manner with other solicitors, lenders, RoS, Revenue Scotland and, indeed, their clients. Once there is a single national missive and standard styles of common conveyancing documents[22] there will be a greater opportunity for solicitors to focus on being a trusted adviser in the process which, in time, will hopefully see the Scottish system of conveyancing retain its uniqueness. There is, at present, a trend towards us having a conveyancing system that is, to all intents and purposes, the same as that which operates in England and Wales, with

21 The Law Society of Scotland, "Introducing the Smartcard," available at www.lawscot.org.uk/smartcard

22 See below.

exchange of contracts and chains of transactions becoming the norm. There is an opportunity now to reverse this trend.

(3) The need for client confidence

As mentioned above, The Law Society of Scotland Smartcard initiative will not have full coverage until October 2015. Commercial solutions are believed to be available however. One such solution is the Yooseful Technology Property Manager™ product.[23] This product is registered under a certification authority through Entrust.[24] To become a certification authority, an organisation must seek accreditation under the T Scheme.[25] T Scheme was initially established to provide a voluntary approval scheme for providers of the cryptographic elements necessary to underpin the use of digital signatures. This is because Government wishes people and organisations to have trust in e-commerce. The digital certificate can be embedded in a mobile phone or in a card and card reader as the case may be and can be used on a "pay as you go" basis. There are benefits of other "wrappers" offered by the providers of the digital signature e.g. indemnity insurance etc.

In essence, it is envisaged that the net effect will be a streamlining of the conveyancing process and thus satisfying the desire for the legal profession to remain as effective gatekeepers of sale and purchase transactions. People want to communicate electronically – and many do it already without fully appreciating the inherent risks that exist when transacting in an insecure manner. They are used to it and expect instant responses. Secure email exchange would be much better so that transactions are safe. It is therefore imperative that there are robust safeguards in place in order that the sale and purchase process can operate smoothly and hopefully help minimise delay and loss. This will be achieved by removing uncertainty with regard to undelivered or intercepted emails; missing deeds; delay in conclusion of missives etc. In what way is that not a good thing?

For the Law Society Secure Digital Signature to be used effectively in a conveyancing transaction, it will require to be integrated with a firm's case management software and other systems. That may not be as simple a

---

23 For more information see Yooseful Technology Limited's website available here: www.yoosefultechnology.com

24 For more information see Entrust®, Inc.'s website available here: www.entrust.com

25 For more information see the Scheme Limited's website available here: www.tscheme.org

process as it sounds and discussions are underway with case management software providers with a view to smoothing integration. Perhaps there is an opportunity for the Law Society to offer a branded secure dealing room or portal to its members as a way to effectively host the platform on which secure transactions can be carried out?

Digital signatures based on digital certification provided by a certification authority allow parties to rely on the validity of the signature. In simple terms, if you trust the certification authority, then you can trust the digital signature. The digital signature will be legally valid and admissible as evidence of the authenticity and integrity of the electronic communication. It will hopefully also speed up the process of concluding missives, and remove problems encountered with regard to delivery of letters concluding the bargain etc.[26]

As with any change in the way things are done, it will take time for digital signatures to become the norm. Put simply, we tend to trust that which we know. I am confident that practice will evolve quickly, however – especially among the younger members of the profession. Why should we and our clients not benefit from a secure way in which to sign and exchange contracts and documents? "Early adopters" will have an opportunity to develop their practices further by embracing this exciting, and entirely logical development.

Any system, whether in ARTL or in the exchange of missives or the signing of documents in a manner designed to replicate as nearly as possible the existing paper-based systems, must be based on client confidence. For so long as members of the public do not have digital signatures of a type that meet the prescribed requirements, the essential underlying element will be the authority given by a client to his/her solicitor or other agent to sign for them using a digital signature. From a policy and security point of view, the holding of a digital signature should be with an individual rather than by a firm or limited liability partnership as a whole as the latter would render the system less secure. There are, however, already developments which might result in the use of digital signatures being extended to any transaction concluded over the internet. This involves the use of a biometric.[27] A biometric solution uses physiology to reinforce the link between the person applying the digital signature and the signature itself and is, perhaps, where we will end up as further technological advances are made.

26 See *Park, Petitioner* 2009 *SLT* 871.

27 See L Reid and M Bromby, "Beyond the Chip and PIN" 53(7) *JLSS* (2008) 50.

Change will happen and it is suggested that it makes logical sense for the whole sale and purchase transaction to be able to be competed electronically from start to finish. Conveyancing Case Management systems are now widely used and it is envisaged that changes to these systems will increasingly make use of the technological developments that exist, especially when, as is the case with Part 10, these are underpinned by legislation. It is essential however that all new systems are introduced with care and attention especially with regard to the importance of client confidence therein. It is this that gives the solicitor an opportunity to remain central to the sale and purchase process as a "trusted adviser."

C. Conveyancing Future

(1) National Land and Property Information database

An essential requirement for an efficient system of transferring ownership of heritable property is the accuracy and availability of information relative to the property being sold and, indeed, neighbouring properties. It is essential that searches of local authority and other records are undertaken prior to the purchase of a property. Unfortunately, however, the quality of records and practices differ from local authority to local authority. This results in uncertainty and increases the potential for error and loss.[28] There are some examples of very good practice in local authorities. One such is the City of Edinburgh's planning and building standards portal.[29] Even that system still has its gaps however e.g. plans are not available in all instances and all current systems suffer from the lack of a uniform addressing database. It is nevertheless an example of what can be achieved. The introduction of the National Gazetteer as a result of a collaboration among 32 local authorities in Scotland was a significant step forward with each property being allocated a Unique Property Reference Number ("UPRN"). There is considerable potential in grouping all relevant data from both public and private sources around the UPRN.

Up to date and readily accessible information on land and property is at the very core of the conveyancing service. It has been argued for many years that it is nonsensical for solicitors to have to have recourse to multiple

28 See *Runciman v Borders Regional Council* 1998 *SLT* 135.

29 This is available at https://citydev-portal.edinburgh.gov.uk

data sets, some of which may not be comprehensive in their coverage or, indeed, be current. This is not in the best interests of either buyer or seller. Why should they be put at risk? It must surely be the case that in today's information-based society that all relevant data on land and property is held in a comprehensive and easily searchable database. This initiative may well be the catalyst for reform that has been required. Without it, the existing systems would grind on with little or no appetite for change. It is suggested that the availability of relevant information which is accurate and comprehensive, can be properly interpreted and can be relied upon and is readily accessible is not only consistent with the aims of Government as far as efficiency is concerned, but is also necessary as part of the Scottish Government's commitment to improve the supply of information for people when making a decision about buying and selling a home. The benefits of a national portal containing all information relative to land and property (other than title information) are significant and are achievable given the political will to do something about the present unsatisfactory nature surrounding the supply of information relative to land and property. Why should this be tolerated in this day and age when it can be avoided?

There have been a number of recent developments which have the potential to significantly improve the way in which information about Scotland's land and property is managed and made available. A number of inter-related initiatives are being, or are about to be, launched, which together with new governance arrangements, suggest that the original aims of the Scottish Land Information Service ("ScotLIS") may finally be realised.

In 2001, those involved with the ScotLIS project[30] produced the following statements of intent:

> The ultimate aim of the ScotLIS project is that of providing an integrated data set where the user obtains information from a range of providers by means of a single search enquiry. This will be facilitated by means of a gazetteer ... The extent to which data from different suppliers will be integrated will be determined in the course of the ScotLIS pilot and through the ongoing development of the service.

ScotLIS never progressed beyond the pilot stage for a number of reasons, mainly to do with the available technology at the time, but also due to the way in which the organisations involved viewed their own information.

30 See http://brymerlegal.blogspot.se/2012/03/joined-up-land-and-property-information.html

Since then, a number of significant events have occurred including legislative change and most markedly the economic downturn which has led to serious review of the way in which the public sector will require to deliver services in future.[31]

In December 2009, Scottish Ministers signed the European INSPIRE Directive which places an obligation on them to publish information on a number of spatial data themes which contain environmental data. Those themes directly related to land and property are Addresses, Geographic Names, Cadastral Parcels and Buildings and the Directive explicitly specifies what information is required to be published and how this must be done using web services. This was a very important step on the road to the goal of joined-up property information.

In 2010, a joint venture was established between the Local Government Association and the Ordnance Survey to deliver a National Address Gazetteer for England and Wales by working collaboratively to combine the best features of the National Land and Property Gazetteer and Ordnance Survey address products. This provided for the inclusion of One Scotland Gazetteer data into the National Address Gazetteer.

The Scottish Government also established a Spatial Information Board with the remit to implement the Scottish Spatial Data Infrastructure/ INSPIRE Directive requirements. The Board's membership is drawn from senior officers from Scottish Government, NDPBs, SOLACE, NHS, AGI Scotland, Edina and the Registers of Scotland. The Board reports to a National Board overseeing public sector reform in Scotland. Five theme groups were established under the Board, with one of these having the remit for Land, Property and Addresses, which include Geographic Names and Buildings and there is a clear reporting structure for land and property related information to Ministerial level. This was one of the key components missing from ScotLIS in 2001, as well as the links to other geospatial initiatives.

Scotland is well placed to develop a land and property infrastructure which will be capable of supporting greatly improved services, including e-Conveyancing and improved asset management.

Unifi Scotland[32] is a think tank that was established a number of years ago to look at ways of improving access to and use of data on Land and Property with a view to having a government-backed definitive source

31 For a more detailed review of the background to ScotLIS see S Brymer, "National Gazetteer for Scotland" (2008) 97 *Greens Property Law Bulletin* 1-3.

32 See http://www.unifiscotland.com/

of information. Its membership includes representatives from The Law Society of Scotland, the Royal Institution of Chartered Surveyors, RoS, the Council of Mortgage Lenders, Ordinance Survey private search companies and representatives of local and national government. The focus of Unifi is to enhance the accessibility, quality and reliability of property information and, in turn facilitate the quicker completion of property transactions. In essence, Unifi seeks to improve the current system. The progressive availability of location-based information and the ability to usefully link various sources of this through definitive addressing and intelligent mapping provides the means to improve decision making, smarten traditional ways of working and draw significant value in a way that has not been possible before. Hopefully all stakeholders will be convinced of the considerable savings that will be achieved and we can move quickly towards converting this vision into a reality.

(2) Comparative example

It is usually the case that someone, somewhere will have done, or is thinking of doing, that which you are considering. Legal systems are no different. One of the attributes of Scots law over the years is the way that it has adapted and learned from other jurisdictions. That has been hugely beneficial and the study of comparative law can bring significant benefits.

One such benefit may be capable of being found in Norway where an innovative land information project has already been introduced by the Norwegian Land Information company.[33] In Norway, the majority of municipalities have pooled their information on land and property with the Norwegian Land Information company, Ambita AS. This information is held digitally and is accessed on a "pay as you go" basis. Considerable benefits have accrued both for local government and for those who rely on the information. It is hoped that it might be possible for a pilot study of such a project to be undertaken in Scotland. This would require collaboration among local authorities, utility companies and the holders of other information on land and property.

The property information portal in Norway is called INFOLAND and it serves as an inter-operable cooperation between public and private sector, collecting layers of information necessary to the various stakeholders in the property segment, be they a private citizen, mortgage lenders and

33 For more information see Ambita AS's website at www.ambita.com.

credit institutions, property solicitors, surveyors, contractors and others. The INFOLAND portal connects information from the planning and property departments of the municipalities in addition to information developed on the back of this from private sector search companies and other government bodies such as environmental offices, Ordnance Survey and others. The principle behind the portal is simple. A one-step search for a property in question and all information relevant to the request is made available. The supplier (the local authority or another information provider in the portal) provides the necessary information either immediately as a pdf to be downloaded or to an email address or – in the case of non-digital documents – to a specified postal address. The simplicity of the portal's front-end function for the searcher covers a multitude of layers that also entail an administration statistic allowing the supplier to follow requested transactions. In the case of payments, a simple arrangement that allows for subscription or for credit card payments is also made available.

In short, the INFOLAND portal has functioned as a single one-stop-shop for all layers of property information in Norway since its launch in 1998 in Stavanger. It provides efficient and timesaving access to information, thereby saving money and speeding up Norwegian property transactions. It is hoped that the same result can be achieved in Scotland.

(3) Lender Exchange

Changes are also currently being made by a number of mortgage lenders with the introduction of Lender Exchange[34] by Decision First Limited, a joint venture company between Decision Insight Information Group and First Title plc. Individual lenders have been communicating their positions to solicitor firms on their lending panels.

Lender Exchange is a web portal which aims to address the issue of multiple lenders seeking similar information from solicitors in order to better manage their panel systems. The aim is to reduce costs and the administrative burden on solicitor firms while also helping the mortgage lenders minimise fraud and negligence through due diligence.

Information is gathered by Decision First and a fee is paid based on the size of the firm. Once in the system, the information need not be further updated unless there is a change to individual details such as an

34 For more information see Decision First Limited's website at www.lenderexchange.co.uk

amalgamation, a finding of professional misconduct etc. The obligation will be on the firm to advise of changes. Leading the way with Lender Exchange are Santander, Lloyds Banking Group and RBS, but the system is open to all mortgage lenders who wish to participate.

Lender Exchange is being promoted by mortgage lenders – not the Council of Mortgage Lenders.[35] Lender Exchange is designed to allow lenders to communicate better with solicitors on their panels by electronic means rather than the present outdated requirement that fax be used. An added benefit might be that solicitors could also be able to communicate in a secure manner with other solicitors on the portal, thus creating a secure dealing room of the type mentioned above on which conveyancing transactions can be carried out. This would be a good example of solicitors and lenders working together, irrespective of any decision with regard to separate representation. This would be a positive step forward but it is dependent upon Lender Exchange being operated in a manner which is seen to be fair to all concerned.

(4) Law Society Working Party on the Future of Conveyancing

Following the Law Society AGM in 2013, a Working Party was established to consider various issues affecting the residential property sector. The Working Party is made up of practitioners and others with interest in the residential property sector and it has managed a full meeting each month since July 2013. Various strands worthy of investigation were identified which, taken together, should enhance the way property transactions are undertaken. These include:

(i) Standard Missives
(ii) Standardised Documentation
(iii) Secure dealing room or portal
(iv) Quality Badge for Conveyancers

The Working Party believes there is a clear role for a vital, progressive legal profession assisting consumers in the sale and purchase of residential property and that solicitors should seek to remain at the core of that process. That goal is best achieved however by the Law Society leading the change process from the front for the benefit of its members and citizens alike. In

35 For more information see the Council of Mortgage Lender's website available here www.cml.org.uk.

so doing, the Law Society is following the lead of countries like Denmark where solicitors made fundamental reforms to the way their role in the house buying/selling process operated following the removal by the Danish Government of the solicitors' monopoly in conveyancing. They now have a thriving property profession and we can usefully learn lessons from their experience.

(5) The Digital Home

With registration happening automatically following completion of an electronic process, there will, in future, be no physical delivery of title deeds. Settlement will therefore become truly symbolic with the keys being the focal point – for as long, of course, as keys are still required. We will have therefore come full circle and are effectively taking sasine! A fully integrated electronic security system covering the property and operated by a personal PIN is already a reality. Who is to say how this will develop? It is conceivable that all information relative to a property could be stored in a memory chip embedded in the property itself perhaps in the form of an In Home Display. This could be a register of all repairs and improvements carried out – including all local authority and other permissions in respect of the works. This would be an up to date record and would replace the Property Questionnaire as part of the Home Report. Until that time however, the keys and supporting documentation such as consents, guarantees, permissions and others will be delivered at settlement. These are important documents and have to be kept safe and it is suggested that these should also be recorded electronically in much the same way as a car log book is maintained.

D. So How Does the Vision Become a Reality?

We are already quite far along the road towards conveyancing transactions being completed electronically. As mentioned above, there are already companies that have developed software which can be utilised to enable agents and solicitors to collaborate, share property information and digitally sign and exchange property contracts.

The 2012 Act will also further enable electronic registration of title in the registers under the management and control of the Keeper of the Registers of Scotland. Additional regulations under the 2012 Act will follow which will e-enable ARTL Mark 2 and other such developments. It is envisaged that this will be by way of a process of evolution rather than revolution however. Practitioners will be given the opportunity to get used to accessing the registers electronically and the move towards a comprehensive ARTL process will thus evolve over time. That time period is finite however. The road map to digital conversion is being prepared.

Over a period of time, the Land Register will be cleansed of real burdens that are no longer valid and subsisting. This will be achieved by solicitors informing the Keeper of their judgment in this regard. Once done, the Land Register will be transparent and fully accessible. This, of course, also fits with the stated aim of Government to have all Scotland mapped and registered in the Land Register by 2024.

It is suggested that the electronic genie is out of the bottle and we have been afforded a glimpse of the future. We have a chance to shape that future however. Is it to be one where the solicitor remains central to the process? I do not see why not. Changes in working practices and, more importantly, in attitudes, will be required however. Conveyancing is a service and we all like to receive good service. Most solicitors provide a very good service and it is suggested that it is now time to focus on how to implement these changes and re-design our businesses accordingly. The heady days of the property boom have passed. During that period, it was almost too easy to make money from buying and selling property for clients. Looking forward, we must surely focus on quality of service and the trusted adviser concept as a means to providing a better service to our clients. I suggest that the effective introduction of changed working practices will assist that goal rather than hinder it.

Once available, e-Conveyancing (in its fullest extent) will make property transactions cheaper and quicker to complete. Such a facility may not speed up the negotiation of missives which, on many occasions, for many often oblique reasons can become very lengthy. It might just act as a catalyst however and we might get back to a situation last seen in the 1970s when missives were often concluded in a short period of time and often on a *de plano* basis. To become a reality however, there has to be a will on the part of everyone involved in the process to embrace the necessary changes and make it happen. The fact of the matter is that clients will expect change and for transactions to be processed in the most efficient way possible. Those who do embrace change once the necessary safeguards are in place should gain a competitive advantage over their rivals.

The digital clock is ticking…

7

The Role of the Expert Witness in Professional Negligence Litigation

Gerald F Hanretty QC

A. Introduction

Expert or skilled witnesses are objectionable. Needless to say, that observation is not directed towards the characters, qualities, learning or experience of those not infrequently called to assist parties and the court in litigation. Rather, the leading of such evidence necessarily results in material being presented to the court which is, by its nature, opinion evidence and accordingly objectionable – and, in the absence of justification, therefore inadmissible.

Issues in relation to the admissibility and use of opinion evidence have long been the subject of debate throughout the English-speaking world. Indeed, in the 21st-century it is worthwhile reflecting upon the observations of J P Taylor in the third edition of his work *A Treatise on the Law of Evidence*:[1]

> Perhaps the testimony which least deserves credit with the jury is that of skilled witnesses. These gentlemen are usually required to speak, not to facts but to opinion; and when this is the case, it is often quite surprising

1 J P Taylor, *A Treatise on the Law of Evidence as Administered in England and Ireland*, 3rd edn (1858) 54.

> to see with what facility, and to what extent, their views can be made to correspond with the wishes or the interests of the parties who call them.

It is likely to be the position that such an observation would be thought by most to remain valid, at least in part. However, what has not much been discussed is the role of the expert in modern dispute resolution other than analyses of the principles to be adopted by experts in the conduct of their duties with only a little practical guidance for practitioners in relation to the choice of experts.

B. The Conventional Analysis

Although litigation by its nature puts in issue partisanship on the part of expert witnesses, in reality, those giving evidence within the realm of professional negligence litigation are highly regarded. In a relatively small jurisdiction like Scotland, it is unsurprising that professional integrity, impartiality and sound judgement are highly prized. Accordingly, challenges to skilled witnesses are most often advanced by challenging the empirical material upon which opinions are advanced or by denouncing the expert opinion as an exercise in usurping the function of the court itself. The importance of instructing expert witnesses who command respect from within their professions cannot be overemphasised.

Of course, the Court jealously guards the role society calls upon it to perform. The classic exposition of the expert's function might be found in the familiar guidance provided by Lord President Cooper in *Davie v Magistrates of Edinburgh*.[2]

More recently, it appears to have been thought necessary to elaborate upon the role of the expert witness. Although discussed within the context of a criminal appeal the observations made in *Wilson v HM Advocate*[3] provide general guidance on the matter. It is worthwhile considering at length the court's opinion in relation to expert evidence in its adoption of Lord President Cooper's *dicta* and its application in a more modern context:[4]

> At this point, in view of the significance of (certain) testimony in this case, we should now consider what we believe to be the proper character of

2 1953 SC 34 at 40.
3 2009 JC 336.
4 *Wilson* at para 58-63.

> expert evidence, and in particular attempt to describe our understanding of its nature and effect on the conclusions we should draw. In general, of course, opinion evidence is not admissible in our criminal courts; witnesses may only under normal circumstances give evidence about matters within their direct knowledge. The evidence of an expert witness is an exception to this rule. It is not possible to provide an absolute direction as to what constitutes legitimate subject-matter for expert opinion. However, two general principles will normally give some guidance. First, the subject-matter under discussion must be necessary for the proper resolution of the dispute, and be such that a judge or jury without instruction or advice in the particular area of knowledge or experience would be unable to reach a sound conclusion without the help of a witness who had such specialised knowledge or experience. Secondly, the subject-matter in question must be part of a recognised body of science or experience which is suitably acknowledged as being useful and reliable, and properly capable of reaching and justifying the opinions offered, and the witness must demonstrate a sufficiently authoritative understanding of the theory and practice of the subject. The nature and scope of expert opinion evidence cannot at any one point in time be exhaustively defined.

The effect of expert opinion evidence can perhaps be described with more precision. The role of the expert witness, and his duties and responsibilities, have been subject to much judicial comment. In *National Justice Campania Naviera SA v Prudential Assurance Co Ltd (The Ikarion Reefer)*,[5] Cresswell J listed a number of such duties and responsibilities, *inter alia*:

1. Expert evidence presented to the court should be, and should be seen to be, the independent product of the expert uninfluenced as to the form or content by the exigencies of litigation.

2. An expert witness should provide independent assistance to the court by way of objective unbiased opinion in relation to matters within his expertise.

3. An expert witness should state the facts or assumptions on which his opinion is based. He should not omit to consider material facts which could detract from his concluded opinion.

4. An expert witness should make it clear when a particular question or issue falls outside his expertise.

To this might be added a requirement that an expert witness should in particular explain why any material relevant to his conclusions is

5 [1993] 2 Lloyd's Rep 68; [1993] FSR 563; [1993] 37 EG 158.

ignored or regarded as unimportant. Although the categories of duty and responsibility described by Cresswell J in the Ikarion Reefer case were concerned with civil matters, these rules are equally applicable to criminal cases.

In addition, particularly in criminal cases, other duties and responsibilities have been recognised by the courts. For example, the court will expect in a criminal matter that an expert's report must state the facts upon which opinions are based, and if assumptions are made, these must be clearly identified. Reasons must be given for conclusions. Whether instructed for the prosecution or defence, the principal duty of an expert witness is to the court, and this overrides any duty he owes to the party which instructed him. Again, explanations should be given for the basis on which all relevant material is either accepted or rejected.

It therefore follows that a judge or jury is not bound by the opinion evidence tendered by an expert witness. There are clear principles under which such evidence is admitted. In *Davie v Magistrates of Edinburgh* Lord President Cooper said (p 40):

> Expert witnesses, however skilled or eminent can give no more than evidence. They cannot usurp the functions of the jury or the Judge sitting as a jury ... Their duty is to furnish the Judge or jury with the necessary specific scientific criteria for testing the accuracy of their conclusions so as to enable the Judge or jury to form their own independent judgment by the application of these criteria to the facts proved in evidence. The scientific opinion evidence, if intelligible, convincing and tested, becomes a factor (and often an important factor) for consideration along with the whole other evidence in the case, but the decision is for the Judge or jury. In particular the bare ipse dixit of a scientist, however, eminent, upon the issue in controversy, will normally carry little weight, for it cannot be tested by cross-examination nor independently appraised, and the parties have invoked the decision of a judicial tribunal and not an oracular pronouncement by an expert.

Although in modern practice (as in the present case), expert evidence is routinely appraised and cross-examined, the position essentially remains that an expert witness's opinion is only a factor (albeit an important one) in the decision of a judge or jury.

It is abundantly clear therefore, and has been for many years in our courts, that an expert witness is not in the position to provide the court with a statement of unqualified conclusions about the question of fact on which his opinion bears. If he does so, the effect of his testimony may well be much diminished. In this context, it is perhaps worth noting that an expert witness is in a particularly privileged position in our courts. Prior to the decision, he is the only person permitted to express an opinion. Other witnesses must confine themselves to facts. Further, an expert witness will routinely rely on assumptions, hearsay evidence, his impression of testimony that he has not heard, and reports, statements and other secondary sources of information, all of which might be incompetent in a court of law if presented as factual evidence. It is therefore of the utmost importance that any expert witness carefully describes the source and assesses the worth of all material on which his opinion is based. We refer to the case of *Gilmour v HM Advocate*[6] (paras 79, 80).

If the approach taken by the court is a paradigm warning to experts in relation to empirical fact lying within the province of the decision-maker, more recent guidance has been given reiterating the court's duty to make findings as opposed to simply adopting an expert's views. In *Kennedy v Cordia (Services) LLP*[7] Lord Brodie considered the admissibility of expert evidence in a personal injuries action arising out of the pursuer's fall in icy conditions:[8]

> In the present case the dispute that had to be resolved was whether, on the basis of the essentially uncontroversial primary facts, as a matter of law, the reclaimers [the defender employers] were under a duty to take a particular precaution (providing attachments to footwear and ensuring their use) and, had they taken that precaution, whether the respondent would have suffered injury. That was something that the Lord Ordinary was fully equipped to do without any instruction or advice; it was squarely within his province as judicial decision-maker. No additional expertise was required. It may be that a judge has personally never carried out a risk assessment of any kind. That does not mean that, having heard evidence of the nature of the activity being assessed and having been provided with a document recording the risk assessment, he cannot determine whether or not the assessment was "suitable and sufficient" in terms of regulation 3(1) of the [Management of Health and Safety at Work Regulations 1999]. It is the job of a judge to hear evidence about matters with which he may previously have been totally unfamiliar and, on the basis of that evidence, come to conclusions of fact and then apply the relevant law to these facts. In *Midland Bank Trust Company Limited v Hett Stubbs & Kemp* [1979] 1 Ch 384 (a case of alleged negligence on the part of a solicitor engaged to carry out a conveyancing transaction) Oliver J was faced with a similar situation to that which faced the Lord

6 [2007] HCJAC 48; 2007 *SLT* 893; 2007 SCCR 417.
7 [2014] CSIH 76.
8 *Kennedy* at para 15.

Ordinary here. In what has become a much-quoted passage, he said this, at p. 402:

> 'I must say that I doubt the value, or even the admissibility, of this sort of evidence, which seems to be becoming customary in cases of this type. The extent of the legal duty in any given situation must, I think, be a question of law for the Court. Clearly if there is some practice in a particular profession, some accepted standard of conduct which is laid down by a professional institute or sanctioned by common usage, evidence of that can and ought to be received. But evidence which really amounts to no more than an expression of opinion by a particular practitioner of what he thinks that he would have done had he been placed, hypothetically and without the benefit of hindsight, in the position of the Defendants, is of little assistance to the Court whilst evidence of the witness's view of what, as a matter of law, the solicitor's duty was in the particular circumstances of the case is, I should have thought, inadmissible, for that is the very question which it is the Court's function to decide'.

C. The Realities of Modern Practice

Bearing in mind the foregoing admonitions, what then is the role of the expert in professional negligence litigation? Perhaps, notwithstanding the quantity of judicial ink addressing the issue, the reality is rather more prosaic. Each of the cases mentioned above in reality identifies the professional obligations incumbent upon experts. They do not, and are not intended to, discuss the pragmatic and practical aspects of the role. Moreover, as society has become more complex and more aspects of business and private life are thought to lie within the province of one profession or another, the need for expert opinion where things are perceived to have "gone wrong" has increased exponentially. Indeed, it is not unreasonable to suggest that in a developed, economically active society there shall be an increasing need for the advice of those who engage in the wide variety of professional activities now commonly encountered. The historical categorisation of "professions" and "trades" is probably an anachronism which fails to address the societal changes wrought by demographic, scientific and clinical advances over the last two centuries. Why might a computer programmer not be asked to explain her decision to write a particular line of code which thereby exposed the computer user to an increased threat from an obscure but identified virus? If the decision was a consequence of a judgement weighing the risks, advantages and disadvantages of such a piece of code, is such not a matter for expert analysis? Of course, such an example demonstrates the need not for one role for the expert witness but rather a multiplicity of roles arising in relation to such a scenario.

Experience suggests that there are at least four and possibly five distinct roles which the expert might be called upon to perform in the context of dispute resolution/litigation. Plainly, much will depend upon the nature of the expertise under scrutiny. In addition, especially within the context of claims against those who have professional indemnity insurance, the professional under challenge will, more often than not, have the benefit of experienced insurers and solicitors. As a corollary, those who feel aggrieved may well require to instruct solicitors who are less familiar with either the profession or professional branch concerned or the constraints of litigation in such a context.

(1) The investigator

If the issue truly arises out of the carrying out of some professional skill or art the detail of which is a mystery to those unskilled in such it must be axiomatic that some investigation will be likely. Obviously, in many cases the basic facts will have been fully explored by the legal teams involved. For example, the allegedly negligent conveyancer's file will have been recovered and pored over. The client's precognition will have addressed the solicitor's mandate. The lender's terms of engagement will have been considered.

In reality, the expert will frequently identify issues which require to be investigated before any concluded view might be taken in relation to breach of duty. Examples might be found of cases where a solicitor's knowledge of his client's intentions in relation to development of a property may or may not be relevant where a material period of time has elapsed during which the possibility of development could reasonably be discounted as a matter to be drawn to the attention of potential lenders.[9] Such knowledge may or may not be apparent to the solicitors instructed but might reasonably be anticipated to be the sort of issue which an expert might, in an appropriate case, bring to the client's and his solicitor's attention.

Likewise, it is not uncommon where losses are sought to be recovered in relation to claims arising out of events many years previously for experts to suggest avenues of attack or defence where law or practice has in the meantime changed. Examples can be found in the field of conveyancing

9 *Leeds and Holbeck Building Society v Alex Morrison & Co* 2001 SCLR 41.

relating to letters of obligation, the necessity for site visits and the requisites for a competent and sufficiently comprehensive report on title. Practice in relation to each of these aspects of day-to-day conveyancing has drastically altered over the last ten years. Diverging views in relation for example to standard forms of clauses in missives has resulted in the need for creation of organisations such as the Standard Missives Joint Working Party of the Edinburgh Conveyancers' Forum. An expert relying on what is perceived to be a standard clause in modern practice would in all likelihood be providing a pretty poor opinion if he or she were to suggest that the Working Party's suggestions are indicative of practice in earlier years.

It also ought to be borne in mind that experts may be engaged not only in relation to whether or not there has been negligence/breach of duty but whether any admitted breach has been causative of loss. In many cases, the quantum of damages will necessarily demand investigation by experts. The input of the forensic accountant exemplifies the role of expert/investigator. Invariably, such an expert will be provided with basic documentation in relation to the performance of individuals or companies. In the real world however such experts frequently advise on the recovery of documents the existence of which is beyond the ken of mere lawyers.

For the avoidance of doubt, it is not suggested that the investigator expert don a forensic trenchcoat and fedora. Indeed, it is no part of the expert's function to effectively dig about to find material which might support his side's position. Such would, having regard to the dicta mentioned above, be anathema. The instructing solicitor must do all within his power to carry through such investigations as the expert identifies. Plainly, steps should already have been taken to ensure that the information initially provided to the expert is as complete as possible. The investigator expert does however require to address the issues in the case and in so doing must take steps to ensure that his opinion satisfies the proper requirements of the court in relation to a presentation of the whole factual matrix necessary for the just determination of the cause.

(2) The gatekeeper

The role of the expert as gatekeeper remains to some extent unrecognised. However, the importance of this role cannot, it is submitted, be underestimated.

Claims of professional negligence have diverse consequences. In the first place, the professional reputation of individuals is invariably placed in the public domain for dissection. In the second place, the ability of individuals to earn a living may well be adversely affected. In the third place, the costs of professional practice may substantially increase in consequence of claims or a claims history. The consequences for individuals and firms can be dire.

It is the first consequence that more often than not has greatest impact on people. Professional men and women often consider the making of a claim against them as a personal attack. He or she might often think of such a claim as being a challenge to his or her *raison d'être*. The emotional consequences might outweigh even a significant pecuniary disadvantage. It follows that such claims ought not ordinarily to be advanced unless they have some proper foundation.

It has been recognised in Scotland for many years that the proper conduct of professional negligence litigation demands that no such claim be advanced before the court unless there is available to the pursuer and his advisers suitably qualified expert opinion that supports the existence of certain professional practices or duties and that same have been breached to the pursuer's detriment. The point has been made forcefully in a number of decisions relating to vexatious litigants. In *Lord Advocate v McNamara*[10] the opinion of the court was delivered by Lord Reed. He made the following remarks in relation to the advancing of claims against professionals in the absence of appropriate opinion evidence:[11]

> As we have explained, these proceedings were based on allegations of professional negligence which were unsupported by the opinion of anyone qualified to express an opinion on that issue. It is not suggested that they were instituted in the expectation that such support could be obtained; nor does there appear to have been any attempt to obtain such support. In those circumstances, we consider that we are entitled to conclude that the proceedings were instituted without any reasonable ground and were vexatious.

More recently, Lord Woolman had cause to discuss the requirements for an expert witness to support a claim in relation to a counter-claim arising out of alleged professional negligence in the related case of *Tods Murray WS v Arakin*.[12] He stated:[13]

10 [2009] CSIH 45; 2009 SC 598.
11 *McNamara* at para 54.
12 2010 CSOH 90.
13 *Arakin* at 90-93.

> The pursuers emphasised the vital importance of a party being in possession of an appropriate expert before making allegations of professional negligence. They contended that in the absence of such a report, it is an abuse of process to institute and persist in such proceedings.
>
> In response, Mr McNamara argued that in respect of some of the allegations, no expert was required. This was most clearly put in the defenders' Note of Argument, which stated "sometimes matters of misconduct are just so blatant they require no experts' view to demonstrate that this is the case."
>
> I reject that approach. In my view, allegations of professional negligence require to have a proper foundation. Without such underpinning, the court is not in a position to make a finding in favour of the defenders (Walkers Evidence, third edition para. 16.3). As a solicitor must always exercise a measure of judgement in fulfilling his duties, it is not enough to say that he has failed to implement his instructions. The allegation must always be buttressed by a report from an appropriate witness, which states that the course taken was one that no solicitor exercising ordinary skill and care would have taken.
>
> In the absence of such a rule, it would be open to a party to make whatever assertions he or she chose, however spurious or mistaken. In my view, that is just what has happened here.

Lest it be thought that the rules in Scotland in relation to the stringency inherent in requiring the production of an expert report are to any extent inconsistent with *Midland Bank Trust Company Limited,*[14] it should be noticed that in England and Wales a not dissimilar approach in relation to the need for expert support is adopted in modern practice.[15] However, for completeness' sake, it should be noticed that an exception is made in that jurisdiction in relation to some claims arising out of negligent conveyancing[16] although same is probably explicable by reference to technical differences in conveyancing practice.

The requirement for an expert report supporting a claim necessarily creates the role of gatekeeper expert. It probably goes without saying that those with a sceptical approach might consider that the necessity for such a role to be borne in mind by the expert witness is indicative of protectionism or cronyism. On the other hand, it is submitted that the views provided by both Lord Reed and by Lord Woolman amply demonstrate the necessity of such a role if the court is to exercise its jurisdiction equitably and efficiently.

14 *Midland Bank Trust Company Limited v Hett Stubbs & Kemp* [1979] 1 Ch 384.

15 *Pantelli Associates Ltd v Corporate City Developments Number Two Limited* [2010] EWHC 3189.

16 *Brown v Gould & Swayne* [1996] EWCA Civ J0124-3.

(3) The mediator

Within the context of disputes relating to professional liability it is, by the nature of things, by no means unusual for experts also to be engaged in mediation practice. However, the individuals concerned will be at pains to recognise the very distinctive role of the mediator in a mediation process from other aspects of their professional practices including the provision of expert opinion.

It is perhaps interesting to observe that the overlap in areas of expertise between mediators and expert witnesses is sometimes thought to be a necessary subject for analysis.[17]

For present purposes the mediator expert remains principally a witness. What has changed in the course of the last 20 years is an increasing reliance by the court upon experts to reduce the scope of dispute. In particular, since the introduction to the Court of Session of commercial actions the court has made demands upon parties to narrow the scope of any controversy and, where appropriate, to demonstrate that steps have been taken towards agreeing evidence.

Rule 47.12 of the Rules of the Court of Session 1994 makes provision for Procedural Hearings in commercial causes. Rule 47.12(2)(h) provides that the court may direct:

> that skilled persons should meet with a view to reaching agreement and identifying areas of disagreement, and may order them thereafter to produce a joint note, to be lodged in process by one of the parties, identifying areas of agreement and disagreement, and the basis of any disagreement.

Needless to say, in many professional negligence claims there will be substantial areas of agreement. However, inasmuch as such disputes not infrequently require to be resolved by reference to the exercise of a professional judgement there will always remain scope for disagreement. This rule nonetheless requires a meeting. Such meetings will, no doubt, be approached in a positive fashion. Experience suggests that such meetings effectively operate as a form of informal mediation. That may well be desirable.

An understandable desire to reduce the scope of disagreement is bolstered somewhat by the provisions of Rule 47.12(2)(i) which provides that the court:

17 See for example C Haselgrove-Spurin, "The role of the mediator," available at http://www.nadr.co.uk/articles/published/mediation/RoleOfTheMediator.pdf

may appoint an expert to examine, on behalf of the court, any reports of skilled persons or other evidence submitted and to report to the court.

The position in the Sheriff Court is arguably even more demanding in as much as rule 40.12(3)(m) of the Ordinary Cause Rules 1993 empowers the sheriff to make any order which the sheriff thinks "will result in a speedy resolution" of the case!

What ought to be borne in mind by expert witnesses is that they cannot indulge in advocacy. To do so would plainly run counter to the whole ethos of the expert witness.

Mention was made above of the significance of professional judgement on the part of those whose actions are being criticised. Inasmuch as professional judgement necessarily connotes the possibility of a range of different actions/advice on the part of the individual concerned it must at least be possible for expert witnesses to effectively mediate in a way which reduces the breadth of the professional judgement challenged. Such a form of "mediation" has the significant advantage of narrowing the issues in dispute to the point where, if appropriate, certain evidence might be agreed or, where possible, compromise arrived at.

A necessary *caveat* must be stated. It is no part of the expert witness role to indulge in negotiation. She cannot enjoy any such mandate. More importantly, notwithstanding the professional obligations upon the expert to assist the court as outlined above, any such expert will nonetheless still require to answer to his client. There will be occasions where the expert witness risks professional embarrassment by failing to observe the limits imposed upon her to confine opinions advanced to the four walls of the litigation concerned and the factual matrix under consideration.

(4) The quantifier

When discussing the role of expert witnesses in professional negligence cases it is inevitable that the focus will be on the merits of the claim. In reality, many litigations focus as much upon the question of causation and the quantum of damages as upon primary liability.

The quantifier expert will be required to opine on the pursuer's position but for the negligence/breach of duty complained of. In many cases, as suggested earlier, the nature of the breach of duty dictates that the quantifier expert shall be one and the same person who speaks to the merits. That will not always be the case. Frequently, within the context for example of clinical negligence claims, a number of areas of expertise arise for consideration. The birth of a baby born with cerebral palsy may well focus upon the action or inaction of an obstetrician. The prognosis for the child, damaged and undamaged, will be addressed by others such as neonatal paediatricians and paediatric neurologists.

Lest it be thought that the quantifier expert's role is in some way lesser than that of those providing opinions on the merits of a claim, the position in the real world is far more demanding. It is frequently the case that at the point in time at which the disgruntled client asserts that the professional's negligence occurred many alternative ways forward might have been in contemplation. It is certainly not uncommon for example for developers of land to consider a number of different possibilities for development when acquiring a site. An error in relation to the extent of the title obtained may require the consideration of a series of different hypotheses as to how the land would otherwise have been developed. For example, planning considerations may have impacted upon the number of plots which might have been marketed. Such might plainly have impacted upon the profit to be generated by the development. Equally, planning conditions may have rendered an otherwise profitable part of a developer's land bank of no worth whatsoever.

Indeed, in certain respects the quantifier expert's function is particularly difficult. The discussion above in relation to the development value of land is an obvious example. The developer will invariably suggest that he would have adopted whatever scheme would have maximised the profit to be generated. The obligation on the expert however will necessarily require him to test that proposition. To fail to do so would be a dereliction of his obligations to the court as well as to his client. But in fulfilling his obligations he will necessarily risk being perceived as taking views adverse to those of his client. Moreover, the quantifier expert will almost invariably also be an investigator expert. It is not always the position that the client assists in providing information which might have a consequence of reducing the value of the claim being advanced. Of course, the preceding observations arise within the context of the expert witness retained on behalf of the claimant. Similar considerations will arise nonetheless for those instructed and retained in respect of the defence of such claims.

Another complicating factor for the quantifier expert arises from the need to consider the quite distinct issue of mitigation of damages. It is trite to observe that the onus of proof in relation to a failure to mitigate damages rests upon the defender. Although issues in relation to mitigation might have been identified by defenders in appropriate cases it will frequently be the quantifier expert who is charged with forming a view on the steps which might properly have been taken by the claimant when presented with the breach of duty hypothetically conceded to have taken place.

(5) The communicator

It is implicit throughout the foregoing that expert witnesses are reasonably anticipated to be well-respected, vastly experienced and of obvious integrity. All of those attributes however are, within the confines of dispute resolution, almost valueless in the absence of an ability to relay complex factual material, explain sometimes ethereal concepts and address all manner of hypotheses which might be advanced in discussion with the decision-maker.

Of particular worth in the expert witness is a demeanour which is empathetic to the role of the decision-maker. Equally, he or she should be capable of communication in a fashion which is neither arrogant nor submissive.

D. The Choice of an Expert Witness in the Real World

It will be apparent that the demands made upon expert witnesses are many and varied. The scepticism which is sometimes applied to expert evidence is, for the most part, balanced by the need to repose confidence in those witnesses skilled in the multiplicity of professional roles found in modern society.

This discussion is intended to broaden issues surrounding the instruction of expert witnesses in professional negligence claims. It highlights the diverse skill set which ought to be found in the well instructed expert's toolbox. It may assist experts in recognising the different roles that they perform at a subconscious level.

Inevitably, professional negligence litigation is testing of all those involved in whatever role and at whatever level. What is most important is that such litigations are conducted in a way which reflects the nature of the issue at hand. Professionalism, propriety, integrity and diligence require to be deployed throughout.

8

The Court and the Conveyancing Expert

Lady Paton

A. The Changing Landscape

The traditional litigation landscape once familiar to the conveyancing expert is undergoing considerable upheaval. The development of automated and electronic technologies, a question-mark over immunity from suit, and the recommendations in Lord Gill's Scottish Civil Courts Review Report,[1] are some of the changes bringing about a new and unfamiliar environment.

B. Automated and Electronic Technologies

Not every lawyer aspires to an automated and paperless world. John Mortimer possibly spoke for many when he observed through his fictional character barrister Horace Rumpole (habitué of the Old Bailey and the Uxbridge Magistrates Court):[2]

> Things, I regret to have to say it, have not improved since those distant days, and many of the faults must be laid at the door of automation. Not only have witnesses changed [replaced, for example, by recording devices]. String quartets, which were once the pride of the tea room, have now been replaced by an abominable form of mechanical music. The toasting fork has given way

1 Report of the Scottish Civil Courts Review (2009), available at http://www.scotcourts.gov.uk/about-the-scottish-court-service/the-scottish-civil-courts-reform

2 J C Mortimer, *Rumpole for the Defence* (1982) 108.

> to an alarming machine that fires singed bread at you like a minute gun. The comforting waitress in black bombazine has become a device that contrives to shoot a warmish and unidentifiable fluid into a plastic cup and over your trousers at the drop of a considerable sum of money. None of these engines is an improvement on the human factor, neither are trials made any easier by the replacement of the living witness with the electronic device.

Nevertheless there is a current trend in the legal world seeking to achieve an automated electronic paperless environment. The Scottish Government has published a paper entitled The Digital Strategy for Justice in Scotland,[3] setting out how digital technology will be used to transform the way in which justice services are delivered in Scotland. The government envisages fully "digitised justice systems" including digital warrants, digital recording of evidence, video-conferencing, and the creation of a secure digital platform to store all information relevant to a case. Cynics might predict that court hearings will soon consist of judges sitting alone surrounded by plasma screens, recording devices, and qwerty-keyboards, with a piece of software instead of a clerk of court, witnesses' evidence taking the form of talking heads on-screen, productions flashing up on a split screen, and lawyers' submissions being transmitted directly from offices or chambers by means of a system such as Skype, phone-conferencing, or Twitter.[4]

That may be too gloomy a view. The judiciary in the Court of Session has expressly welcomed much of the government's digital initiative. In an address at the launch of the Digital Strategy, Lady Dorrian described current problems being experienced in the courts, and possible digital solutions, pointing out *inter alia* that:[5]

> Cases are becoming more complex, with a greater array of technical and forensic evidence that requires analysis and careful presentation in court. Video evidence needs time to be examined thoroughly. Witnesses who are cited for court may not turn up on the appointed day. There may be issues around the timely disclosure of evidence. All of these factors might be mitigated by the application of digital solutions – as evidence can be collected and shared electronically, for example, or witnesses reminded of their need to attend court by text or e-mail, as now happens. [...]
>
> In any modern society, the administration of justice must retain the trust and confidence of the people it serves. And it will only do that if it keeps

3 Scottish Government, The Digital Strategy for Justice in Scotland (2014).

4 Something similar to the future envisaged by the Rt Hon Lord Justice Brooke, "The Courts and Judiciary in 2024" in *Now and Then, A Celebration of Sweet & Maxwell's Bicentenary* (1999) Ch 8.

5 Victoria Quay, Edinburgh, 20 August 2014, available at http://www.scotland-judiciary.org.uk/26/1301/Speech-by-Lady-Dorrian-at-the-launch-of-The-Digital-Strategy-for-Justice-in-Scotland

> pace with the times, and remains relevant to the experience of the people and organisations it serves. We are now in an era, according to research published earlier this month, when Britons spend more time using technology devices than they do sleeping. If people and businesses communicate instantly by e-mail, Skype, or Facebook, they will expect public services to do likewise. [...]
>
> [D]igital innovation will allow greater transparency in proceedings, make it easier for people to participate in the system – whether making applications, submitting documents, giving or providing evidence, paying fines – wherever they are and at a time that suits them. [...]
>
> Changes in technology and changes in procedures cannot happen in isolation – they must be accompanied by changes in the attitude and behaviours of those using the new technology. It is very encouraging that the Digital Strategy has been the product of wide-spread collaboration across the justice system; this suggests that there is a willingness to embrace change in all quarters, at least at the leadership level. It is vital that this willingness is spread further, and that is best done by making real – for all those involved – the benefits that innovation will bring.

Certainly it must be acknowledged that a wealth of information can be stored, transported, and accessed by the use of computers and electronic technology. Pen-drives and USB sticks are becoming more common in court: thus pleadings, submissions, notes of appeal, notes of argument, case reports, statutes, rules of court and productions can be contained in an item measuring about 4cm by 2cm, easily portable and easily inserted into a computer, giving access at any time and any place to all these materials. Text-books, rule-books, bench-books, codes of conduct and other guidance can be accessed by a DVD disc, or directly online. Search and cut-and-paste facilities available on computers are very helpful to court-users. General electronic functions such as email and texting are undeniably useful, for everyone, and are currently being used for court work including solicitors' firms enrolling ancillary motions in court cases. Thus the new technology, albeit not entirely welcomed by every generation of court-user, is currently being actively incorporated into the court system.

The "wide-spread collaboration across the justice system" referred to in Lady Dorrian's address is already taking place in the world of conveyancing. For example, in October 2002 the Keeper of the Registers of Scotland consulted four conveyancing professors[6] in a project which resulted in the digital "Automated Registration of Title to Land" (ARTL).[7]

6 Professors Stewart Brymer, George Gretton, Roderick Paisley and Robert Rennie (Professor Kenneth Reid was not involved because he was at that time a full-time commissioner with the Scottish Law Commission). See S Brymer, G Gretton, R Paisley and R Rennie, "Automated Registration of Title to Land" (2005) JR 201-50.

7 R Rennie and S Brymer, *Conveyancing in the Electronic Age* (2008); S Brymer and I Davis,

Dispositions may be electronic, as may missives (fax or email and possibly text). Electronic signatures are now permitted.[8] Since the coming into force of the Land Registration etc (Scotland) Act 2012, a title to land may never appear as a tangible deed: its provenance may be digital and it may remain digital throughout its life. For some lawyers, these developments may give rise to anxiety and nostalgia for the traditional working environment of documentary missives, parchment-like dispositions, storage in deed-boxes, title searches in the Register of Sasines, and face-to-face settlement meetings at solicitors' offices during which deeds and cheques physically changed hands. But the new world is here, and the combination of a paperless court system and electronic conveyancing may mean that any conveyancing expert wishing to assist the court should be IT-literate,[9] reasonably skilled in computers and electronic devices, familiar with current electronic conveyancing practices, and able to give evidence (supported by productions) by video-link. Thirty years ago, those skills and qualifications were not even contemplated, far less required of a conveyancing expert. Some experts might benefit from further training, and may find themselves experiencing a steep learning curve.

C. A Question-mark over Immunity from Suit

A further upset for conveyancing experts has arisen in the context of immunity from suit. For many years it has been a well-established principle that an expert witness taking part in court proceedings has civil immunity in relation to his evidence. As explained by the Court of Appeal in *Stanton v Callaghan*:[10]

> (i) an expert witness who gives evidence at a trial is immune from suit in respect of anything which he says in court, and that immunity will extend to the contents of the report which he adopts as, or incorporates in, his evidence; (ii) where an expert witness gives evidence at a trial, the immunity which he would enjoy in respect of that evidence is not to be circumvented by a suit based on the report itself; and (iii) the immunity does not extend to

---

"Automated Registration of Title to Land ('ARTL')" in R Rennie (ed), *The Promised Land: Property Law Reform* (2008) Ch 9; G L Gretton and K G C Reid, *Conveyancing*, 4th edn (2011) para 8.23-8.25.

8 Requirements of Writing (Scotland) Act 1995, ss9B(1) and (2), as introduced by the Land Registration etc. (Scotland) Act 2012, s97(2). For discussion, see R Rennie and S Brymer, "A Bold Step Forward" 2012 *JLSS* 32-33; R Rennie and S Brymer "E-missives: What Now?" 2014 *JLSS* 18-19.

9 J Irving, "Survival in the IT Age" 2000 *JLSS* 18-19.

10 [2000] QB 75 at 100.

> protect an expert who has been retained to advise as to the merits of a party's claim in litigation from a suit by the party by whom he has been retained in respect of that advice, notwithstanding that it was in contemplation at the time when the advice was given that the expert would be a witness at the trial if that litigation were to proceed.

That was the position in Scotland: the immunity enjoyed by expert witnesses was part of a greater immunity enjoyed by those involved in court cases.[11]

However the law has changed, certainly in England. The Supreme Court in *Jones v Kaney*,[12] by means of what might be seen as judicial legislation,[13] decided by a majority of three to two that an expert witness giving evidence in court should not be immune to an action for professional negligence.[14] Lord Hope and Lady Hale dissented. Lord Hope saw no principled basis for removing immunity from expert witnesses. He relied upon the Scottish case *Watson v McEwan*,[15] pointing out that *Watson* remained binding in Scotland, and that witness immunity in Scotland was a devolved matter. Thus the accepted view is that the decision in *Jones* is not binding in Scotland, where *Watson* remains binding until appropriate legislation is enacted by the devolved Parliament.[16] While some may agree with Lord Phillips, who led the majority in the Supreme Court, that experts will not be discouraged from giving opinions or evidence if immunity is removed,[17] many would disagree.[18] Accordingly the approach adopted by the majority of the

11 Stair, *Inst* 4.1.5.

12 [2011] UKSC 13; [2011] 2 AC 398.

13 R Rennie, S Brymer and D Reid, "The End of Immunity for Expert Witnesses?" 2012 Scottish Law Gazette 37-40.

14 Thus overruling *Stanton v Callaghan* (n 10).

15 [1905] AC 480.

16 Rennie et al (n 13).

17 R Jackson and J Powell, *Professional Liability* (7th ed) by J Powell and R Stewart (2011) para 2-110; Rennie et al, "The End of Immunity" (n 13), although the authors went on to identify a potential problem as follows: "If ... the evidence of the expert for the client [is] clearly rejected by the court, the likelihood is that the client will be found liable in expenses. One hopes that the removal of immunity (should it ever come to Scotland) would not then result in a subsequent claim against the expert on the losing side. If that were the case, would we all then be hunting for an elusive super expert able to say that no expert of ordinary competence could ever have given that particular opinion?"

18 Including the Earl of Halsbury LC in *Watson v McEwan* (n 15); Salmon J in *Marrinan v Vibart* [1963] 1 QB 234 at 237; Lord Wilberforce in *Roy v Prior* [1971] AC 470 at 480; Simon Brown LJ in *Silcott v Commissioner of Police of the Metropolis* (1996) 8 Admin LR 633 at 637; Lord Hoffmann in *Taylor v Director of the Serious Fraud Office* [1999] 2 AC 177 at 214; and Lord Hope in *Jones* (n 12) at para 165: "It is one thing to be liable to a wasted costs order at the instance of the court itself, or to proceedings by a professional body for professional misconduct. It is quite another to be at risk of worthless but possibly embarrassing and time-consuming proceedings by a disgruntled and disaffected litigant in person."

Supreme Court in *Jones v Kaney* must bring a frisson of apprehension to those in Scotland offering their services as expert witnesses, even although the effect of the decision has not hitherto come north of the border.

D. Case Management and the Conveyancing Expert

Following upon the success of the new rules of court for personal injuries actions,[19] there has been general recognition that a similar case management approach would be beneficial in other types of cases. As is noted in Lord Gill's Report of the Scottish Civil Courts Review:[20]

> We are satisfied that, with the exception of certain specified types of action, all actions in the Court of Session and the sheriff court should be subject to judicial case management. On the lodging of defences, a case should be allocated to the docket of a particular judge or sheriff. A case management hearing should be fixed shortly thereafter. This would normally take place by means of a telephone conference call. Parties would make submissions as to further procedure and any other matters arising, such as disclosure of documents. The judge or sheriff would identify the factual and legal issues in the case and decide what form of case management is most appropriate. In complex cases this may take the form of active judicial case management akin to the commercial model ... with further case management hearings as the case progresses. In straightforward cases the court might decide that a timetable and related orders akin to the case-flow procedure under Chapter 43 would be appropriate. In that event, no further case management hearings would be required. In certain cases a mixture of these techniques would be appropriate.

One outcome of increased case management might be the ordering of experts to hold discussions, exchange reports and/or prepare a minute of admissions or a joint statement.[21] Thus the modern conveyancing expert should be prepared to participate in such a meeting, treading the fine line between fulfilling his duty to the court while protecting his client's interests (a task made more difficult by being in a private consultation without the immediate supervision of the presiding judge.)[22] As Lord Hope commented in *Jones v Kaney*:[23]

---

19 Rules of the Court of Session 1994, Ch 43.

20 Report of the Scottish Civil Courts Review (n 1), Ch 5, para 48.

21 A L Stewart, "Evidence," in *The Laws of Scotland: Stair Memorial Encyclopaedia*, Reissue (2006) para 179; and see the procedure adopted in *Jones* (n 12).

22 For example, one expert might seek to exert pressure on the other: cf *Jones* (n 12).

23 *Jones* (n 12), para 156.

> [I]t is plain that the paid expert owes duties to the client by whom he is being paid. If he agrees for a reward to prepare a report and to present himself in court to give evidence, he is obliged to do those things and to take reasonable care when he is doing so. He must make the necessary investigations and preparations for the giving of that evidence. Nevertheless when it comes to the content of that evidence his overriding duty is to the court, not to the party for whom he appears. His duty is to give his own unbiased opinion on matters within his expertise. It is on that basis that he must be assumed to have agreed to act for his client. It would be contrary to the public interest for him to undertake to confine himself to making points that were in the client's interest only and to refrain from saying anything to the court to which his client might take objection.

E. The Conveyancing Expert and Alternatives to Court

Lord Gill's Report of the Scottish Civil Courts Review notes that:[24]

> ADR [alternative dispute resolution] in general provides a valuable way in which the burden on the civil courts can be lifted. More importantly, it provides an opportunity for dispute resolution in cases where the confrontational process of litigation is inappropriate. It is therefore a valuable complement to the work of the courts. [...]
>
> Mediation may, in some cases, offer advantages over litigation, particularly in cases where it is important to preserve relationships. [...]
>
> [Quoting, with approval, Dame Hazel Genn] "ADR cannot supplant the machinery of justice precisely because, in civil cases, the background threat of litigation is necessary to bring people to the negotiating table ... a well-functioning civil justice system should offer a choice of dispute resolution methods."

Conveyancing disputes concerning boundaries, real burdens, titles, servitudes, prescriptive possession and other similar problems, are classic examples of disputes which respond well to these flexible, less formal, dispute-resolution procedures. The opinion of a respected conveyancer will frequently resolve the issues, without the need to go to court. Meetings and joint consultations can assist in achieving a mutually acceptable outcome. By contrast, formal court proceedings can be protracted, wearing, and expensive, as Rennie has pointed out:[25]

> [E]ven if [clients] win, there will be expense involved on an extrajudicial basis... If matters go to court [it should be emphasised to clients] that civil litigation is for the very rich or very poor and that if they lose they will be

24 Report of the Scottish Civil Courts Review (n 1), ch 7, para 20-22.

25 R Rennie, "Boundary Ddisputes Rrevisited" 2013 *SLT (News)* 189-94, at 193.

liable not only for their own expenses both judicial and extrajudicial but for the other side's judicial expenses.

Thus a valuable ADR service is currently being provided by practising conveyancers, professors, and other members of academic staff.[26] The result is not only the satisfactory resolution of many disputes, but also a great saving of resources, both the courts' and the parties'. In this context, the conveyancing expert can be regarded as, in effect, assuming the mantle of "the court."

F. In a Changing Landscape, some Classic Principles Remain

It is some comfort that, amidst all the changes and upheavals, certain well-established principles continue to apply in relation to the role of the conveyancing expert in court.

(1) Assistance for the court

Once in court, the conveyancing expert is not the final arbiter. His role is to provide assistance to the judge.[27] As Lord Justice-Clerk Cooper emphasised in *Davie v Magistrates of Edinburgh*[28] (a case involving scientific evidence):[29]

> Expert witnesses, however skilled or eminent, can give no more than evidence. They cannot usurp the functions of the jury or judge sitting as

---

26 See, for example, D Cusine, *Conveyancing Opinions of JM Halliday* (1992); R Rennie, *Opinions on Professional Negligence in Conveyancing* (2004).

27 Even although instructed and paid by one party. See however the reservations expressed in F Davidson, *Evidence* (2007) para 11.27; and the views stated in I Macphail, *Evidence* (1987) at para 17.27: "It is sometimes maintained that the system whereby in adversary procedure each party adduces its own expert evidence is objectionable... In [certain] countries ... the court is permitted to select experts to inform it of their opinion based on their own particular knowledge and experience. Recently, in countries whose practice is based on an adversary rather than an inquisitorial system, the question whether the device of the court expert should be adopted has been widely discussed. It is not generally employed in Scotland, where conflicts of opinion between experts are adjudicated upon frequently and apparently without embarrassment by both judges and juries. (Footnote 90: A rare example, if not a unique case [of a court expert] is *Irvine v Powrie's Trs* 1915 SC 1006, where the professor of chemistry in Edinburgh University was appointed by the court for the limited purpose of supervising the parties' experts while they removed specimens of paper and ink from a registered deed which the pursuer sought to reduce on the ground of forgery.)"

28 1953 SC 34.

29 *Davie* (n 28) at 40.

> a jury, any more than a technical assessor can substitute his advice for the judgment of the court...Their duty is to furnish the judge or jury with the necessary...criteria for testing the accuracy of their conclusions, so as to enable the judge or jury to form their own independent judgment by the application of these criteria to the facts proved in evidence. The...opinion evidence, if intelligible, convincing and tested, becomes a factor (and often an important factor) for consideration along with the whole other evidence in the case, but the decision is for the judge or jury. In particular the bare *ipse dixit* of [an expert], however eminent, upon the issue in controversy, will normally carry little weight, for it cannot be tested by cross-examination nor independently appraised, and the parties have invoked the decision of a judicial tribunal and not an oracular pronouncement by an expert.

The court frequently has to choose between the evidence of two expert witnesses.[30] But the court is also entitled reject the evidence of both,[31] and further is not bound to accept the conclusions of one party's expert witness simply because no counter evidence was led by the other party.[32]

(2) Standing and experience

It is essential that the expert's qualifications and experience are established, to enable the court to be satisfied that the witness is truly skilled and experienced in the relevant area.[33] Davidson explains that:[34]

> It is for the court to be satisfied that a particular individual tendered as an expert does have sufficient relevant expertise to assist the court, and if this is not established, the evidence of that witness is not admissible, even if the opposing party raises no objection.[35]

---

30 See, for example, *Leeds & Holbeck Building Society v Alex Morison & Co (No 2)* 2001 SCLR 41. The party bearing the onus of proof may fail if a judge is unable to decide between conflicting expert accounts: *Pickford v Imperial Chemical Industries plc* [1998] 1 WLR 1189, Lord Hope at page 1200A-B.

31 *Assessor for Lothian Region v Wilson* 1979 SC 341; *Armour v Thyssen Edelstahlwerke AG* 1986 *SLT* 452, 1989 *SLT* 182 (IH); *Beaton v HM Advocate* 1993 JC 35 at pages 39H-40A.

32 *Davie* (n 28).

33 In the Law Society of Scotland Code of Practice for expert witnesses, available at http://www.expertwitnessscotland.info/codepract.htm, potential expert witnesses are warned *inter alia* that: "2. Instructions should be accepted only in matters where the expert (a) has the knowledge, experience, expertise, qualifications, or professional training appropriate for the assignment." Note however that professional qualifications are not always essential: Davidson, *Evidence* para 11.12.

34 *Evidence* at para 11.13.

35 For recent examples of expert evidence tendered but ruled inadmissible, see *Kennedy v Cordia (Services) LLP* [2014] CSIH 76 (evidence from a health and safety expert ruled inadmissible in a slipping on ice case); *Snowden and Jennings v HM Advocate* [2014]

In some jurisdictions, for example England[36] and the USA,[37] there is procedure whereby the judge operates as a "gatekeeper" in that, during some procedure or hearing prior to the proof or trial, he determines *inter alia* whether or not a person who is to be invited to give evidence as an expert has the necessary expertise and qualifications and what areas of evidence may be addressed. That procedure has not yet reached Scotland. In Scottish courts, the exercise of "setting up" an expert is normally carried out during the proof (or trial), by the lodging of the witness's *curriculum vitae*, and the leading of evidence from the witness about his qualifications, experience, publications and particular expertise. A recent judicial consideration of this practice can be found in *Hainey v HM Advocate*[38] where Lord Clarke observed:[39]

> While the trial judge does not act as a gatekeeper ... he has a continuing role as referee, or umpire, throughout the trial to ensure that it is conducted fairly and that evidence from a person claiming specialist knowledge and expertise, who clearly does not have such expertise and knowledge, is disregarded by the jury.[...]
>
> It is to be noted that in England and Wales, the rules of procedure require that where there is to be medical evidence led and relied upon it should be considered at a pre-trial hearing. 'The pre-trial process is of particular importance. Without robust pre-trial management, the real medical issues cannot be identified and, absent such identification, a judge is unlikely to be able to prevent experts wandering into unnecessary, complicated and confusing details; accordingly, a judge who is to hear a case of this type should deal with all pre-trial hearings, save for those in which no issue of substance arise. By the time a trial starts, the essential medical issues which the jury have to resolve, and the expert evidence, identifying the source on which the evidence is based, should all be clear' (see Archbold, *Criminal Pleading, Evidence and Practice 2012*, at 1380).
>
> It may be that the time has come for some thought to be given to providing for such an approach in Scotland in such cases.

While a proof before a single judge concerning a conveyancing matter presents a rather different context from a trial before a jury involving complex medical and forensic evidence, these *dicta* emphasise the

---

HCJAC 100 at paras 18, 44 and 67 (evidence from a senior lecturer in psychology ruled inadmissible in the context of identification).

36 Civil Procedure Rules 1998, r35 (see Davidson, *Evidence* para 11.31).

37 See, for example, the leading case of *Daubert v Merrell Dow Pharmaceuticals Inc* (1993) 509 US 579, discussed in Davidson, *Evidence* para 11.15-11.17.

38 2014 JC 33.

39 *Hainey* (n 38) para 49 and 52.

importance of appropriate qualifications and/or experience, and the limiting of the evidence to the relevant area of expertise.[40]

(3) Presence in court

A conveyancing expert (or indeed any expert) should not be present in court during another expert's evidence. If it is thought that an expert would benefit from hearing certain witnesses to fact, a motion should be made seeking the judge's permission for the expert to sit in court during that evidence. If it is found that an expert has *per incuriam* been present in court without permission listening to evidence given by others, that may seriously undermine his own evidence.[41]

(4) Duties

Key guidelines for any professional appearing in court to give evidence as an expert witness have been usefully summarised by Cresswell J in *National Justice Compania Naviera SA v Prudential Assurance Co Ltd (The Ikarian Reefer) (No1)*[42] as follows (omitting case references):

> The duties and responsibilities of expert witnesses in civil cases include the following:
>
> (i) Expert evidence presented to the court should be, and should be seen to be, the independent product of the expert uninfluenced as to form or content by the exigencies of litigation. […]
>
> (ii) An expert witness should provide independent assistance to the court by way of objective unbiased opinion in relation to matters within his expertise.... An expert witness in the High Court should never assume the role of an advocate.
>
> (iii) An expert witness should state the facts or assumption upon which his opinion is based. He should not omit to consider material facts which could detract from his concluded opinion. […]

---

40 There may be finely-balance decisions in this context: see, for example, *McTear v Imperial Tobacco Ltd* 2005 2 SC 1, para 5.15-5.18; *Main v McAndrew Wormald Ltd* 1988 *SLT* 141 (medical witnesses held entitled to refer to published papers by epidemiologists, although not themselves epidemiologists).

41 Although there are differing views on this matter: see, for example, Davidson, *Evidence*, para 11.26; A L Stewart, "Evidence," in *The Laws of Scotland: Stair Memorial Encyclopaedia*, Reissue (2006) para 174.

42 [1993] 2 Lloyd's Rep 68 at 81.

(iv) An expert witness should make it clear when a particular question or issue falls outside his expertise.

(v) If an expert's opinion is not properly researched because he considers that insufficient data is available, then this must be stated with an indication that the opinion is no more than a provisional one.... In cases where an expert witness who has prepared a report could not assert that the report contained the truth, the whole truth and nothing but the truth without some qualification, that qualification should be stated in the report.

(vi) If, after exchange of reports, an expert witness changes his view on a material matter having read the other side's expert's report or for any other reason, such change of view should be communicated (through legal representatives) to the other side without delay, and when appropriate to the court.

(vii) Where expert evidence refers to photographs, plans, calculations, analyses, measurements, survey reports, or other similar documents, these must be provided to the opposite party at the same time as the exchange of reports.

These principles are to a large extent echoed in the Law Society's Code of Practice for expert witnesses,[43] which provides *inter alia*:

Independence

11. Experts will bear in mind that:

    (i) When giving evidence at court, the role of ... an expert witness, is to assist the court and remain independent of the parties.

12. Experts will disclose to [instructing] solicitors at the start of each project any personal or financial or other significant circumstances which might influence work for the client in any way not stated or implied in the instructions, in particular:

    (i) Any directorship or controlling interest in any business in competition with the client;

    (ii) Any financial or other interest in goods or services (including software) under dispute;

    (iii) Any personal relationship and/or professional relationship, and the nature thereof, with any individual involved in the matter;

43 Code of Practice (n 33).

(iv) The existence but not the name of any other client of the expert with competing interests;

(v) Whether the expert has worked with the expert instructed by the opposing party (if known).

13. Any actual or potential conflict of interest must be reported to the solicitor as soon as it is raised or becomes apparent and the assignment must be terminated.

Despite the existence of such guidelines, difficulties can arise. A recent action for damages for alleged professional negligence[44] illustrates a failure fully to comply with principles 12(c) and 13 of the Code of Practice. In that case, property consultants and architects/planners gave evidence in court concerning the loss which the pursuers alleged they had suffered. Lord Woolman felt obliged to make the following observations:[45]

> During cross-examination, Mr A [of Keppies, Glasgow, Architects and Planners] disclosed that although there is no formal association, his firm has had links with the defenders since 2004. The name "Keppie" appears on the main door of the defenders' offices. Keppie has used rooms within to hold meetings. The defenders' website states that Keppie is able to offer planning services.
>
> Individuals must think carefully before accepting instructions to act as an expert witness. The court expects them to be scrupulously impartial. In this instance, Mr A's links with the defenders should have been notified at a much earlier stage.

Another illustration of a problem (in effect a breach of the third proposition of *The Ikarian Reefer*) was referred to in *McTear v Imperial Tobacco Ltd*[46] at para 5.10. An expert witness in a criminal trial[47] had made an assumption which was neither justified nor disclosed to the court. Lord Justice General Emslie stated that, as a result, the witness had been discredited. He observed:[48]

> This was, in our judgment, conduct on the part of an expert witness which demonstrated a complete misunderstanding of the role of scientific

44 *Hawthorne v Anderson* [2014] CSOH 65; and see too *Liverpool Catholic Archdiocese Trs v Goldberg (No 3)* [2001] 1 WLR 2337 at page 2340, where the court refused to admit the evidence of an undoubted expert who was also a long-standing friend of the defendant

45 *Hawthorne* (n 44) at para 84 and 85.

46 *McTear* (n 40).

47 *Pierce v HM Advocate* 1981 SCLR 783.

48 *Pierce* (n 47), quoted with approval by Lord Caplan in *Elf Caledonia Ltd v London Bridge Engineering Ltd*, 2 September 1997, unreported at 225, referred to by Lord Nimmo Smith in *McTear* (n 40) at 139.

witnesses in the courts, and a lack of the essential qualities of accuracy and scientific objectivity which are normally to be taken for granted.

G. Conclusion

In conclusion, much is expected of both the court and the conveyancing expert in the twenty-first century. Neither can afford to rely solely upon traditional or well-established practices or technology. Each must acquire new competences which were not even envisaged in the latter part of the twentieth century, yet each must retain and abide by the well-tried principles and practices expected of both court and expert when an expert witness gives evidence. The result is a challenging but fascinating and ever-developing area of the law.

9

Islamic Mortgages

Professor George Gretton

A. Theory, Practice and Fun

In most countries property law is, or at least is seen as being, dry and dull. And in most countries links between property law theorists and property law practitioners are weak. Not so here. Far from being dry and dull, property law in Scotland is, and is seen as being, exciting, fun and often – in a good sense – funny (thanks, Robert) funny. Strong links exist between theory and practice (thanks again, Robert). This paper has no laughs, but has something in it of practice and theory.

B. Introduction

I hesitate to write on Islamic mortgages for a good reason: I am unqualified to do so. To be qualified one would need to unite three qualities: knowledge of property law, knowledge of Shari'a[1] law, and knowledge of what is happening in practice. I have some of the first, but little of the second or third. So why this paper?

The main answer is that – as far as I can see – there is hardly anything published on the subject. There is a large literature on Islamic finance, all of which mentions the Islamic mortgage, but none of which seems to get

1 Variously transcribed into the Latin alphabet. Other forms are "Sharia," "Shari'ah," "Sharia'a" and "Shariah," where English is the destination language, and yet other forms for other destination languages, such as French *Charia* or *Chari'a*, or German *Scharia* or *Schari'a*.

down to brass tacks – at least as far as the legal systems of the UK are concerned. The two standard English texts on mortgage law pass over the subject in complete silence.[2] The Scottish monographs are silent. If there is a periodical literature I have not found it, though there is one exception, and, to boot, a Scottish exception: Graham Burnside has written on the subject.[3] I find this paucity of discussion odd. Someone needs to do something. Islamic mortgages are not common in Scotland (less common, I think, than in England) but they are not unknown.

A subsidiary reason is that the internet is full of nonsense on the subject. Of course, the internet is full of nonsense on *every* subject, but with most subjects one can, with a bit of effort, navigate to reliable sources. Not so, as far as I can see, with Islamic mortgages in the UK context. Even seemingly respectable sites have dubious material. Here for instance is *The Guardian* on 29 June 2008:[4]

> Imagine a mortgage lender who allows you to take all the increase in the price of your home when you sell, but is prepared to share any loss if the property has fallen in value. Such a deal may seem too good to be true in the current property market, but it is exactly what a handful of banks specialising in Islamic home loans are offering.

Is that really true? I don't want to target *The Guardian*, and quote it here precisely because it is usually a respectable source, but here it goes again, on 29 October 2013, under the intriguing heading "Facts are sacred":[5]

> Islamic finance is all about sharing risk between financial institutions and the individuals that use them. To do that, the two parties are tied into a longer-term relationship with each other that is supposed to shift incentives and avoid cut and run financial deals. So, for example, sharia-compliant mortgages mean that the bank and the borrower share the risks of repayment rather than charging any form of interest.

Hmmm.

2 W Clark (ed), *Fisher and Lightwood's Law of Mortgage*, 13th edn (2011) (at the time of writing, a 14th edition is in the offing, but is not yet available to me); I Clarke (ed), *Cousins on the Law of Mortgages*, 3rd edn (2010).

3 "Unveiling the Islamic Mortgage" 2005 *JLSS* Dec/58; "Islamic Finance: A Scottish Lead?" 2009 *JLSS* Aug/56.

4 H Qureshi, "Sharia-compliant mortgages are here – and they're not just for Muslims," available at http://www.theguardian.com/money/2008/jun/29/mortgages.islam

5 M Chalabi, "Islamic finance for beginners," available at http://www.theguardian.com/news/datablog/2013/oct/29/islamic-finance-for-beginners. "Facts are sacred" is a heading used in the Guardian's "datablog," in reference to C P Snow's aphorism "comment is free, but facts are sacred."

So: despite my lack of qualifications for the subject, and conscious of the inadequacies of what follows, I offer some thoughts on the Islamic mortgage, mainly with reference to Scots law. Lastly by way of throat-clearing, the subject is larger than could be covered in a short paper such as the present. Indeed, it would be a good subject for a PhD. But half a loaf is better than no bread.

C. Prohibition of Interest

Judaism forbade interest, and that prohibition was received into its two daughter religions, Christianity and Islam.[6] In Christian countries the prohibition was generally accepted not only as a religious rule but also as a matter of positive law. Eventually, however, the legal ban was abandoned everywhere, though at different times in different countries.[7] In Scotland the ban ended with the Reformation (1560).[8] Turning to Islamic countries, in some (for example, Turkey) the law now permits interest: in those countries that accept Shari'a law as part of positive law, interest is legally impermissible. Pious Muslims, and Muslim organisations, seek to avoid interest, whether as debtors or as creditors.[9] Some non-Islamic financial institutions also offer what they claim to be Shari'a-compliant financial products. Such products will usually have been given the approval of a Shari'a compliance board composed of experts in Islamic theology.

The question is not whether interest should be limited to reasonable levels.[10] In Shari'a, all interest, reasonable or unreasonable, is forbidden. What is forbidden is not the lending of money, but interest: loans are

6 There are also roots in Greek philosophy, especially Aristotle.

7 For an illuminating history of the European position from Roman to modern times see R Zimmermann, *The Law of Obligations* (1996) 166-77.

8 I know of no legislation lifting the ban. What happened at the Reformation was that a number of canon law rules, which had been accepted as part of the common law, were simply abandoned, other examples being the celibacy of the clergy and the prohibition of divorce. The first statute on the law of interest that I know of was the Act 1587 c 52 (APS iii 451 c 35) providing that the maximum lawful rate of interest was to be 10%. The Act expressly said that its provisions were not applicable to transactions entered into before its date. Thus between 1560 and 1587 interest was permitted and there was no maximum lawful rate. As far as I know the history of the subject (in Scotland) has never been fully studied.

9 Though in practice many Muslims do in fact borrow and lend at interest.

10 Legal limits on interest rates have been and remain common. For instance in the Roman Empire the maximum permitted rate was 12%. For a study of the current situation, see U Reifner, S Clerc-Renaud, and R A M Knobloch, Study on Interest Rate Restrictions in the EU: Final Report (2010), available at http://ec.europa.eu/internal_market/finservices-retail/docs/credit/irr_report_en.pdf

permissible so long as they are at zero interest. Nor is there any objection, in the Islamic tradition, to security for a loan. For example, there would be no objection to X lending Y money, secured by standard security – so long as the loan is interest-free. And there's the rub: whilst loans between friends and relatives are commonly interest-free, in the world of commerce no one will lend without a return. Indeed, to lend without a return is to transfer net value from lender to borrower: it is like a donation. Achieving a return without using interest is the challenge for Islamic finance, and various workarounds have been developed. (As they were in medieval Europe.[11]) How Muslims and Muslim organisations deal with the fact that interest often runs on debts *by force of law*,[12] I do not know, but that is another story.

(1) Other rules

Islamic theology imposes other restrictions, too, such as the prohibition of contracts involving uncertainty or speculation. Thus conventional insurance is forbidden, though as with interest there exist workarounds, which achieve by the back door what cannot be achieved through the front door. Another theological principle is that one transaction cannot be made conditional on another.[13] I do not understand, and so cannot explain this principle, but its influence is evident.

D. Circumventing the Prohibition

A workaround involves structuring the transaction as something other than a contract of loan. Some other type of contract has to be identified, to bring about the actual results of a loan contract. The three main workarounds[14] are to structure the transaction as (i) a contract of lease, this being called *ijara*, or (ii) a contract of sale, this being called *murabaha*, or (iii) a contract

11 The parallels are striking. In medieval Europe the ban on interest was circumvented easily, just as it is in the Islamic tradition.

12 There is a body of law (some of it common law and some of it statutory) whereby interest can run where a debt is not paid when due, including (but not limited to) such matters as judicial interest, interest on overdue tax, and the Late Payment of Commercial Debts (Interest) Act 1998.

13 Whether this is a separate principle, or an aspect of the previous principle, I do not know.

14 One comes across references to other Arabic terms, but it may be (I do not know) that all such other terms boil down to one of the three mentioned in the text.

partnership, this being called *musharaka*.[15] Before looking at these, a few words on terminology.

(1) Terminology: "mortgage," "debtor," "lender"

Although the terms "Islamic mortgage" and, less commonly, "Halal mortgage" are in standard use, lenders offering these products tend to prefer the term "home purchase plan," no doubt because the term "mortgage" suggests the existence of a contract of loan. (Still, the term "home purchase plan" does not work well, because it suggests that the finance is available only for house purchase. In fact it is also available where a person already owns property and wishes to raise money on the back of it.) For the same reason, the terms "debtor/borrower" and "creditor/lender" tend to be avoided. This is easily achieved, by using such terms as "the customer," "the bank" etc. In this paper, however, this terminology is not adopted.[16]

(2) Workaround (i): *ijara*

In the first type of workaround, *ijara*, the lender acquires the property and leases it to the borrower for the mortgage term, such as 25 years. The contract confers on the borrower a right to acquire ownership at the end of the term. In short, the arrangement is one that, for moveables, would be called hire-purchase, though this analogy seems never to be remarked upon.[17] Whether this method has been used to any extent in Scotland I do not know, but it is common in England. The entry in HM Land Registry shows the lender as owner, and shows the borrower as holding a registered lease.[18] The lease is usually charged to the lender by the borrower, but one may wonder how much this really adds to the lender's security, given that the lender has in any event the fee simple, coupled with all the rights of a landlord if a tenant is failing to pay the rent.

The "rent" covers both the interest and the capital payments. The rent does not relate to the value of the property, as would be the case in a genuine

15 These three terms are variously transliterated.

16 And for convenience in this context I use the term "mortgage" even though it is not the right term for Scots law. I beg forgiveness.

17 Hire purchase is itself a workaround, arising from a different cause, namely the inadequacy of chattel mortgage law in England, and its complete absence in Scotland.

18 Except in the unusual case of a very short-term mortgage, where the lease term will be too short to be registrable.

lease. For instance, a buyer who puts down a 50% deposit on the property would be paying less rent than a buyer of an identical property who puts down only a 30% deposit. The rent is reviewed periodically, but not in line with the changing value of the property, as would happen with a genuine rent, but in line with changing market interest rates. Typically the "rent" is linked either to LIBOR[19] or to Bank of England lending rate. The aim is to achieve, as closely as possible, the effects of a conventional mortgage.

(3) Workaround (ii): *murabaha*

In the second type of workaround, *murabaha*,[20] the lender buys the property and then immediately resells it to the borrower at a higher price, the price to be paid in instalments over a period of years. (15 years seems to be a common period for this kind of mortgage.) For instance, the property is bought by the lender for £200,000, and immediately resold to the borrower for £300,000.[21] (The difference depends partly on the length of the mortgage term and partly on market interest rates at the time of the transaction.) This latter price is paid in instalments. At the end of the mortgage term, the lender conveys title to the borrower. The "price" is in reality, though not in name, a mix of two elements: capital repayments and interest. One drawback to this scheme is that the interest rate is non-variable, for the re-sale price is fixed at the outset.

I have said that there is first a transfer by the original seller to the lender, and a later transfer by the lender to the borrower. But one could imagine a modified structure, whereby there are at the outset two transfers, one by the original seller to the lender, followed (perhaps the next day) by the transfer by the lender to the borrower, coupled with a mortgage back to the lender by the borrower. But whether this happens at all in practice I do not know. Finally, while this type of mortgage is used in England, I am not aware that there has been any use of it in Scotland.

---

19 London Interbank Offered Rate.

20 Also transliterated as *murabahah*.

21 This paper is about private law, not public law, but it may be noted that double tax is not payable: Land and Buildings Transaction Tax (Scotland) Act 2013 sch 7. These provisions reproduce ss 71A-73AB of the Finance Act 2003, the latter remaining in force south of the border. The exemptions apply not only to *murabaha* mortgages but to any Islamic mortgage involving double transfer.

(4) Workaround (iii): *musharaka*

The third type of workaround is the *musharaka*,[22] and this is of particular importance because my impression is that it is the main form in use in Scotland.[23] The word means "partnership," and the broad idea is that borrower and lender own the property as partners. It is, however, not a partnership in any sense of that term known to Scots (or English) law. Thus it is not a partnership at common law, or under the Partnership Act 1890, the Limited Partnerships Act 1907, or the Limited Liability Partnerships Act 2000. In what sense it could be described as a partnership in any sense of that word is not easy to see. Nevertheless this arrangement is marketed as being a partnership.

The only form that seems to be used in the UK is the "diminishing *musharaka*," in which borrower and lender in some sense (see below) co-own the property, and the borrower buys the lender's shares over a period of time, eventually ending up with 100%. In the meantime the borrower pays the lender interest on the diminishing balance, this interest taking the nominal form of rent. As in a conventional "repayment mortgage," the borrower's periodical payments to the lender include both capital and interest, the latter being named rent. As with the *ijara* mortgage, the rent is kept under regular review, and is linked to LIBOR or to Bank of England rate. The diminishing *musharaka* mortgage seems to be the main form of Islamic mortgage in use in Scotland.

Transferring a slice of ownership from lender to borrower every month or quarter or year would be awkward and expensive, and whilst numerous websites say that that is what happens, I am sceptical. The diminishing *musharaka* is the only type of Islamic mortgage where I have been able to study the documentation in detail. I am very much obliged to the Islamic Bank of Britain plc, which seems to have the main share of this area of finance in Scotland, for providing me with that documentation. What happens (at least under the IBB's Scottish documentation) is that the property is held by the debtor as trustee, and the borrower and lender have beneficial interests under the trust. As the borrower gradually repays

22 Also transliterated as *musharakah*.

23 I am most grateful to the Islamic Bank of Britain plc for providing me with its full style documentation for Islamic mortgages in Scotland.

the lender, the beneficial shares change, until eventually the borrower has a 100% share of the beneficial interest. As in the other types of Islamic mortgage, the regular payments are in substance payments of capital plus interest. The interest is called an "occupancy payment." There is a standard security over the property in favour of the bank. Though this is granted by the debtor as trustee (for title is held as trustee) it secures the obligations owed by the debtor as an individual. Thus in property law terms, this has the same structure as a conventional standard security: ownership held by the borrower, and a subordinate real right of security is held by the lender. Once the borrower has acquired 100% of the beneficial interest, the bank discharges the standard security. Of the three types, the diminishing *musharaka* comes the nearest to being the same as a conventional mortgage in everything but name.

In England, by contrast, it seems that title is usually vested in the lender, with the lender then granting a lease to the borrower in respect of the lender's beneficial share of the property. The difference between this and *ijara* is perhaps not clear to those not expert in Islamic theology.

E. Shared Risk?

It is commonly said that in Islamic finance there must be risk-sharing. This statement as such is not very informative, since in all finance there is risk-sharing: in a conventional loan, the borrower runs the risk of not being able to pay, with unfortunate consequences, and the lender runs the risk of not being paid, also with unfortunate consequences. "Sharia-compliant mortgages mean that the bank and the borrower share the risks of repayment rather than charging any form of interest."[24] As far as I can see that is not true. If the borrower defaults, the bank sells the property and takes what is due. If there is a shortfall, the borrower remains liable. I cannot be sure that this is universally the position: that would require more research than I have been able to undertake. But it may be noted that the more a financial deal protects the borrower, the more expensive it is going to be.

It seems that in an Islamic mortgage the lender and borrower are supposed to share the burden of maintenance, presumably on the basis of risk-sharing. But again this can be circumvented. For instance in the

24 See above.

IBB documentation, the borrower is bound to maintain the property, and the bank the binds itself to pay the borrower the "service change amount" (defined as "the expenses incurred by you in providing the services" – that is, maintaining the property). But at the same time any such amount is automatically met by a "supplemental occupancy payment" due by the borrower to the bank, which is of precisely the same amount.[25] There is also an obligation on the borrower to insure the property. (How that fits in with the prohibition of insurance in Shari'a law I do not know.)

F. The 20-Year Issue

The Land Reform (Scotland) Act 1974 provided that residential leases could not be for longer than 20 years.[26] That is a problem if an Islamic mortgage involves a lease, as in the *ijara*, and the term of the loan is over 20 years. How significant the problem is depends to some extent on how one interprets the rather complex provisions of the 1974 Act. It seems that the rule has in fact been a reason why there has (as it seems) been little attempt to use *ijara* mortgages in Scotland, though it should be noted that the rule in the 1974 Act does not affect non-residential property. In the IBB documentation for "diminishing *musharaka*" the interest is labelled not "rent" but an "occupancy payment" and one imagines that the 1974 Act is the reason for that terminology. Whether such words make any difference is perhaps open to debate: for instance in an English case in 1985 the House of Lords held that language designed to prevent an agreement being characterised as a lease will fail in its purpose if the agreement is in reality a lease.[27] There is an irony here: in the 1985 case an arrangement that was in reality a lease was being dressed up in the documentation as not being a lease: in (some types of) Islamic mortgages what is in reality not a lease is being dressed up in the documentation as being a lease. Although one might speculate as to what would happen if a court were to say that "occupancy payment" means rent, with the result that the 1974 Act is engaged, that is surely unlikely since (unlike the 1985 case) the underlying intention of the parties is not a tenancy anyway.

---

25 This is, at least, how I understand the documentation. The documentation is sometimes unclear to me, but the same is true of the documentation for conventional secured loans.

26 Sections 8-10. Some exceptions were introduced by the Housing (Scotland) Act 2010 s 138 but the basic rule remains. It may be added that the 1974 Act did not apply to pre-existing leases.

27 *Street v Mountford* [1985] AC 809.

The period of 20 years crops up quite often in property law, and one such instance is the rule that a standard security is redeemable after 20 years regardless of the terms of the agreement.[28] It is occasionally suggested that this rule might have negative consequences for Islamic mortgages, but in fact the rule has no greater significance for Islamic mortgages than it does for conventional mortgages,[29] and accordingly nothing more will be said here.

G. The "Lease between Co-owners" Issue

If property is co-owned, it cannot be leased to one of the co-owners.[30] Whilst this is a background issue worth noting, its importance for Islamic mortgages is probably limited. In the first place, in Islamic mortgages it does not seem that the property is in fact co-owned between borrower and lender (despite what one reads on the internet): as far as I can see title is always held (in Scotland at least) either by the borrower (solely) or by the lender (solely). In the second place, the rule does not prevent an arrangement whereby one co-owner has exclusive occupation, paying the others a periodical sum in return. That is perfectly possible: the rule merely says that such an arrangement is not a lease. Finally, it is perhaps open to debate how the rule would work out if something called a "lease" were to be entered into between those holding the *beneficial interest* under a trust. But as has been said, that seems to be rare or unknown in Scottish Islamic mortgages.

H. The "Only by Standard Security" Issue

In the years before 1970, the usual way of securing a loan over heritable property was the "*ex facie* absolute disposition." Here title was vested in the lender, and the debtor's right was a contractual: to occupy the property, and, after paying off the loan, with interest, to have the property conveyed to him/her. In the language of Roman law, this was *fiducia cum creditore.*

28 Land Tenure Reform (Scotland) Act 1974 s 11. The Housing (Scotland) Act 2014 s 93 confers power on the Scottish Ministers to alter this period.

29 That is also the view of the Scottish Government. See Scottish Government, Consultation on Proposals to Exempt Certain Heritable Securities from the "20 Year Security Rule" (2014), available at http://www.scotland.gov.uk/Resource/0046/00461603.pdf

30 *Clydesdale Bank v Davidson* 1998 SC (HL) 51.

The arrangement could happen in either of two ways. In the first place, Donald Debtor might own the property and then convey it to a lender. In the second place, and this was commoner in practice, it was used as acquisition finance: Donald Debtor wanted to buy a house, and would conclude missives, but would direct the seller to convey, not to him, but to his lender.

There was thus a gap between substantive reality (debtor = in reality owner, bank = in reality merely secured lender) and legal reality (bank = owner, debtor = contractual occupier). This came to be seen as undesirable. The Conveyancing and Feudal Reform (Scotland) Act 1970 did two things.[31] First, it created a new form of heritable security, the standard security. Secondly, it banned the *ex facie* absolute disposition. The reform took root. Standard securities remain with us to this day, and *ex facie* absolute dispositions are now just a memory for the old and not even a memory for the young. As a result, few today remember the prohibition. The prohibition is phrased briefly:[32]

> A grant of any right over land or a real right in land for the purpose of securing any debt by way of a heritable security shall only be capable of being effected at law[33] if it is embodied in a standard security. Where for the purpose last-mentioned any deed which is not in the form of a standard security contains a disposition or assignation of land or of a real right in land, it shall to that extent be void and unenforceable...

This prohibition seems to strike at some types of Islamic mortgage, where heritable property is granted in security of a debt, otherwise than by standard security. An argument could be set up that the statutory prohibition affects only grants by debtor to creditor, and that grants by a third party to the creditor are unaffected, which would be the state of affairs, for the *ijara* and the *murabaha*, in acquisition finance, i.e. where Donald Debtor is seeking to buy property and asks the seller to convey to the bank. This is not the place

31 To speak of just "two things" is of course to oversimplify.

32 Conveyancing and Feudal Reform (Scotland) Act 1970 s 9(3) and part of (4). It is quoted here in its amended form. The contrast between the brevity of this prohibition and the prolixity of the 1974 prohibition of long leases over residential property is striking.

33 Though not pertinent to this paper, I cannot resist mentioning that these two words ("at law") have always puzzled me. Presumably they were included for *some* purpose. At law – as opposed to what? Equity? This is not entirely a joke. Note that the passage says "at law" not "in law." English equity lawyers use the contrasting terms "*at* law" and "*in* equity."

to discuss that argument;[34] I will only mention that in 1970 it was taken for granted that the statutory prohibition applied to both types of case, with the result that the *ex facie* absolute disposition wholly disappeared.

The issue is most serious for the *ijara*: this seems to be exactly the sort of thing that the section 9 prohibition was aimed at. As for the *murabaha*, the argument is a good deal weaker, because although the property is conveyed to the creditor, it is then immediately conveyed to the debtor. What about the diminishing *musharaka*? If the typical English form were adopted, whereby title is vested in the bank, the section 9 prohibition would seem to apply, but, as mentioned, this form does not seem common in Scotland. Might the section 9 prohibition apply to the form described above, used in Scotland? The property itself is not granted to the bank in security of a debt, so probably the section 9 prohibition is not engaged. However, the wording of the section 9 prohibition is broad, and could be read as covering even the grant, by way of security, of even a beneficial share of property.

It might be said that the section 9 prohibition is irrelevant to Islamic finance, because the section 9 prohibition is about security for loan finance, and Islamic mortgages do not use the contract of loan. That argument does not work. Section 9 is not tied to loans but to "debt,"[35] and all Islamic mortgages use debt.

Finally on this subject, the section 9 prohibition is not some quirky fossil rule. There is a strong argument of public policy in its favour: that for the owner of heritable property to be the party that is in reality merely a lender, is an unacceptable subterfuge: the transaction should show its face.

I. The Consumer Protection Issue

Consumer protection is one of the themes of modern law. Consumers are protected[36] in credit transactions, in tenancy agreements, in standard securities and in many other areas. In a conventional mortgage, consumers are protected in a number of ways, including the provisions of the Conveyancing and Feudal Reform (Scotland) 1970, as amended over

34 Discussion of section 9 would take a paper to itself. It is curious that, as far as I know, it has never been subject to any published examination in detail. Furthermore, the report that led to section 9 said rather little about it. (Report on Conveyancing Legislation and Practice (Cmnd 3118: 1966), chaired by Robert's great predecessor, Jack Halliday.)

35 Defined in the broadest way: s 9(8)(c).

36 The quality of the protection is of course open to debate, but that cannot be discussed here.

the years. Are Islamic mortgages subject to the same level of consumer protection as conventional mortgages? In the case where title is vested in the debtor, and the creditor's enforcement rights are based on a standard security, the answer would seem to be affirmative. But in those structures where title is held by the lender,[37] consumer protection is weakened. The modern law on protecting mortgage debtors is based on the assumption that what is involved is a standard security.[38] If there is no standard security, and title is held by the bank, the consumer protection provisions are not engaged. If the structure is that of an *ijara* mortgage, the creditor has title and the debtor has a lease; that may engage the consumer protection provisions of lease law, but the protections are not the same. In *murabaha* it is not apparent to me that there would be any protection at all, apart from generic consumer credit protection.

J. Second Mortgages

Property can be encumbered by more than one standard security. Indeed, there is in theory no limit to the number that can be granted, though I do not recall ever having seen more than four. Subject to one or two qualifications, they rank by order of creation of the real right, which is to say by date of registration. There is no conceptual difficulty about multiple standard securities, for the groundwork lies in the theory of property law that we have inherited from the civilian tradition: the grant of a subordinate real right leaves ownership where it was. One of the drawbacks of the old *ex facie* absolute disposition was that second mortgages were problematic. A workaround was created whereby the debtor's personal right to a future conveyance (after paying off the loan) was assigned by way of security.

The same problems, and indeed perhaps even more intractable, would arise for Islamic mortgages where title is held by the lender. Whether some workaround would be possible, I do not know. If it is not possible, that is a negative. If it is possible, it would inevitably be artificial and cumbersome, as was the case with the old *ex facie* absolute disposition.[39] Even where

37 Structures that may fall foul of the section 9 prohibition (see above).

38 Much the same is true I think in English law.

39 Given the problems with the old *ex facie* absolute disposition, it may be wondered why it was in such common use until 1970. The short answer is that although there were alternatives, whereby the creditor had a subordinate real right and the substantive owner was also the legal owner (as in a standard security), these alternatives had significant technical disadvantages.

title is not held by the lender, there would be problems. Thus in the IBB diminishing *musharaka* the registered owner is the debtor but *qua* trustee, the beneficial interest being divided between debtor and lender. How one could pin a second mortgage on to that I am is unclear to me.

K. Insolvency Risk

In a conventional mortgage, the possible future insolvency of the creditor is not a risk for the debtor. If Donald Debtor borrows £100,000 from the Bank of Unst, Fetlar and Yell,[40] secured by standard security, and in the next financial crisis the bank becomes insolvent, and, like Lehman Brothers, is allowed to collapse, Donald Debtor is not sucked into that collapse, because he owns his property. That is one of the benefits of the system of subordinate real rights. But if property is owned by Bank of Unst, Fetlar and Yell, Donald has a problem.[41] The subject is complex, involving, among other things, the question of whether Donald can successfully argue that the bank owns the property as implied, or as constructive, trustee. That issue would require a whole paper to itself. I merely note it here as another example of the problems that may arise from adopting an artificial structure.

L. Impediments?

Holyrood:

> S2W-16368 – Brian Adam (Aberdeen North) (SNP) (Date Lodged Tuesday, May 10, 2005):
>
> To ask the Scottish Executive whether any impediments exist in Scots law to the provision of Islamic mortgages and, if so, what action it will take to remove these.
>
> Answered by Hugh Henry (Thursday, May 19, 2005):
>
> The Scottish Executive is not aware of any impediment in Scots law which prevents the provision of Islamic mortgages.

---

40 Actually too good a name to waste of a mere bank, I'm sure you'll agree, Robert. In future this will be a law firm. Everyone who knew them agrees that Messrs Unst, Fetlar and Yell (all LLB (Glas)) not only had a sound knowledge of the law of Scotland, but were shrewd men of business, whose success in legal practice was affected neither by Mr Unst's occasional grumpiness, nor by Mr Yell's excitable disposition.

41 Which, however, is not the case for the IBB Scottish mortgage.

An answer that has the merit of brevity. Given what has already been said in this paper, there is no need here to discuss the answer substantively, but something should be said about the question. "Impediment"? The word suggests something undesirable. Someone (such as myself) with the view that Islamic mortgages, when compared with conventional mortgages, might be undesirable, would not use such language.

M. Conclusion

Islamic mortgages aim at the same practical reality as conventional mortgages. Different words are used, to conceal the reality. That, at least, is how it seems to me. If interest-bearing mortgages are a bad thing, then Islamic mortgages are a bad thing, for Islamic mortgages are, apart from the wrapping, interest-bearing mortgages. But if, on the other hand, interest-bearing mortgages are not a bad thing, then it is better that they should be done in an open manner, and not by artificial means, producing both complexity and pitfalls. And finally, whilst I am no expert in Islamic theology, I note that those who do have such expertise frequently criticise Islamic mortgages as being mere shams.[42] What they say (albeit that I do not subscribe to Islam) makes more sense to me than the promotional brochures and videos of the institutions that offer what they call Shari'a-compliant finance, brochures and videos that the mainstream media and politicians should have a slightly more critical attitude towards.

42 Here is a sample: (i) http://www.islamicawakening.com/viewarticle.php?articleID=1291; (ii) http://sunnahonline.com/library/contemporary-issues/115-islamic-ijara-mortgages-by-hsbc-and-other-banks; (iii) http://www.islamicmortgages.co.uk/index.php?id=258; (iv) http://www.islamicparty.com/commonsense/hlmort.htm

10

Enforcing Repairing Obligations by Specific Implement

Professor Angus McAllister

A. Repairing Obligations

Repairing obligations in leases may either be owed by the landlord to the tenant or vice versa, depending upon which of them has responsibility for the repair in question. Which party owes the obligation is likely to vary according to the type of lease. At common law, all landlords of urban leases have an obligation to provide subjects in a tenantable or habitable condition, and to maintain them in a like condition throughout the let.[1] However, most commercial leases are granted on a full repairing and insuring (FRI) basis, contracting out of the common law and making repairs the responsibility of the tenant.

The opposite is true in the case of residential leases: it is not normally possible to contract out of the landlord's common law obligation because it has been strengthened and considerably reinforced by statute.[2] In all residential tenancies, the landlord has a duty to provide a house that is

1 J Rankine, *A Treatise on the Law of Leases in Scotland*, 3rd edn (1916) 241; for other references, including the institutional writers, see A McAllister *Scottish Law of Leases*, 4th edn (2013) paras 3.12 and 3.40.

2 There may be a partial exception to this in the case of private sector residential tenancies under s 18 of the Housing (Scotland) Act 2006, which allows limited contracting out of statutory repairing obligations.

wind and watertight and in all other respects reasonably fit for human habitation at the commencement of the tenancy and to keep it that way throughout its currency.[3] The slight discrepancy in wording between the common law and statutory wording is probably due to the fact that the latter is taken from the equivalent English provision; however, it has been held that there is no significant difference between the common law and the statutory formulations.[4]

The repairing obligations of private sector residential landlords (collectively known as "the repairing standard") extend much further and are spelled out in greater detail, beyond the basic habitability requirement, which mirrors the common law obligation and applies to social tenancies.[5]

In agricultural leases, both the landlord and the tenant have repairing obligations, e.g. their respective obligations regarding the maintenance of fixed equipment.[6]

B. Enforcement by Specific Implement

In principle, it ought to be possible for either party to enforce a repairing obligation by specific implement, by means of a decree *ad factum praestandum*, compelling the other party to fulfil the broken obligation. Specific implement is a primary breach of contract remedy in Scotland.[7] There are a number of situations where it cannot be used (e.g. for the payment of money), but where it is competent it is a right which the court has the discretion to refuse only in exceptional circumstances; these include situations where it would be impossible to enforce, or where its imposition would cause exceptional hardship to the recipient. Damages would then be the appropriate alternative remedy. In such cases the onus is on the defender to aver and prove that it would be inequitable for implement to be granted.[8]

---

3 Housing (Scotland) Act 2006 ss 13(1)(a) and 14(1) (private sector tenancies); Housing (Scotland) Act 2001, Sch 4, para 1 (social tenancies).

4 *Galloway v Glasgow City Council* 2001 HousLR 59; *Todd v Clapperton* [2009] CSOH 112, 2009 *SLT* 837.

5 Housing (Scotland) Act 2006 s 13(1)(b)-(f).

6 Agricultural Holdings (Scotland) Act 1991, s 5; Agricultural Holdings (Scotland) Act 2003 s 16.

7 For a general discussion of specific implement, see WW McBryde *The Law of Contract in Scotland*, 3rd edn (2007) para 23-01 to 23-37.

8 *Salaried Staff London Loan Co Ltd v Swears & Wells Ltd* 1985 SC 189; 1985 *SLT* 326.

This contrasts with the situation in England, where damages is the primary remedy, and specific performance (the nearest English equivalent of specific implement) is an equitable alternative that the court only has the discretion to grant in cases where damages would not be a sufficient remedy. As Lord Watson observed in the leading case of *Stewart v Kennedy*:[9]

> In England the only legal right arising from a breach of contract is a claim of damages; specific performance is not a matter of legal right, but a purely equitable remedy, which the Court can withhold when there are sufficient reasons of conscience or expediency against it. But in Scotland the breach of a contract for the sale of a specific subject such as landed estate gives the party aggrieved the legal right to sue for implement, and although he may elect to do so, he cannot be compelled to resort to the alternative of an action of damages unless implement is shown to be impossible... Even where implement is possible, I do not doubt that the Court of Session has inherent power to refuse the remedy on equitable grounds, although I know of no instance in which it has done so.

There are past examples of specific implement being used successfully to enforce a repairing obligation.[10] However, the few reported cases are more likely to be examples of failure, and it is necessary to consider the reasons for this.

C. Problems of Specification

The main problem seems to have been the need for precision, the traditional rationale being that breach of an order *ad factum praestandum* could result in penal consequences (at one time most likely imprisonment), and so the defender had to be absolutely clear about what needed to be done in order to obey it:[11]

> In pronouncing decree *ad factum praestandum*, the Court has to bear in mind the consequences and sanctions of such a decree. Failure to implement such a decree exposes a defender to the penalty of imprisonment which it is in

9 (1890) 17 R (HL) 1. See also *Co-operative Insurance Society v Argyll Stores (Holdings) Ltd* [1998] AC 1 at 9-10; [1997] 2 WLR 898 and *Beardmore v Barry* 1928 SC 101; 1928 *SLT* 143.

10 *Marianski v Jackson* (1872) 9 SLR 80.

11 *Middleton v Leslie* (1892) 19 R 801 at 802 per the Lord President; see also *Fleming & Ferguson Ltd v Paisley Magistrates* 1948 SC 547 at 557 per Lord Cooper, 1948 *SLT* 457; D M Walker *Civil Remedies* (1974) at p 270; McBryde, *Contract* (n 7) para 23.13 and 23.14. The need for precision was thoroughly re-examined in *Retail Parks Investments v Royal Bank of Scotland (No2)* 1996 SC 227, 1996 *SLT* 669, discussed below in relation to keep-open obligations.

> the power of the pursuer to put in force. I therefore think that in the case of decrees which may be thus enforced, or which expose a defender to penal consequences, it is right that the court should so express the decree that the defender shall be in no doubt regarding the obligation he has to discharge.

For example, an action requiring a residential landlord to comply with the common law obligation to maintain the subjects in a tenantable or habitable condition, according to the traditional view, would be likely to fail for want of specification if framed in such broad terms. Instead, it would be necessary to give precise details of the repairs required, thereby placing a substantial burden upon the pursuer, one which in practice would prove extremely difficult to overcome.[12]

It should be noted right away that the spectre of imprisonment was greatly weakened some time ago by Section 1 of the Law Reform (Miscellaneous Provisions) (Scotland) Act 1940, which (in the case of natural persons) sanctions imprisonment only in cases where the breach is wilful, and gives the court the discretion to impose an alternative penalty. Moreover, imprisonment was never an option in the case of corporate bodies such as companies or local authorities, and it is now clear that the imposition of a fine is an appropriate alternative in such cases.[13]

D. Keep-open Obligations

However, much of the case law relating to the enforcement (or attempted enforcement) of repairing obligations is very old, and virtually all of it predates the considerable development in the law of specific implement deriving from another area of lease law, the enforcement of so-called keep-open obligations in commercial leases. In the substantial body of case law

---

12 The case law is extremely sparse and often lacking in depth or detail, but see, for example, *Renfrew District Council v McGourlick* 1987 *SLT* 538 (an attempt to enforce a local authority's repairing obligations by utilising the statutory nuisance provisions, but in which Lord McCluskey analysed at some length the problems of specification attending a decree *ad factum praestandum* in this context); *Traynor v Monklands District Council* 1988 GWD 8-327; *Gunn v Glasgow District Council* (1990) 1 SHLR 213; *Nicol v Glasgow District Council* (1990) 1 SHLR 229 (The single volume of Scottish Housing Law Reports (SHLR) was published jointly in 1991 by Shelter (Scotland) and the Legal Services Agency. *Gunn* was successfully appealed to the Inner House, but only on the issue of damages – see 1992 SCLR 1018). For a useful discussion of the legal problems encountered in the housing sector see M Dailly "The Law of Specific Implement" (1993) SCOLAG 102.

13 See *Postel Properties Ltd v Miller and Santhouse plc* 1993 *SLT* 353 at 357 per Lord Sutherland.

on this topic the remedy of specific implement has come under intensive judicial scrutiny, and the courts have addressed many of the same difficulties that have prevented the enforcement of repairing obligations.

From the 1980s onwards, cases began to arise of tenants in shopping centres who ceased to occupy shops that were trading unprofitably. This was invariably in breach of the standard lease condition requiring the tenant to occupy and trade from the subjects in terms of the lease's use clause. The tenant would continue to pay rent, but would cut its overheads by closing down the unprofitable branch.

There was never any doubt that such a tenant was in breach of contract and that the landlord could claim damages and/or rescind the lease. However, damages could be difficult to quantify and there was no point in ending the lease of a property that could not be re-let. Instead, landlords tried to resort to specific implement, in order to compel the tenant to re-occupy and continue trading from the shop.

At first specific implement was thought to be incompetent in such cases, for the familiar reasons involving specification.[14] How could the court grant a decree *ad factum praestandum* for an activity which (like carrying out repairs) involved performing, not a single action, but a large number of actions? Moreover (unlike the situation with repairs) enforcing keep-open provisions involved compelling the tenant not merely to carry out a once-and-for-all action or number of actions, but a series of actions that would continue for a period of years until the lease came to an end.

However, this position was reversed by the Inner House of the Court of Session in the leading case of *Retail Parks Investments v Royal Bank of Scotland (No 2)*,[15] a decision that has been followed in a number of subsequent cases. The court granted an order of specific implement compelling the Royal Bank to re-open their branch in the Sauchiehall Centre in Glasgow and to continue conducting their business there for the remaining seven years of their lease.

While recognising that each case had to be decided on its own merits, Lord McCluskey was able to formulate some general statements of the legal considerations to be kept in mind when assessing the competence of an action *ad factum praestandum*. Several of these are relevant to the present discussion:[16]

14 *Grosvenor Developments (Scotland) plc v Argyll Stores Ltd* 1987 *SLT* 738.
15 1996 SC 227; 1996 *SLT* 669.
16 Ibid 1996 *SLT* 669 at 678 per Lord McCluskey.

(i) The material wording of the contract must make it certain what the defender has to achieve in order to fulfil the obligation, though this will not by itself guarantee the granting of a decree of specific implement.

(ii) An order of specific implement may require a number of distinct acts in order to secure compliance. However, the more numerous the required acts, the more necessary will it be to find terms for the order that will satisfy the need for adequate precision.

(iii) An order may specify the end to be achieved but leave open the precise means whereby that end is to be achieved, thereby allowing a degree of flexibility.

(iv) In considering the necessary degree of precision (bearing in mind that breach of the order could have serious, including penal, consequences) the court should consider the commercial realities which form the background to the undertaking of the parties' mutual obligations. In *Retail Parks* the defenders were a large commercial organisation that freely undertook the obligation with legal advice, and they had already occupied the subjects for the purpose stated in the lease for nearly 20 years without any apparent difficulty or misunderstanding. When seeking to enforce repairing obligations, one could make a similar comment, for example, about large residential landlords, such as local authorities, housing associations or private letting organisations with many properties and many years of experience.

(v) Even if the defenders experienced difficulties in knowing what was required of them, the matter would have to come before the court again before any penalty for breach could be imposed. The court would have to be satisfied that the breach was wilful and any imprecision in the wording of the order would be exposed; if satisfied that the breach was not wilful, the court could even give the defenders a further opportunity to comply before imposing a penalty.

E. The English Position

As noted above, in England specific performance is a purely equitable remedy that will only exceptionally be granted. It has been argued in the past that the distinction between the English and Scottish positions is more apparent in theory than in practice.[17] It has been suggested that the main difference in practice is that in Scotland, but not in England, there is a presumption in favour of specific implement,[18] though the circumstances

17 See E McKendrick, "Specific Implement and Specific Performance – A Comparison" 1986 *SLT (News)* 249; McBryde, *Contract* (n 7) para 23-09.

18 Walker, *Civil Remedies* (n 12) 276.

in which both remedies are likely to be denied, and those where they may be granted tend to be similar. A notable exception is keep-open obligations, where the landlords' remedy is still confined to damages, a position confirmed by the House of Lords in *Co-operative Insurance Society Ltd v Argyll Stores (Holdings) Ltd.*[19] Interestingly, however, the court made a distinction between court orders requiring a defendant to carry on an activity, such as running a business, and orders which require him to achieve a result, such as the enforcement by specific performance of building contracts and repairing obligations.[20]

The English action is therefore supposedly more restricted in scope than the Scottish one, but can, nevertheless, encompass the enforcement of repairing obligations. Admittedly, English house tenants are given statutory assistance by section 17 of the Landlord and Tenant Act 1985 which specifically facilitates the use of specific performance to enforce repairing obligations against residential landlords. There is no statutory equivalent of this in Scotland. Nevertheless, given the wider scope of the Scottish remedy indicated in the keep-open cases, it would seem strange if it could not be successfully used to enforce repairing obligations.

F. Keep-open Decrees

If we look at the actual wording of the decrees granted in keep-open cases, we find a degree of generality and even vagueness that would never have been contemplated under the old law. In *Retail Parks Investments* the Royal Bank was ordered *inter alia* "to use and occupy the premises as bank offices" and to keep them open for business during "all normal business hours." In *Co-operative Wholesale Society Ltd v Saxone Ltd*[21] the defenders were ordered "to keep the subjects open as a high class shop" for the sale of "footwear, hosiery, and handbags of all descriptions." In Lord Hamilton's view the expression "high class shop" was "a familiar commercial expression readily capable of objective assessment."[22] In *Highland and Universal Ltd v Safeway Properties Ltd (No 2)*[23] the expressions "high class retail store" and "normal

19 [1998] AC 1; [1997] 2WLR 898.

20 1998 AC 1 at 13 per Lord Hoffmann. For a general discussion regarding the competence of specific performance to enforce repairing obligations in England, see *Rainbow Estates Ltd v Tokenhold Ltd and Another* [1999] Ch 64.

21 1997 *SLT* 1052; 1997 SCLR 835.

22 1997 *SLT* 1052 at 1055.

23 2000 SC 297; 2000 *SLT* 414

hours of business" were again held, for the purposes of a decree *ad factum praestandum*, to be sufficiently precise phrases with an easily ascertainable meaning. And in *Oak Mall Greenock Ltd v McDonald's Restaurants Ltd*[24] decree was granted ordaining McDonald's to keep the restaurant in question open as "a quick service restaurant for the consumption of food and non-alcoholic drink both on and off the Leased Premises." In applying the guidelines laid down in *Retail Parks*, Lord Drummond Young observed:[25]

> In framing an order for specific implement of a lease or other contract, commercial realities must be taken into account. In particular, it must be presumed that, when they agreed on the terms of their contract, the parties considered the expressions used by them to be sufficiently precise to let them know what had to be done. Consequently, if the order for implement essentially repeats the provisions of the contract, it is inherently likely that the parties will know what [it] means and what must be done to comply with its terms.

Unmoved by the hardship that would be experienced by the McDonald's organisation by having to keep open a restaurant that had been trading at a loss for almost four years, his lordship decided that this was not an exceptional case where the court should exercise its discretion to refuse specific implement.

As already noted in relation to Lord McCluskey's comments in *Retail Parks*, Lord Drummond Young's observation could equally apply to the repairing obligations owed by many social and private landlords.

G. *Pik Facilitites v Shell UK*

In *Pik Facilities Ltd v Shell UK Ltd and Another*[26] a specific implement action to enforce a commercial tenant's repairing obligation failed because the lease had ended. However, the case did not fail because of lack of specification or precision. Lord Kingarth concluded, though without any great enthusiasm, that the pursuers' pleadings were adequate in this respect. This case is significant as it is an isolated example following in the wake of the keep open decisions in which an action of specific implement almost succeeded.

---

24 2003 GWD 17-540.

25 Ibid at para 6.

26 2005 SCLR 958

H. Third Party References

Rule 29(2) of the Ordinary Cause Rules for the Sheriff Court provides as follows:[27]

> 29.2 – Remit to person of skill.
>
> (1) The sheriff may, on a motion by any party or on a joint motion, remit to any person of skill, or other person, to report on any matter of fact.
>
> (2) Where a remit under paragraph (1) is made by joint motion or of consent of all parties, the report of such person shall be final and conclusive with respect to the subject-matter of the remit.

The remit of technical detail to a person of skill has a long history at common law, and has been used in the past in order to determine the detailed measures required to fulfil repairing obligations in leases. In *Barclay v Neilson*[28] the Inner House, finding that the landlord of a farm was obliged to carry out such repairs and make such additions as were necessary to enable the tenant properly to cultivate the farm according to the terms and conditions of the lease, ordered:

> Of consent remit to Mr John Dickson, Saughton Mains, to visit the said farm, and report to the Court what additions and repairs are necessary for that purpose…

In the words of the Lord President:[29]

> I do not think that this is a case for a proof at large, and I take the liberty of suggesting that, if neither of the parties have anything to say against it, the proper course will be to have the amount of additions and repairs which are necessary to enable the tenant to cultivate the farm in a proper manner settled by a remit to a man of skill.

This procedure would therefore appear to have the potential to help get round some of the problems of specification involved in framing an action *ad factum praestandum*. However, two difficulties immediately arise, both inherent in what was said above.

27 Act of Sederunt (Sheriff Court Ordinary Cause Rules) 1993, SI 1956. For a discussion of this procedure see T Welsh (ed), *Macphail's Sheriff Court Practice*, 3rd edn (2006) para 13.27-13.34.

28 (1878) 5 R 909; see also *Brock v Buchanan* (1851) 13 D 1069.

29 (1878) 5 R 909 at 911 per the Lord President.

(1) Rule 29(1) makes it absolutely clear that such a remit can only be made on matters of fact, and not on questions of law. This principle is also long established at common law. In *Quin v Gardner & Sons Ltd*[30] it was held that a remit requiring construction of the contract in question was incompetent because it involved a question of law. In the context of repairing obligations in leases, in was held in *McFarlane v Crawford*,[31] applying *Quin*, that a crave framed in the following terms was incompetent:

> to remit to a person of skill (a) to inspect the premises at 19 Duncan Street; (b) to report to the Court the present condition thereof, and whether the premises are wind and water tight and in good repair and in a proper tenantable and habitable state; and (c) if not, what repairs are necessary to make the premises thoroughly wind and water tight, and otherwise put them into good repair and a proper tenantable and habitable condition…

In the words of Sheriff Welsh:[32]

> [T]he lease being silent as to the obligation of the defenders for the upkeep of the premises, the reporter would require to inform himself what the common law implied in such circumstances; that is to say, he would require to apply his mind to a question of law at the outset of his investigations. Having informed himself upon this matter, he would then require to find out the state of the facts. He would next require to apply his mind to the construction of the defenders' legal obligation for upkeep, and consider whether that obligation applied to each or all of the matters of fact which he so found. In short, the Court is asked to remit a mixed question of law and fact, which is, in my opinion, incompetent. The question of the nature and extent of the defenders' obligation for upkeep is a question of law for the consideration of the Court.

Presumably the same objection would apply whatever the source of the repairing obligation, whether it involved interpretation of the common law, or the construction of a statutory or lease provision.

(2) Under Rule 29(2) a remit is not conclusive unless it is made jointly by both parties or with the consent of both. The wording would appear to exclude a remit by the sheriff *ex proprio motu*.[33] If made by only one party, therefore, the other could object (presumably a likely occurrence) and the expert's findings would not be conclusive. The matter would have to go

30 (1888) 15 R 776.

31 1919 35 Sh Ct Rep 78; see also *Maclagan v Marchbank* (1911) 2 *SLT* 184; (1911) 27 Sh Ct Rep 282.

32 *McFarlane v Crawford* 1919 35 Sh Ct Rep 78 at 79 per Sheriff Welsh.

33 Welsh, *Macphail* (n 28) para 13.29.

back to the court for determination, and possibly involve the competing testimony of expert witnesses. This is consistent with the decision in *Barclay v Neilson* referred to above. The main issue in that case was whether the landlord owed the repairing obligation at all. The court having decided that he did, there appeared to be no difficulty with obtaining the consent of both parties to the remit.

I. Specific Performance of Statutory Duty

Section 45 of the Court of Session Act 1988[34] provides *inter alia*:

> The Court may, on application by summary petition ...order the specific performance of any statutory duty, under such conditions and penalties (including fine and imprisonment, where consistent with the enactment concerned) in the event of the order not being implemented, as to the Court seem proper.

This Scottish use of the term "specific performance" appears to be distinct from specific implement, but to operate in a similar way, though only in relation to the enforcement of a statutory duty:[35]

> Those who invoke this remedy must, I think, be careful to aver a clear statutory duty which those on whom its performance is incumbent have refused, or unduly delayed, to perform; and to state in precise terms the order which, by their prayer, is sought from the Court. Such an order is more or less equivalent to the English mandamus, as to the nature and application of which there is much authority in England.

There is therefore the same need for precision that was noted above in relation to specific implement.[36]

This procedure could, in theory at least, provide an alternative remedy in cases where a repairing obligation is imposed by statute. This excludes commercial leases, where such obligations derive from the common law or the terms of the lease, but not residential leases where, as we saw above, the

34 Re-enacting s 91 of the Court of Session Act 1868. The cases quoted below relate to the 1868 Act. For an example of a petition under the 1988 Act see *Magnohard Ltd v United Kingdom Atomic Energy Authority* 2004 SC 247, 2003 *SLT* 1083. For a general discussion of this remedy see Walker, *Civil Remedies* (n 12) 271-74.

35 *Carlton Hotel Co Ltd v Lord Advocate* 1921 SC 237 at 246 per Lord Dundas, 1921 1 *SLT* 126. Regarding the comparison with mandamus, see also *Sons of Temperance Friendly Society, Petitioners* 1926 SC 418 at 426 per Lord President Clyde, 1926 *SLT* 273.

36 In this regard see also *Fleming & Ferguson Ltd v Paisley Magistrates* 1942 SC 547 at 557 per Lord Cooper; 1948 *SLT* 457.

landlords' repairing obligations largely derive from statute. In particular, it might be used to enforce the obligation to provide a house that is wind and watertight and in all other respects reasonably fit for human habitation at the commencement of the tenancy and to maintain it in that condition throughout currency of the lease.[37]

The procedure has been held to be competent against a local authority,[38] against a friendly society,[39] (which arguably could extend to other bodies regulated by statute, such as housing associations) and (in the opinion of Professor Walker) "against a private person such as an employer who is subject to a statutory duty."[40] This last category could presumably also extend to private landlords under an assured tenancy and registered social landlords other than local authorities or housing associations.

While the availability of this remedy seems worth pointing out, it has the obvious disadvantage of only being competent in the Court of Session.[41] It therefore offers no clear advantage over raising an action *ad factum praestandum* in the sheriff court and, as we will see below, in the case of private sector residential tenancies the repairing standard enforcement order (RSEO) probably remains the best remedy.

J. Repairing Standard Enforcement Orders (RSEOs)

In relation to private sector residential tenancies only[42] the Housing (Scotland) Act 2006 introduced the Repairing Standard and set out the obligations of landlords regarding compliance with it.[43] In addition to the requirement to provide and maintain a house that is wind and watertight and reasonably fit for human habitation (the "habitability" obligation), which is also owed by social landlords and mirrors the common law obligation,[44] it goes into much more detail about the structure and exterior

37 Housing (Scotland) Act 2006 ss 13 (1)(a) and 14 (1) (private sector tenancies); Housing (Scotland) Act 2001, Sch 4, para 1 (social tenancies).

38 *T Docherty Ltd v Monifieth Burgh Council* 1970 SC 200, 1971 *SLT* 13.

39 *Sons of Temperance Friendly Society, Petitioners* 1926 SC 418, 1926 *SLT* 273.

40 Walker *Civil Remedies* (n 12) 272. However, Professor Walker cites no authority in support of this view.

41 Court of Session Act 1988 s 51.

42 Mostly assured and short assured tenancies under the Housing (Scotland) Act 1988, but also a diminishing number of regulated tenancies under the Rent (Scotland) Act 1984. For a general description of these and a brief historical background see McAllister *Leases* (n 1) para 17.1-17.4

43 Housing (Scotland) Act 2006 ss 13 and 14.

44 Ibid s 13(1)(a).

of the house, sanitary, heating and other installations, the safety of fixtures and appliances supplied by the landlord, and fire safety.[45]

The 2006 Act also provides a statutory mechanism for the enforcement of the landlord's repairing obligations. If a tenant believes that the landlord has failed to comply with the repairing standard, he or she can apply to the Private Rented Housing Panel (formerly the Rent Assessment Panel), whose chairman may refer the matter to a private rented housing committee (formerly a rent assessment committee).[46] The constitution of each private rented housing committee, consisting of a chairman and two other members, is determined by the president of the Rent Assessment Panel.[47] A Committee will usually be made up of a lawyer acting as chairperson, a chartered surveyor and a lay member. Lay members come from a diverse range of backgrounds and many of them are acknowledged experts in housing issues.[48]

If a committee decides that a landlord has failed to comply with the repairing standard, it has the power to issue a repairing standard enforcement order (RSEO) requiring the landlord to carry out any necessary work and make good any damage caused by it within a reasonable deadline of at least 21 days.[49] A landlord who fails to comply with an RSEO is guilty of an offence and may be subject to a fine.[50]

It will be noted right away that RSEOs are effectively a statutory form of specific implement. It will also be noted that the constitution of a private rented housing committee makes it well placed to overcome some of the difficulties with specific implement, as it is not only qualified to decide questions of law, but also to address problems of specification, effectively taking on the role of expert witness.

Since 3 September 2007, when the relevant part of the 2006 Act came into force,[51] a surprisingly large number of RSEOs have been granted. Between that date and 31 October 2014, 1167 decisions by private rented housing committees relating to repairs have been reported. 864 of these concern breaches of the habitability obligation contained in section 13(1)

45 Housing (Scotland) Act 2006 s13(1)(b)-(f).
46 Ibid s 22.
47 Rent (Scotland) Act 1984 sch 4, paras 5 and 6 (as amended).
48 See the website of the Private Rented Housing Panel, available at www.prhpscotland.gov.uk.
49 Housing (Scotland) Act 2006 s 24.
50 Ibid s 28.
51 Ibid (Commencement No. 5, Savings and Transitional Provisions) Order 2007, SSI 270.

(a) of the Act, the one which also applies to social tenancies and mirrors the landlord's common law obligation. In some of them the committee has refused to grant an order, and others deal with matters like the variation of an order (usually by extending the deadline), but a large proportion of the reports are of orders which have been granted.[52]

The following is an example of a recent order:[53]

> NOTICE TO
>
> Colin Todd
>
> Whereas in terms of their decision dated 21st May 2014, the Private Rented Housing Committee determined that the Landlord has failed to comply with the duty imposed by Section 14 (1)(b) of the Housing (Scotland) Act 2006 and, in particular, that the Landlord has failed to ensure that the property is wind and watertight and in all respects reasonably fit for human habitation and that installations in the Property for the supply of water, gas and electricity and for sanitation, space heating and heating water are in a reasonable state of repair and in proper wording order.
>
> The Private Rented Housing Committee now requires the Landlord to carry out such work as is necessary for the purposes of ensuring that the Property meets the repairing standard and that any damage caused by the carrying out of any work in terms of this Order is made good.
>
> In particular the Private Rented Housing Committee requires the following:
>
> 1. The landlord has to ensure that a suitably qualified heating engineer inspect the heating system with regard to providing a report on whether or not it has sufficient and proper thermostatic control and thereafter to comply with any recommendations of the engineer.
> 2. The landlord is to ensure that the bath panel and its trim are properly fitted.
> 3. The landlord is to carry out work to ensure that the front door is wind and water tight.
>
> The Private Rented Housing Committee order that these works must be carried out and completed within twenty-eight days of the date of service.

A typical report will not only contain the order itself, but will give a detailed account of the committee's determination, including the background of the case, a summary of the issues, an account of the evidence, the committee's findings in fact and the reasons for their decision.

52 Reports of the decisions of the private rented housing committees can be found on the Panel's website, available at www.prhpscotland.gov.uk.

53 *Cameron v Todd*, 21 May 2014, reported at www.prhpscotland.gov.uk.

It is submitted that a landlord receiving such an order, coupled with the committee's detailed account of their decision, will be left in no doubt about what is required of him or her in order to avoid incurring a penalty. At any rate, any landlord or tenant aggrieved by the decision of a private rented housing committee may appeal to the Sheriff by summary application within 21 days of being notified of the decision.[54] If any such appeals have raised substantive legal issues, none of them have made it into the casebooks.

It is difficult to escape the conclusion that RSEOs, in sharp contrast with their common law counterparts, have been remarkably successful in the enforcement of repairing obligations.

K. Conclusions

Specific implement, as a remedy to enforce repairing obligations in leases, has long fallen into disuse because of its long history of failure, mainly due to problems of specification and the fear of the unfair imposition of penal consequences. For a number of reasons that have been set out above, it is submitted that the remedy is worth reconsidering and has the potential to be a much more useful tool for both landlords and tenants when enforcing repairing obligations. In particular:

(i) The greater flexibility enabled by the keep-open decisions has addressed many of the fears regarding specification and possible penal consequences. It is worth pointing out that part of the perceived problem with keep-open decrees was not only that they related to a large number of actions, but also that these actions extended over a lengthy period of time. Repairing obligations present only the first and not the second of these difficulties. As Lord Hoffmann pointed out in *Co-operative Insurance Society Ltd v Argyll Stores (Holdings) Ltd*[55] (in relation to the supposedly more restricted English remedy of specific performance) a distinction can be made between court orders requiring a defendant to carry on an activity, and those designed to achieve a result. And one of the examples which he gave of the latter was the enforcement of repairing obligations by specific performance.[56]

(ii) The possibility of delegating technical details to a person of skill could go some way to addressing any remaining problems of specification,

54 Housing (Scotland) Act 2006 ss 64(4).
55 1998] AC 1; [1997] 2WLR 898.
56 1998 AC 1 at 13 per Lord Hoffmann.

provided that care is taken to confine any such remit to questions of fact. Even if the objection of one of the parties prevents the expert's decision being final, the court could nevertheless be given considerable assistance in wording a suitable decree.

(iii) Repairing standard enforcement orders have proved to be a formidable tool by means of which private sector residential tenants can compel their landlords to carry out necessary repairs. They have operated in a similar way to specific implement, without apparently throwing up any substantial legal difficulties. The decisions of the private rented housing committees (which include legal expertise) have been thoroughly documented and their experience could provide valuable guidance for the courts in framing decrees *ad factum praestandum*. There seems no reason in theory why social tenants and commercial landlords should remain the poor relations.

The greatest potential for the revival of specific implement is probably in the case of residential tenants in the social sector, who do not of course have recourse to the Private Rented Housing Panel. Problems of disrepair in residential property have a long history in social as well has private housing, one of the most notorious examples being the severe dampness frequently experienced in sub-standard council housing.[57] For the tenant of such a property, who possibly has limited opportunities to move elsewhere, damages alone may not be an adequate remedy, and the ability to compel the landlord to carry out repairs could be invaluable.

We noted above the remarks of Lord McCluskey in *Retail Parks* that the defenders were a large commercial organisation that freely undertook their obligation with legal advice, and that they had already occupied the subjects for the purpose stated in the lease for nearly 20 years without any apparent difficulty or misunderstanding. A similar comment could be made about social landlords, particularly local authorities and housing associations. As well as being large organisations who freely undertook their obligations with legal advice, one would expect them normally to have extensive experience and expertise in executing repairs. And the meaning of "wind and water tight and in all other respects reasonably fit for human habitation" (and its common law equivalent) has been thoroughly explored in legal precedent, mainly because the statutory formulation is identical to its English counterpart, and has been so for more than 100 years.[58]

57 Problems thoroughly examined in P D Brown and A McIntosh *Dampness and the Law* (1987).

58 See for example the leading English case of *Summers v Salford Corporation* [1943] AC 283, [1943] 1 All ER 68.

It is also worth pointing out that the model tenancy agreement for Scottish secure tenancies recommended by the Scottish Executive[59] elaborates substantially upon the basic habitability obligation prescribed by statute, including many of the obligations spelled out in the repairing standard introduced for the private sector by the Housing (Scotland) Act 2006, and also setting out in detail the landlord's repairing obligations in relation to dampness, condensation and mould. In cases where a social landlord has adopted this model, therefore, the enforcement rights of tenants have been even more strengthened.

Specific implement has perhaps less potential in the case of commercial leases. As noted above, the standard commercial lease is the tenant's FRI (full repairing and insuring) lease, by which the landlord's common law repairing obligation has been passed on to the tenant. It is also standard for commercial leases to provide that, in the event of the tenant failing to carry out repairs, the landlord may step in and carry them out at the tenant's expense. This right also provides the legal justification for the landlord presenting an outgoing tenant with a bill for dilapidations. In these circumstances, specific implement may not be the most effective and convenient remedy. However, there may still be cases where the possibility of specific implement may be useful, for example in cases where commercial landlords may be short of the funds to carry out the repairs themselves.

In any case, any further development of the common law can only enhance the enforcement potential of repairing obligations in all types of lease. We have seen above how the development of specific implement deriving from the keep-open issues in commercial leases can be applied to assist with the enforcement of repairing obligations in residential leases. There is no reason why this type of cross-fertilisation could not work in the opposite direction, with the result that new precedents in the residential sector could establish principles applicable in other areas of lease law. Landlords and tenants of commercial and agricultural leases could therefore also benefit in the longer term.

As we saw above, specific implement is a primary remedy for breach of contract in Scotland, there is a presumption in favour of it being available, and the onus is upon the defender in any case to show why it should be denied. It is hoped that the above discussion may help to make that onus more difficult to overcome.

59 Scottish Executive "Model Scottish Secure Tenancy Agreement" (revised version July 2002), available at www.scotland.gov.uk/publications.

11

A New Era in Conveyancing: Advance Notices and the Land Registration etc. (Scotland) Act 2012

Ann Stewart

For decades, property lawyers in jurisdictions other than Scotland expressed astonishment that Scottish solicitors effectively underwrote their seller client's obligation to a purchaser to provide, after settlement, records in the property and personal registers that would be clear of any entry, deed, decree or diligence, which was either prejudicial to the validity of, or was an encumbrance on, the seller's title to the property. Solicitors did this by granting to the purchaser, by way of formal letter to the purchaser's solicitor, a firm's undertaking either that the records would be clear, or to clear them if they were not. The "letter of obligation," the document by which this apparently reckless practice was effected, was an invariable feature of the Scottish conveyancing landscape.

But that has all now changed. The Land Registration etc. (Scotland) Act 2012 introduced a new concept to Scottish conveyancing – the advance notice procedure – which has transformed the way in which property transactions are conducted, and in the vast majority of cases has eliminated the requirement for any letter of obligation.

A. Letters of Obligation

(1) Historical background

The origin of the practice of granting a letter of obligation at settlement may be said to be lost in the mists of time. As early as 1900 James Sturrock,[1] in an annotation to a lecture by Professor Allan Menzies on searches in conveyancing transactions, refers to a case in 1896[2] in which Mr Gordon, the law agent, sold the property "and granted the usual obligation to produce a search showing a clear record." Although in that case, the law agents themselves had had an interest in the property and signed the disposition as consenters, the fact that, four years later, Sturrock describes the granting of a letter of obligation as "usual" indicates that this was already standard practice. This is in spite of the fact that there is no legal obligation on a seller's solicitor to give a letter of obligation.

Is it necessary to delve back further to identify the origins of this practice? Arguably, over a century of practice must be compelling enough evidence that this was firmly embedded in Scottish conveyancing tradition. Later conveyancing manuals allude to this practice as being "general and almost universal"[3] and "usual practice."[4]

(2) What is the function of a letter of obligation?

Until recently, the letter of obligation was a "little understood, but vital, part of any transaction."[5] There is an intrinsic weakness in the conveyancing process, for which the letter of obligation was the plaster cast. The weakness arises because of a hiatus in the succession of steps in the conveyancing process around settlement.[6]

---

1 J S Sturrock, *Conveyancing According to the Law of Scotland* (1900) 935, based on the Lectures of Allan Menzies, Professor of Conveyancing at the University of Edinburgh between 1847 and 1856.

2 *Dryburgh v Gordon* [1896] 24 R 1.

3 J Burns, *Conveyancing Practice According to the Law of Scotland*, 4th edn (1957) 302.

4 J M Halliday, *Conveyancing Law and Practice in Scotland*, 2nd edn (1997) 515.

5 J H Sinclair and E Sinclair, *Handbook of Conveyancing Practice in Scotland*, 5th edn (2006) 181.

6 "Settlement" is the term used for the steps that take place on the date of entry when the price is paid by, and the disposition is delivered to, the purchaser and (usually) entry is taken by him. In commercial property transactions this is often referred to as "completion."

The "gap" period

A seller is required to exhibit clear searches in the property and personal registers before settlement of the purchase takes place. The existence of any adverse deed, or an inhibition against the seller that predates the missives, will be disclosed in such searches, and usually steps have to be taken to discharge such entries before the purchaser will proceed to completion and pay the price. Those searches must be ordered up and exhibited to the purchaser's solicitors as close as possible to the date of entry, but before settlement takes place. Such searches can only disclose the state of play of the registers at a date that pre-dates settlement. The date to which the searches are certified may also pre-date the date of settlement, perhaps by two or more days. So there is a gap between the date to which the Registers have been searched, and the date on which the purchaser hands over the price.

There is another, consecutive gap that occurs between settlement and the date on which the purchaser registers his title and obtains a real right to the property. While it is possible, immediately following completion of the transaction, to take the delivered deed to the Land Register and present it in person (and this does happen reasonably frequently), in the majority of cases, following completion there is a delay, perhaps only of a day or two, while the post completion formalities are dealt with, any stamp duty land tax[7] paid, and registration forms completed, before the disposition in favour of the purchaser arrives at the Registers and is entered onto the records. Professional practice guidance permits a period of up to fourteen days after settlement within which to present the purchaser's application for registration.[8] Solicitors whose offices are not located in Glasgow or Edinburgh usually have no choice but to submit applications by post or through legal document exchange arrangements, or resort to the expense of a courier.

During this gap, or invisibility period, there are risks. A competing deed could be presented for registration before the purchaser's disposition is presented. Until comparatively recently, the possibility of the seller being sequestrated or going into liquidation or administration during the

7 To be replaced in Scotland on 1 April 2015, by land and buildings transaction tax.

8 Law Society of Scotland, Rules and Guidance, Section F, Division C – Letters of obligation and advance notices, para 3, available at http://www.lawscot.org.uk/rules-and-guidance/section-f-guidance-relating-to-particular-types-of-work/division-c-conveyancing/guidance/letters-of-obligation-and-advance-notices/

gap period also posed a serious risk. To provide protection against the occurrence of these risks – particularly insolvency or the emergence of a rival deed – the letter of obligation historically stepped into the breach.

The guarantee of clear records

It is unusual for a solicitor to bind himself personally, and thus be liable to incur personal liability, in respect of the obligations of his client. Generally when conducting a transaction, it will be beyond any doubt that the solicitor is acting as the agent for a disclosed principal. Missives are entered into by solicitors "for and on behalf of our client." The letter of obligation was a clear exception to this general rule.

The letter of obligation was, in effect, a guarantee that the registers would be clear of any competing deeds or decrees and diligences affecting the seller. Although the styles of wording used varied slightly depending on whether the transaction involved recording in the General Register of Sasines (now unlikely, since all transfers of property[9] will induce a first registration in the Land Register, where the seller's title is in the Sasine Register), or in the Land Register, the effect was the same: if any deed, decree or diligence appeared on the records that would prejudice the purchaser's title, then provided these had not been created by or against the purchaser, the firm was obliged to remove them. The firm's exposure under a typical letter of obligation was a maximum of fourteen days, or until the purchaser's deed was registered, if earlier.

The undertaking

The undertaking given in a typical letter of obligation (for a sale of registered property) would say:

> With reference to the settlement of this transaction today, we undertake to clear the records of any deed, decree or diligence (other than such as may be created by, or against, the Purchaser) which may be recorded in the Personal Registers or to which effect may be given in the Land Register in the period from [date of certification of Form 12 or 13 Report (search)] to fourteen days after today's date inclusive (or to the earlier date of registration of the

---

9 Following the introduction of the 2012 Act on 8 December 2014, all conveyances, whether for valuable consideration or not, induce a first registration in the Land Register, if the title to the property is still in the Sasine Register.

Purchaser's interest in the Property) and which would cause the Keeper[10] to make an entry on, or qualify her indemnity in, [the Title Sheet to be updated] [the Land Certificate to be issued] in respect of that interest.

(3) Minimising risk to the seller's solicitor

Professional indemnity insurance

That the solution to the gap period, and the underwriting of these risks, was taken on by the solicitor profession in Scotland (which appears to be the only jurisdiction in which such a mechanism was used) seems, on the face of it, perverse. If there is a risk associated with a process, then the obvious solution is to arrange insurance to protect against that risk. In fact, title indemnity insurance cover was available in situations where no letter of obligation was to be granted, although it was not routinely obtained.

However, insurance cover was and remains available, albeit indirectly, for the gap period risks. It takes the form of the professional indemnity insurance that all firms of solicitors have to take out to be able to practice. The Master Policy is arranged by the Law Society of Scotland, to provide indemnity for solicitors against a variety of types of professional liability, arising out of business which is customarily carried on or transacted by solicitors in Scotland. This includes claims arising out of letters of obligation. Solicitors make a contribution annually to the Law Society for the cost of this insurance which sets a mandatory limit of indemnity, currently £2 million, for each firm. Individual firms can, and do, arrange their own top-up cover for protection in the case of claims of higher amounts. Since letters of obligation were given in commercial property transactions involving tens or hundreds of millions of pounds, such top-up cover was essential for firms with a commercial property practice.

Professional indemnity insurance cover was and remains available for a letter of obligation or other undertaking by the firm in any circumstances. However the letter of obligation was given a benign treatment under Special Conditions that apply to the Master Policy if it is "classic."[11]

---

10 The Keeper of the Registers of Scotland.

11 That "benign" treatment continues beyond 8 December 2014, at least for the PI insurance year 2014/2015. Whether it will continue beyond November 2015 is up to the insurers.

The classic letter of obligation

The wording of the classic letter of obligation had to contain the components of the style wording above, including the fourteen day time limit, although there was no mandatory style. Before granting the letter of obligation, the seller's solicitor had to comply with certain conditions, designed to ensure that any risk of a claim was minimised.

The conditions were:

- A search in the property and personal registers must have been obtained immediately before settlement. What was meant by "immediately before" was not always clear, but Law Society Guidance indicated that the searches in both registers could be up to seven days' old (equivalent to five working days), counting back from the date of settlement to the date to which the search was certified as being correct.[12] In residential property transactions there was a requirement under the Council of Mortgage Lenders Scottish Solicitors' Handbook[13] for the search in the personal registers to be no more than three working days old.
- The client had to be asked to confirm whether or not there were any outstanding securities.
- The solicitor issuing the letter of obligation had to be unaware of any other security; and
- Where the undertaking was a firm's undertaking to deliver a discharge of a standard security, the solicitor granting the obligation had to have sufficient funds to pay off the loan.

Provided these conditions were complied with for a letter of obligation, then even in the case of a claim which had to be met from professional indemnity insurance, the excess that the firm in question was required to pay in the event of any claim (the "self-insured amount") was nil, and there was no adverse impact on any premium loading or discount for that firm. If a letter of obligation was given in classic terms, but the conditions had not been complied with (known as a "failed classic"), then the normal self-insured amount applied. Obligations which fell outside the "classic"

12 Law Society of Scotland, Rules and Guidance, Section F, Division C – Letters of obligation, para 4, available at http://www.lawscot.org.uk/rules-and-guidance/section-f-guidance-relating-to-particular-types-of-work/division-c-conveyancing/guidance/letters-of-obligation-and-advance-notices/

13 Available at http://www.cml.org.uk/cml/handbook/scotland. No changes have been made to the CML Handbook to reflect any changes in practice relating to the coming into force of the provisions of the Land Registration (Scotland) Act 2012, although individual lenders are left to make whatever arrangements they consider are required.

obligations to clear the records or deliver an executed discharge (known as "non-classic") resulted in the application of a double excess if a claim was made and met[14] as well being taken into account for any discount or loading to Master Policy premiums for the firm in question.[15]

An unpopular arrangement

It probably goes almost without saying that the letter of obligation was extremely unpopular with solicitors in Scotland, but it had for many years been an unavoidable evil, due in large part to the effect of professional custom and tradition, and it is a not an understatement to say that, without the letter of obligation as an integral part of the settlement procedure, the conveyancing process as we knew it would have collapsed.

While, as already noted, a solicitor had no legal obligation to grant a letter of obligation, Law Society guidance had moved from the position held several decades ago that no letter of obligation had to be given unless the missives expressly provide for it, to the recent view of the Conveyancing Committee of the Law Society that "conveyancing transactions should be settled with a letter of obligation being granted by the solicitor personally" and "[w]hile there is no legal obligation to give a letter of obligation where missives are silent, there is a professional duty on a solicitor to grant a letter of obligation unless the solicitor advises to the contrary at the earliest possible opportunity."[16]

In recent years there had been increasing unwillingness on the part of solicitors to grant letters of obligation in certain circumstances. In transactions where the solicitor acted for an insolvency practitioner in a sale, for example, the practice had evolved of flatly refusing to give any letter of obligation. This was in part due to the refusal by insolvency practitioners to accept any personal liability. The letter of obligation was equally unpopular with insurers, and this was exacerbated in the late 1980s and early 1990s by the increased incidence of second standard securities over residential properties which were granted unknowingly by home owners. These securities were usually granted at the time of making home improvements, such as installation of double glazing

14 Known as a "double deductible."
15 But see n 11
16 Law Society of Scotland, Rules and Guidance, Section F, Division C – Letters of obligation.

or replacement kitchens, with the owner being under the impression that they were being asked to sign some credit agreement, unaware that the "agreement" would then be registered against their title. The preponderance of such second standard securities led to the requirement to make proper enquiry of the client as to the granting of other securities, and the prudent conveyancer would include an enquiry about carrying out any home improvements.

Against a background of increasing concern, it was clear that something would need to be done. One only needs to look at the legal systems of other countries and jurisdictions, including our closest neighbour, England, and to certain advance warning systems that were already operating in Scotland – the most obvious being the notice of letters of inhibitions procedure[17] – to see the prospects of a solution in some form of priority notification procedure, linked to the registration of deeds and documents in the Registers of Scotland.

B. The New System of Advance Notices

(1) The genesis of the Scottish Advance Notice

The Scottish Law Commission, always innovative in bringing forward new approaches to old problems, had already decided to include the thorny topic of land registration reform in its Sixth Programme of Law Reform,[18] at the request of the Keeper of the Registers of Scotland. There then followed a series of Discussion Papers[19] on a wide range of aspects of land registration, which had been introduced in Scotland by the Land Registration (Scotland) Act 1979. The third of these Discussion Papers, which dealt with a miscellaneous collection of issues, first flagged the prospect of a priority notice scheme.[20]

That early consideration of how a priority notice procedure in Scotland could work drew from a number of other jurisdictions for inspiration, both selecting and rejecting elements of other systems to consider how best to

17 Introduced by the Titles to Land Consolidation (Scotland) Act 1868, s155.

18 (Scot Law Com No 176, 2000).

19 Discussion Paper on *Land Registration: Void and Voidable Titles* (Scot Law Com DP No 125, 2004), Discussion Paper on *Land Registration: Registration, Rectification and Indemnity* (Scot Law Com DP No 128, 2005) and Discussion Paper on *Land Registration: Miscellaneous Issues* (Scot Law Com DP No 130, 2005).

20 DP on *LR: Miscellaneous Issues* (n 19) part 7.

tailor the system for Scotland. The DP identified the key advantages of a scheme of advance notices.[21] Uppermost is the certainty of success against the threat of a competing title (or the comfort that there are no competing titles) that a priority notice system would bring,[22] coupled with the reduction of exposure to risk from letters of obligation that would follow as a consequence.[23]

However the DP also identified disadvantages to such a system, citing arguments that it could be regarded as unnecessary[24] – the imminent introduction of ARTL[25] would enable the instantaneous signing, payment for and delivery of conveyancing documents, removing the risk from a competing deed. It was, however, recognised in the DP that ARTL would not necessarily be suitable for all types of transaction, and might not therefore be a sufficient solution.[26] It has proved to be the case that, although there have been many transactions completed under ARTL, it can only cope with transactions that are a dealing of the whole of an already registered interest, and its application, since introduction, has been largely confined to residential transactions and remortgages.

Another criticism of a priority notice system identified in the DP was that it would be disproportionate.[27] The level of risk from insolvency has in any event decreased, since a trustee in sequestration is no longer able immediately to complete a title to property in the bankrupt's estate following on appointment, but must wait for a period of 28 days to elapse.[28] While there may be risks attendant with the liquidation or administration of a company, the Scottish Law Commission did not consider these to be either considerable or insurmountable.

The original proposal for priority notices in the DP suggested backdating the effective date of registration of the protected deed to

21 DP on *LR: Miscellaneous Issues* (n 19) para 7.21-7.28.
22 Ibid para 7.22-7.24.
23 Ibid para 7.25-7.27.
24 Ibid para 7.29-7.30.
25 Automated Registration of Title to Land, a system by which the transfer document (disposition) is created within an electronic system, digitally signed and electronically delivered, thus eliminating the gap period. ARTL was subsequently introduced, but it is (currently) limited in the types of deeds and transactions that it can facilitate.
26 DP on *LR: Miscellaneous Issues* (n 19) para 7.30.
27 Ibid para 7.31-7.33.
28 Bankruptcy and Diligence etc. (Scotland) Act 2007, s 17.

the date of registration of the notice.[29] This would be similar to the way inhibitions work: a notice of letters of inhibition is registered,[30] which provides a period of twenty one days in which the inhibition itself can be registered on condition that the schedule of inhibition is served on the debtor after registration of the notice.[31] If registration takes place within this period, the effective date of the inhibition is backdated to the date of service of the schedule of inhibition. If registration does not take place, the notice lapses.

Applying this backdating effect to priority notices would mean that a real right in the property could, retrospectively, be obtained prematurely.[32] The priority notice would always be registered before the date of entry, and sometimes could be registered before conclusion of missives. To adopt this model would mean that ownership) would pass to the purchaser before settlement, but so too would liabilities incidental to ownership. It is easy to see why these proposals were not generally supported at the time.

However pressure on, and dislike of, the system of letters of obligation continued to grow. By the time the Scottish Law Commission was preparing its Report on Land Registration[33] it had already received representations, including from the Law Society of Scotland, to look again at a priority procedure for land registration. The Report proposed a much more straightforward system of advance notices,[34] that this time received a considerable degree of support from the profession.

The Report also contained a draft Land Registration Bill,[35] which was the starting point for the Land Registration etc. (Scotland) Act 2012. The Bill introduced to the Scottish Parliament on 1 December 2011[36] differed in some material (and minor) respects from the draft Bill prepared by the Scottish Law Commission, but the proposals for a system of advance notice were largely intact.

29 DP on *LR: Miscelluneous Issues* (n 19) para 7.19-7.20.
30 Titles to Land (Consolidation) (Scotland) Act 1868, s 155.
31 Ibid. The addition of service of the schedule of inhibition on the debtor was amended by the Bankruptcy and Diligence etc. (Scotland) Act 2007, s 149, after the publication of the DP.
32 DP on *LR: Miscellaneous Issues* (n 19) para 7.34.
33 Scot Law Com No 222, 2010.
34 Report on *Land Registration* (n 33) part 14.
35 Ibid vol 2.
36 Available at http://www.scottish.parliament.uk/parliamentarybusiness/Bills/44469.aspx

(2) The statutory system of Advance Notices

The principles of Advance Notices

The statutory structure for advance notices in conveyancing transactions adopts the principles for providing a period of priority protection for deeds that are intended to be granted and intended for registration in the Land Register.[37] The key elements of the advance notice procedure are:

(i) An advance notice relates to a specific deed that a granter intends to grant to another person.

(ii) An advance notice has to be applied for by the person who intends to grant the deed, and who may validly grant the deed, or by a person who has the consent of the person who may validly grant the deed.[38]

(iii) Once registered, the advance notice provides a period of thirty-five days' protection to the grantee, from any competing deeds, or other subsequent advance notices, that are registered against the property during that period, or an inhibition registered against the granter during the protected period.

(iv) The protected period starts the day after the date of registration of the advance notice.

(v) A second advance notice (and third (and potentially an unlimited number of advance notices))[39] can be applied for, but subsequent advance notices provide a separate, not a continuous, period of protection.

The detail of the Advance Notice protection

The introduction of Advance Notices is a major transformation for conveyancing practice in Scotland, and one that many in the profession would regard as long overdue.

The Advance Notice concept is similar to, but not exactly the same as, the priority period which currently exists for registration of documents in the Land Registry of England and Wales. In England and Wales it is tied in with a register search. The system that now applies in Scotland

37 See generally Land Registration etc. (Scotland) Act 2012, Part 4. Specific provisions are discussed in detail below.

38 There is something of a conceptual non sequitur in the way the legislation has been drafted, discussed further below.

39 There is nothing in the legislation about multiple consecutive advance notices for the same deed, but in theory this is technically possible although, in practice, unlikely.

borrows from both the English system[40] and the system that applies in Germany.[41]

It should be borne in mind that the advance notice procedure is voluntary. There is no compulsion to use it, but the advantages of it over the flawed and precarious letter of obligation alternative are compelling.

Under the provisions of the 2012 Act, it is possible to apply to the Keeper for an advance notice in respect of a deed that a person intends to grant.[42] For a fee of £10,[43] an advance notice application can be submitted,[44] for example when a seller has agreed to sell a piece of his land, and consequently will be granting a disposition in favour of the purchaser.

The advance notice application is submitted to the relevant register in advance of the completion date for the transaction, and once it is registered, it provides a period of protection of thirty-five days (beginning with the day after the advance notice is registered in the relevant register)[45] in which any competing deed, or another advance notice, would not have priority.[46]

So, for example, if the seller registers an advance notice for a disposition over his property that he intends to grant in favour of the purchaser, and then some other person presents a competing disposition for registration in respect of the property in question, although the competing disposition would be entered onto the Register initially, the existence of the earlier advance notice would prevent the competing disposition from prevailing, provided always that the purchaser with the benefit of the advance notice submits his disposition for registration within the thirty-five day period of protection.

However, if the purchaser fails to submit his disposition within the thirty-five day period, in that case, the earlier registered disposition will take effect at the expiry of the thirty-five day period.

Advance notices apply to other types of deed, such as a standard security or deed of servitude, and also to a registrable lease or sub-lease,

40 The Land Registration Act 2002 and Land Registration Rules 2003.
41 German Civil Code BGB, Articles 883 to 888.
42 Land Registration etc. (Scotland) Act 2012, s 56.
43 The Registers of Scotland (Fees) Order 2014, SSI 2014/188, sched 1, para 3(b).
44 Land Registration etc. (Scotland) Act 2012, s 57.
45 Ibid, s 58.
46 Ibid, ss 59-61.

but the deed must be a bilateral one,[47] that is, with a granter and a grantee.[48] Unilateral deeds, such as a local authority charging order, are not covered, nor actually are they likely to have need of advance notice protection.

Only a person who intends to grant the deed and may validly grant the deed can apply for an advance notice.[49] However, a person with the consent of such a person may also apply.[50] The statutory wording is a little problematic in a situation where the purchaser wants to register an advance notice for a deed that the purchaser plans to grant as part of the purchase transaction, for example, a standard security in favour of its heritable creditor. Only the purchaser can *intend* to grant that deed, but there is an argument that the purchaser may not *validly grant* the deed until it is the owner, therefore it needs the consent of the seller to apply for the advance notice. But in these circumstances, the seller cannot *intend to grant* the standard security by the purchaser, so neither of the parties can fulfil the two part statutory requirement: (i) intention to grant and (ii) ability validly to grant, at the time of applying for the advance notice. However, unless the effect of the statutory provision is to permit a purchaser to apply for an advance notice of this type, its inclusion in the 2012 Act is pointless. The Registers are in no doubt that the intention of the legislation was that a purchaser would be able to register an advance notice for a standard security it intends to grant, if it has the consent of the seller, and that they will accept such applications.[51]

An application for an advance notice can be made for a title that is recorded in the General Register of Sasines, as well as for titles that are registered in the Land Register.[52] As all dispositions, whether for valuable consideration or not, induce a first registration under the provisions of the 2012 Act, if the title is still in the Sasine Register, advance notices can be recorded in the Sasine Register in those cases. For a title that is already in

47 Note however that it is not currently possible to apply for an advance notice for any bilateral deed. Renunciation of leases and section 75 agreements are two obvious examples of deeds that are conspicuous by their absence from the current advance notice application system.

48 Land Registration etc. (Scotland) Act 2012, s 56(1).

49 Ibid, s 57(1) and (2)(a).

50 Ibid, s 51(2)(b).

51 Registers of Scotland. *Land Registration etc. (Scotland) Act 2012 General Guidance – Advance Notices*, available at https://www.ros.gov.uk/about-us/2012-act/general-guidance/advance-notices

52 Land Registration etc. (Scotland) Act 2012, ss 59 and 60.

the Land Register, the advance notice will be registered in the application record of the Land Register.

If for any reason settlement of the transaction is delayed, it is possible to apply for another advance notice giving the purchaser (or other grantee as appropriate) another thirty-five day period of protection. However, it is important to note that this is not an extension of the first advance notice period: it is a separate period of protection. So, in the example above, the competing disposition submitted during the first thirty-five day period would remain on the Register and the second priority period will not protect against it. The competing disposition would of course show up on a search of the Register, which it is recommended be obtained up to a date when the advance notice to be relied on by the purchaser is disclosed in that search. That search would also disclose the competing disposition alerting the purchaser to its existence. This would mean that the purchaser ought not to proceed to settlement without requiring the seller to take steps remedy the position, should he still wish to buy the property. In the face of a competing disposition, no purchaser would be expected to proceed.

Once an advance notice is on the application record of the Land Register, or in the Sasine Register, it is possible to apply to have it discharged, while it is current (i.e. during the thirty-five day period).[53] The circumstances where this will be necessary may occur from time to time, but as a general rule there is no need formally to discharge an advance notice. It will expire automatically at the end of the thirty-five day period, and the Keeper will remove it from the application record in the Land Register, and archive it.[54] Most advance notices will therefore simply be allowed to lapse. If an applicant wants to have an advance notice discharged, it must obtain the consent of the person in whose favour the notice has been registered (e.g. the purchaser). This will ensure that the protection given by an advance notice is not cancelled without the knowledge and permission of the person benefitting from the protection.

One innovative effect of an advance notice is that, if an inhibition is registered against the granter of the deed during the protected period, provided the protected deed is registered during the protected period, it

53 Land Registration etc. (Scotland) Act 2012, s 63.

54 Ibid, s 62. An advance notice recorded in the Sasine Register will always be shown on that Register. While a formal discharge of such an advance notice can be recorded, it will be evident from the date of recording of the advance notice when its protection will have expired after thirty-five days.

will not be affected by the inhibition.[55] This could mean, in circumstances where an advance notice is submitted before conclusion of missives and the inhibition is also registered before a contract was in place, but after the protected period of the advance notice has begun, that nonetheless the purchaser's deed would be protected, and he could complete the purchase. This represents a change in the law of inhibitions,[56] although it is unlikely that this particular convergence of circumstances will happen very often.

There are some entries in the Registers that an advance notice does not affect. Notices of potential liability for costs under the Tenements (Scotland) Act 2004[57] or the Title Conditions (Scotland) Act 2003[58] are specifically carved out from the effect of the advance notice protection.[59] Scottish Ministers have the power to specify other deeds that should prevail despite the existence of an advance notice on the Register.[60]

(3) Conveyancing procedures for Advance Notices

The statutory provisions relating to advance notices provide what advance notices are, who may apply for them and what their effect will be. But they are voluntary, and therefore there is nothing in the 2012 Act that sets out how they are to be used in a transactional context. So it has been up to the conveyancing profession to work out how to use the advance notice procedure in practice.

The (PSG)[61] took on the task of considering how this would work in practice, and it produced a recommended form of wording for offers[62] that sets out the steps for parties to a typical sale and purchase transaction to take to implement the advance notice procedure. In doing so, the PSG wanted to ensure that the new process, that is now becoming an integral part of

---

55 Land Registration etc. (Scotland) Act 2012, s 61.

56 Under the previous law, an inhibition registered before conclusion of missives would prevail against the rights of the subsequent purchaser. Only sales completed in implement of missives concluded before the inhibition is registered are currently unaffected in these circumstances.

57 Tenements (Scotland) Act 2004, s 12(3).

58 Title Conditions (Scotland) Act 2003, s 10(2A).

59 Land Registration etc. (Scotland) Act 2012, s 61(3).

60 Ibid, s 61(3)(b).

61 A group of four commercial property lawyers, including the writer, from four of the major Scottish firms, who have worked together for over a decade to produce agreed form standardised commercial property documents which are available to the profession to access on the PSG website at www.psglegal.co.uk

62 PSG Offers to Sell incorporating 2012 Act wording are available to download at http://www.psglegal.co.uk/offer_to_sell.php

conveyancing procedure, would be clear, and also as straightforward as possible. Although PSG styles are produced from the perspective of the commercial property lawyer, the PSG form of words, and general approach, has also been adopted (with some minor modifications) in standard form residential missives.[63]

Practical issues that the PSG had to consider in formulating the new wording included:

(i) What is the optimum time in the transaction to submit the advance notice application?

(ii) Should the provision of an advance notice be compulsory or optional?

(iii) How should the requirements for consent be addressed?

(iv) How should the possible need for a second advance notice be tackled? and

(v) Who pays the cost of the advance notice application?

The optimum time to obtain an advance notice

The purchaser (or other grantee) will want advance notice protection to subsist until the application to register the deed in question has actually been submitted to the registers and has entered the application record. So the protection needs to extend beyond the settlement date, even if the purchaser's solicitor is going to personally present the deed for registration, and potentially for up to fourteen days after – or whatever reasonable period of time is appropriate. In reality it may be a lot closer to settlement before the advance notice application is lodged, to make sure that the maximum period of protection is available after settlement.

The PSG wording provides for submission of the advance notice application not earlier than five working days before settlement. This allows as much of the protected period as possible to cover the period after settlement, in case of delays, or rejection of the application first time around.

It is however a bit of a balancing act, and the parties to the transaction should be prepared to be flexible to suit the circumstances of the transaction. The Scottish standard clauses set out a longer period of ten days before the

63 The Scottish Standard Clauses for residential property transactions. For examples see http://www.lawscot.org.uk/rules-and-guidance/section-f-guidance-relating-to-particular-types-of-work/division-c-conveyancing/advice-and-information/scottish-standard-clauses/

date of entry in residential offers. The PSG approach proceeds on the basis that the more of the protected period that continues after settlement will mean that if the application for registration were to be rejected for some reason, there would be a good chance that the presenting solicitor could correct whatever was wrong with the application and re-submit it, all still within the protected period of the advance notice.

Compulsory or optional?

The approach recommended by the PSG is that the seller should be bound to apply for an advance notice. The advantages to a purchaser of the advance notice protection are obvious, but some sellers might question why they should have to make this application, which they may not consider to be of any benefit to them. However, while the protection is principally for the purchaser against any competing deeds, it also brings certainty for the seller, since, once a search has been obtained disclosing the advance notice, the seller can relax for the rest of the protected period too, and the protection provides greater certainty around settlement, compared to the step into the unknown that the gap period presented.

The form of the advance notice should be adjusted with the purchaser, since the advance notice will only protect the specific deed to be granted by that seller to that purchaser. The purchaser will want to be sure that the purchaser's details on the application are correct. Practitioners will need to bear this in mind, in case of a last minute substitution of a nominee to take title to the property. An advance notice that does not refer to that nominee will not protect a deed in its favour.

The requirement for consent

Only the seller can apply for an advance notice for the disposition to the purchaser, because of the requirement in the 2012 Act that only a person who intends to grant, and may validly grant the deed can make the application.[64] So, if there is a requirement for an advance notice for a standard security that the purchaser intends to grant, or for any other deeds that the purchaser intends to grant – for example, where the purchaser is planning a back-to-back sub-sale – the consent of the seller will be needed

64 Land Registration etc. (Scotland) Act 2012, s 57(1).

to make that application. To avoid the requirement in each transaction for specific consent to be sought each time (with the possibility that it is then withheld by the seller) the PSG wording builds in automatic consent of the seller to any application for an advance notice that the purchaser wants to submit. This allows these applications to go ahead at a time to suit the purchaser, without further reference to the seller.

One aspect of the procedure that a purchaser intending a back-to-back (i.e. simultaneous) sub-sale needs to consider is the approach to take where the purchaser does not want the seller to know about the sub-sale. Care would need to be taken in relation to applying for an advance notice for the proposed sub-sale disposition, because that advance notice will show up in any search obtained by the seller after the advance notice has been registered, alerting the seller to its existence. The alternative would have to be either that that no advance notice application can be made, or that the timing of the application for the sub-sale deed advance notice will need to be later than the period covered by the search, meaning that it would need to be a last minute application.

The automatic consent of the purchaser to the discharge of the advance notice, should this ever be required, has also been built in to the PSG offer. If the advance notice has to be discharged, this is likely to be because the original purchaser has withdrawn or failed to complete the transaction, so obtaining consent at that time could be problematic, although there may be a need to discharge an advance notice if it transpires that the purchaser's name is incorrectly stated, or, as anticipated above, a last minute substitution of a nominee is made. A discharge in the case of a failed purchase may only be necessary if there is an immediate requirement to apply for another advance notice in favour of a new purchaser, with an imminent settlement date. The second purchaser will want to have the first advance notice removed, as otherwise it would have priority over any advance notice registered for the second purchaser. In most cases, however, it will simply be a case of allowing the first advance notice to expire at the end of its thirty-five day period.

Additional advance notices

The PSG wording provides for a seller to obtain a second advance notice in a transaction, if the purchaser requests it. This could be necessary, if the first advance notice has been obtained too soon, or if there is a delay in completing the transaction and the protected period is due to expire in only a few days after the postponed settlement date.

Who pays?

The cost of the advance notice should be met by the seller. The application is made by the seller, so the seller is responsible for paying the fee for the application to the Registers. The cost is only £10, and it would cost much more than that in administrative time to recover that sum from the purchaser and process it. While the advance notice provides the purchaser with protection, it is protection against the possible acts of, and deeds granted by, the seller, or decrees or diligence done against the seller, so it seems a fair arrangement in all the circumstances.

If the purchaser wants to submit an advance notice application for any deeds it intends to grant, it should meet the cost of those, and of any discharge of such advance notices, if the seller requires it in cases where the transaction does not proceed.

If a second advance notice is required in the transaction, it should be paid for by whichever of the seller or the purchaser is responsible for the delay. Although there can be disagreement sometimes about the party to which any delay is attributable, this provision will cater for most circumstances, where the position is usually clear.

(4) Timing issues for advance notices

The PSG wording proposes submitting the application for an advance notice not earlier than five working days before completion. In terms of transactional timing, this also really means not *later* than five working days before completion as well. This timescale pre-supposes that a search (now called a legal report) in the property and personal registers has already been obtained, and the parties have seen and dealt with anything relevant that it discloses. As soon as the advance notice application has been made, a continuation legal report can be ordered, immediately before completion. That continuation report will disclose the advance notice,[65] and the purchaser can complete the transaction in the knowledge that protection is in place.

Timing will also be important if there is a delay in settlement, or if the purchaser's application for registration is rejected immediately. If the parties have allowed as much of the protected period as possible to

65 The advance notice can also be viewed on Registers Direct (an online system allowing viewing access to information in the Registers of Scotland).

be extant after completion, then this may be sufficient to turn around a rejected application and submit it again before the expiry of the protected period. Correctly counting the number of days could become important: the thirty-five day period does not start until the day after the day the notice is entered in the application record, or recorded in the Sasine Register, where applicable.

(5) The application process

Application types

Applications for an advance notice are created electronically, within a system built by the Registers of Scotland, access to which is by secure login.[66]

The online form is simple and easy to complete. It requires details of:

(i) the granter of the deed,

(ii) the grantee of the deed,

(iii) the type of transaction (first registration, dealing of whole, transfer of part),

(iv) the type of deed, and

(v) details of the property (including the title number if it is registered, or an adequate conveyancing description (sufficient to identify the boundaries of the property concerned) if it is not).

However not all advance notice applications can be submitted electronically – some have to be printed out.

The advance notice system will accept four types of application:[67]

(i) A first registration – this is where the advance notice is in respect of the grant of a deed that will take the property out of the Sasine Register, and transfer it to the Land Register. However the advance notice has to be recorded in the Sasine Register, as the title to the property is not yet in the Land Register – that will only happen when the intended deed is actually presented for registration.

(ii) An intended deed that applies to the whole of a registered interest.

(iii) An intended deed that applies to part only of a registered interest, and

66 Registers of Scotland, *Guidance* (n 51).
67 Ibid.

(iv) Where an extant advance notice requires to be discharged. This will only be necessary if it needs to be removed from the application record, or its discharge needs to be shown in the Sasine Register during the currency of the thirty-five day period.

It has transpired that the online system for creation of advance notices does not have the ability to save drafts of advance notice applications, meaning that it is not possible for the purchaser to approve the seller's electronically created draft. As such approval is recommended, so that the purchaser's solicitor can ensure that his client's details are correct, Word version drafts of the advance notice forms have been created by the PSG, to allow adjustment of the terms of the application to be made between the parties, then copied and pasted directly into the online form. As an immediate solution to the shortcomings of the online system, these draft forms have helped to maintain transactional momentum in the early days of adjusting to the 2012 Act. However, it would be just as acceptable, as the profession becomes more familiar with the content of advance notice applications, for these details to be adjusted by email.

Submission of advance notice applications

Where an advance notice is sought for a deed relating to a property to which title is still in the Sasine Register, in which case the deed will, when presented for registration, induce a first registration, it is necessary to print the advance notice form, sign and date it and submit it in paper form.[68] This is because the advance notice has to be recorded in the Sasine Register, and every writ to be recorded in the Sasine Register has to be "impressed with a stamp or seal,"[69] which can only be done in hard copy. Electronic submission would not be competent, since a hard copy print of that submission would not be the original. An application for discharge of an advance notice that is recorded in the Sasine Register must also be printed, signed, dated and submitted in hard copy.[70]

If the advance notice relates to a deed which will transfer part of a registered interest, then a plan to identify that part has to accompany

68 Registers of Scotland, *Guidance* (n 51)
69 Land Registers (Scotland) Act 1868, s14.
70 Registers of Scotland, *Guidance* (n 51).

the application (unless the part is a flat in a flatted building, where it is the whole building that is shown as a single unit on the cadastral map).[71] The plan must sufficiently identify the property to allow it to be plotted immediately onto the cadastral map. Submission of a plan can be done by way of uploading an electronic plan, including a plan in pdf format, to the advance notice system, or by providing co-ordinates for the plot, or, if the part to be transferred is a plot in a development that has Development Plan Approval,[72] then all that is required is the Development Plan number and the relevant plot number in the development. If the plan is not available in some electronic format, then the advance notice application has to be printed, signed, dated and submitted in hard copy, with a suitable paper plan, signed and docqueted as relative to the advance notice application.[73]

An advance notice application for a deed that relates to the whole of a registered title, and an application for a discharge of an advance notice in the Land Register, can be submitted electronically.[74] An application for a discharge must refer to the allocated advance notice number for the advance notice to be discharged, which will then enable automatic pre-population of the discharge application form with other details from the original advance notice.[75] Exceptions to electronic submission of these types of advance notice application are only permitted in certain circumstances: where the online submission system is "down" for a forty eight hour period, or longer; where the person applying for the advance notice is the applicant who is not using a solicitor (it is expected that such applications will be rare); or if the applicant does not have access to a computer (possible in remote areas of Scotland where internet access is unavailable).

Where the property affected by the advance notice application is partly Sasine Registered and partly Land Registered, two advance notice applications are required, one for each register.[76] However if the title to

71 Land Registration etc. (Scotland) Act 2012, s 56(d)(iii).The cadastral map is the name given to the map, maintained by the Registers of Scotland showing the extent of all registered titles. See the 2012 Act, s 11.

72 Development Plan Approval is a service offered by Registers of Scotland to developers (e.g. house builders), that will identify and resolve any title extent issues in advance of the sale of individual houses (or plots) from the development. The development is approved and allocated a reference number and the location of each plot in the development is allocated a plot number.

73 Registers of Scotland, *Guidance* (n 51).

74 Ibid.

75 Ibid.

76 Ibid.

the property is in the Land Register and encompasses more than one title number, only one application is required, and can be submitted electronically, referring to each title number affected, unless the transfer relates to part only of one or more of the titles, and a plan showing the extent to be transferred cannot be uploaded electronically (or Development Plan Approval, or co-ordinates are not available).

Acknowledgement of advance notice applications

Electronic submissions of advance notice applications receive an email acknowledgement confirming that submission has been successful.[77] Once the advance notice has been entered on the application record, which should be the same day as submission, provided the application record is still open (meaning usually receipt of the application before 4pm), a second email is sent, confirming that it has been registered.

Paper submissions to the Land Register receive an email acknowledgement, whereas submissions to the Sasine Register are acknowledged by letter.[78]

Email acknowledgements include a pdf of the completed advance notice form, together with an application number and an advance notice number, and, where the advance notice relates to part of a registered plot, a pdf plan showing the extent that has been delineated on the cadastral map is included with the acknowledgement.

The thirty-five day period starts the day after registration. The acknowledgement notifies the applicant of the start and finish dates of the protected period.

C. The Future is Here

A new era of conveyancing started on 8 December 2014. But the fun doesn't stop here. The appetite for land reform at the Scottish Parliament appears to be unabated, with a Bill currently progressing through the Parliament that will see the community right to buy extended to the whole of Scotland,

77 Registers of Scotland, *Guidance* (n 51).

78 Ibid. The logic of this is unclear. Acknowledgement by letter is stated to be "in accordance with usual Sasine practice." It is to be hoped that in practice email acknowledgement will be adopted, with the letter is sent as an email attachment.

not just rural areas,[79] and the passing of a Bill that enables counterpart execution of deeds and effective delivery by electronic means.[80]

The Law Society of Scotland has set up a Working Party on the Future of Conveyancing, with a remit to take forward a variety of initiatives to ensure that conveyancing procedures in Scotland keep pace with modern practice, as well as harnessing the benefits of technology. The Working Party will be looking at standards, processes and standardisation, to make the sale and purchase of property a better experience for the consumer and for the practitioner. There is plenty of scope for improvement and, in most quarters, an appetite for change for the better.

With the advent of the advance notice system, will the traditional letter of obligation become a thing of the past? Early experiences of advance notice applications have not been entirely trouble free. Rejection of applications, with greater frequency than the profession anticipated, or delays in processing applications, has produced situations where recourse has had to be made to a hybrid form of letter of obligation – the gap now being the date of last search or settlement and the start of the protected period – admittedly a much shorter gap, usually no more than a day or two. But this, like all new procedures should settle down with time, and the profession cannot count on the benign treatment of letters of obligation under the Master Policy continuing indefinitely.[81]

And there will still be circumstances anyway, in which a letter of undertaking will have to be given in conveyancing transactions. The advance notice procedure will not cover the situation where a discharge of the seller's standard security is not available at settlement (an increasingly common occurrence, in both commercial and residential transactions). While the default position in commercial property transactions is to insist on delivery of a discharge at completion, undertakings to deliver a discharge are routinely given at residential settlements. How long that can continue, and whether the Working Party can find a way to tackle that issue are challenges for the future.

It is clear that the ghost of Mr Gordon[82] would have considerable difficulty in recognising the post-designated-day conveyancing landscape, but there can be no doubt that more change, and for the better, awaits us all.

79 The Community Empowerment (Scotland) Bill.
80 The Legal Writings (Counterparts and Delivery) (Scotland) Bill.
81 See n 11.
82 The solicitor who gave the undertaking in *Dryburgh* (n 2).

Permissions

All chapters in this book were first published in EIC&PL, by Open Book Publishers; hereby published with permission under the Creative Commons Attribution License or equivalent. Every chapter published in this book has been scrutinized by our experts. Their significance has been extensively debated. The topics covered herein carry significant findings which will fuel the growth of the discipline. They may even be implemented as practical applications or may be referred to as a beginning point for another development.

The contributors of this book come from diverse backgrounds, making this book a truly international effort. This book will bring forth new frontiers with its revolutionizing research information and detailed analysis of the nascent developments around the world.

We would like to thank all the contributing authors for lending their expertise to make the book truly unique. They have played a crucial role in the development of this book. Without their invaluable contributions this book wouldn't have been possible. They have made vital efforts to compile up to date information on the varied aspects of this subject to make this book a valuable addition to the collection of many professionals and students.

This book was conceptualized with the vision of imparting up-to-date information and advanced data in this field. To ensure the same, a matchless editorial board was set up. Every individual on the board went through rigorous rounds of assessment to prove their worth. After which they invested a large part of their time researching and compiling the most relevant data for our readers.

The editorial board has been involved in producing this book since its inception. They have spent rigorous hours researching and exploring the diverse topics which have resulted in the successful publishing of this book. They have passed on their knowledge of decades through this book. To expedite this challenging task, the publisher supported the team at every step. A small team of assistant editors was also appointed to further simplify the editing procedure and attain best results for the readers.

Apart from the editorial board, the designing team has also invested a significant amount of their time in understanding the subject and creating the most relevant covers. They scrutinized every image to scout for the most suitable representation of the subject and create an appropriate cover for the book.

The publishing team has been an ardent support to the editorial, designing and production team. Their endless efforts to recruit the best for this project, has resulted in the accomplishment of this book. They are a veteran in the field of academics and their pool of knowledge is as vast as their experience in printing. Their expertise and guidance has proved useful at every step. Their uncompromising quality standards have made this book an exceptional effort. Their encouragement from time to time has been an inspiration for everyone.

The publisher and the editorial board hope that this book will prove to be a valuable piece of knowledge for researchers, students, practitioners and scholars across the globe.

List of Contributors

Dr Ross G Anderson

John King

Professor Roderick R M Paisley

Kenneth Swinton

Lord Gill

Professor Stewart Brymer

Gerald F Hanretty QC

Lady Paton

Professor George Gretton

Professor Angus McAllister

Ann Stewart

Index

www.ingramcontent.com/pod-product-compliance
Lightning Source LLC
LaVergne TN
LVHW051047220926
848485LV00001BA/35
* 9 7 8 1 6 3 9 8 9 5 4 4 1 *